Adobe®
PHOTOSHOP® CS5
INTRODUCTORY

Gary B. Shelly

Joy L. Starks

COURSE TECHNOLOGY
CENGAGE Learning™

SHELLY
CASHMAN
SERIES®

Australia • Brazil • Japan • Korea • Mexico • Singapore • Spain • United Kingdom • United States

COURSE TECHNOLOGY
CENGAGE Learning™

Adobe® Photoshop® CS5: Introductory
Gary B. Shelly, Joy L. Starks

Vice President, Publisher: Nicole Pinard

Executive Editor: Kathleen McMahon

Product Manager: Crystal Parenteau/
    Aimee Poirier

Associate Product Manager: Aimee Poirier

Editorial Assistant: Lauren Brody

Director of Marketing: Cheryl Costantini

Marketing Manager: Tristen Kendall

Marketing Coordinator: Stacey Leasca

Print Buyer: Julio Esperas

Director of Production: Patty Stephan

Senior Content Project Manager: Jill Braiewa

Developmental Editor: Amanda Brodkin

QA Manuscript Reviewers: Susan Whalen

Copyeditor: Camille Kiolbasa

Proofreader: Kim Kosmatka

Indexer: Alexandra Nickerson

Art Director: Marissa Falco

Cover and Text Design: Lisa Kuhn, Curio Press, LLC

Cover Photo: Tom Kates Photography

Compositor: PreMediaGlobal

For product information and technology assistance, contact us at
Cengage Learning Customer & Sales Support, 1-800-354-9706

For permission to use material from this text or product,
submit all requests online at **cengage.com/permissions**
Further permissions questions can be emailed to
permissionrequest@cengage.com

Library of Congress Control Number: 2010930069
ISBN-13: 978-0-538-47389-7
ISBN-10: 0-538-47389-4

Course Technology
20 Channel Center Street
Boston, Massachusetts 02210
USA

Cengage Learning is a leading provider of customized learning solutions with office locations around the globe, including Singapore, the United Kingdom, Australia, Mexico, Brazil, and Japan. Locate your local office at:
international.cengage.com/region

Cengage Learning products are represented in Canada by Nelson Education, Ltd.

For your course and learning solutions, visit **www.cengage.com**

To learn more about Course Technology,
visit **www.cengage.com/coursetechnology**

Purchase any of our products at your local college bookstore or at our preferred online store **www.cengagebrain.com**

Credits
Chapter 1: Fig 1-1: Fred Starks; Fig 1-85: Mali Jones; Fig 1-86: John J.Mosesso/NBII.Gov; Fig 1-87: NASA/JPL-Caltech/Harvard-Smithsonian CFA; Fig 1-88: National Park Services; Fig 1-90: Misty Vermaat; Case and Places 1: Katie Starks; Cases and Places 2: Fred Starks; Cases and Places 3: Jeffrey Olson Sgt. Floyd Monument Sioux City Iowa **Chapter 2:** Fig 2-1: Fred Starks; Fig 2-73, 2-74, 2-75: Kevin Marshall; Fig 2-76, 2-77, 2-78, Cases and Places 1: Fred Starks; Cases and Places 3: Katie Starks **Chapter 3:** Fig 3 -1: Fred Starks; Fig 3-77, 3-78, 3-80: Kevin Marshall; Figure 3-79 Fred Starks

Printed in the United States of America
1 2 3 4 5 6 7 16 15 14 13 12 11 10

Adobe PHOTOSHOP CS5
INTRODUCTORY

Contents

Appendices

Preface

The Shelly Cashman Series® offers the finest textbooks in computer education. We are proud of the fact that our previous Photoshop books have been so well received. With each new edition of our Photoshop books, we have made significant improvements based on the comments made by instructors and students. The Adobe Photoshop CS5 books continue with the innovation, quality, and reliability you have come to expect from the Shelly Cashman Series.

For this Photoshop CS5 text, the Shelly Cashman Series development team carefully reviewed our pedagogy and analyzed its effectiveness in teaching today's student. Students today read less, but need to retain more. They not only need to be able to perform skills, but to retain those skills and know how to apply them to different settings. Today's students need to be continually engaged and challenged to retain what they're learning.

With this Photoshop CS5 text, we continue our commitment to focusing on the user and how they learn best.

Objectives of This Textbook

Adobe Photoshop CS5: Introductory is intended for a course that offers an introduction to Photoshop and image editing. No previous experience with Adobe Photoshop CS5 is assumed, and no mathematics beyond the high school freshman level is required.

The objectives of this book are:

- To teach the fundamentals and more advanced features of Adobe Photoshop CS5

- To expose students to image editing and graphic design fundamentals

- To develop an exercise-oriented approach that promotes learning by doing

- To encourage independent study and to help those who are working alone

The Shelly Cashman Approach

A Proven Pedagogy with an Emphasis on Project Planning
Each chapter presents a practical problem to be solved, within a project planning framework. The project orientation is strengthened by the use of Plan Ahead boxes, that encourage critical thinking about how to proceed at various points in the project. Step-by-step instructions with supporting screens guide students through the steps. Instructional steps are supported by the Q&A, Experimental Step, and BTW features.

A Visually Engaging Book that Maintains Student Interest
The step-by-step tasks, with supporting figures, provide a rich visual experience for the student. Call-outs on the screens that present both explanatory and navigational information provide students with information they need, when they need to know it.

Supporting Reference Materials (Quick Reference, Appendices)
The appendices provide additional information about the application at hand, such as the Help Feature and customizing the application. With the Quick Reference, students can quickly look up information about a single task, such as keyboard shortcuts, and find page references of where in the book the task is illustrated.

Integration of the World Wide Web
The World Wide Web is integrated into the Photoshop CS5 learning experience by (1) BTW annotations; (2) a Quick Reference Summary Web page; and (3) the Learn It Online section for each chapter.

End-of-Chapter Student Activities
Extensive end of chapter activities provide a variety of reinforcement opportunities for students where they can apply and expand their skills through individual and group work.

Instructor Resources
The Instructor Resources include both teaching and testing aids.

Instructor's Manual Includes lecture notes summarizing the chapter sections, figures and boxed elements found in every chapter, teacher tips, classroom activities, lab activities, and quick quizzes in Microsoft Word files.

Syllabus Easily customizable sample syllabi that cover policies, assignments, exams, and other course information.

Figure Files Illustrations for every figure in the textbook in electronic form.

PowerPoint Presentations A multimedia lecture presentation system that provides slides for each chapter. Presentations are based on chapter objectives.

Solutions to Exercises Includes solutions for all end-of-chapter and chapter reinforcement exercises.

Test Bank & Test Engine Test Bank includes 112 questions for every chapter, featuring objective-based and critical thinking question types, including page number references and figure references, when appropriate. Also included is the test engine, ExamView, the ultimate tool for your objective-based testing needs.

Additional Activities for Students Consists of Chapter Reinforcement Exercises, which are true/false, multiple-choice, and short answer questions that help students gain confidence in the material learned.

Book Resources

- 🔒 **Instructor's Manual**
- 🔒 **PowerPoint Presentations**
- 🔒 **Solutions to Exercises (Windows)**
- 🔒 **Syllabus**
- 🔒 **Test Bank and Test Engine**
- **Additional Student Files**
- **Data Files for Students (Windows)**

Content for Online Learning

Course Technology has partnered with Blackboard, the leading distance learning solution provider and class-management platform today. The resources available for download with this title are the test banks in Blackboard- and WebCT-compatible formats. To access this material, simply visit our password-protected instructor resources available at www.cengage.com/coursetechnology. For additional information or for an instructor username and password, please contact your sales representative. Other formats are also available.

CourseNotes

Course Technology's CourseNotes are six-panel quick reference cards that reinforce the most important and widely used features of a software application in a visual and user-friendly format. CourseNotes serve as a great reference tool during and after the course. CourseNotes are available for software applications, such as Microsoft Office 2010, Word 2010, PowerPoint 2010, Excel 2010, Access 2010, and Windows 7. There are also topic-based CourseNotes available for Best Practices in Social Networking, Hot Topics in Technology, and Web 2.0. Visit www.cengage.com/ct/coursenotes to learn more!

Adobe Photoshop CS5 30-Day Trial Edition

A copy of the Photoshop CS5 30-Day trial edition can be downloaded from the Adobe Web site (www.adobe.com). Point to Downloads in the top navigation bar, click Trial downloads, and then follow the on-screen instructions. When you activate the software, you will receive a license that allows you to use the software for 30 days. Course Technology and Adobe provide no product support for this trial edition. When the trial period ends, you can purchase a copy of Adobe Photoshop CS5, or uninstall the trial edition and reinstall your previous version. The minimum system requirements for the 30-day trial edition is a Intel® Pentium® 4 or AMD Athlon® 64 processor; Microsoft® Windows® XP with Service Pack 3, Windows Vista® Home Premium, Business, Ultimate, or Enterprise with Service Pack 1 (Service Pack 2 recommended), or Windows 7; 1GB of RAM; 1GB of available hard-disk space for installation; additional free space required during installation (cannot install on removable flash-based storage devices); 1024×768 display (1280×800 recommended) with qualified hardware-accelerated OpenGL graphics card, 16-bit color, and 256MB of VRAM; Some GPU-accelerated features require graphics support for Shader Model 3.0 and OpenGL 2.0; DVD-ROM drive; QuickTime 7.6.2 software required for multimedia features; and broadband internet connection required for online services.

About Our Covers

The Shelly Cashman Series is continually updating our approach and content to reflect the way today's students learn and experience new technology. This focus on student success is reflected on our covers, which feature real students from Bryant University using the Shelly Cashman Series in their courses, and reflect the varied ages and backgrounds of the students learning with our books. When you use the Shelly Cashman Series, you can be assured that you are learning computer skills using the most effective courseware available.

Textbook Walk-Through

Plan Ahead boxes prepare students to create successful projects by encouraging them to think strategically about what they are trying to accomplish before they begin working.

Step-by-step instructions now provide a context beyond the point-and-click. Each step provides information on why students are performing each task, or what will occur as a result.

Overview

As you read this chapter, you will learn how to edit the photo shown in Figure 1–1a on the previous page by performing these general tasks:

- Customize the workspace.
- Display and navigate a photo at various magnifications.
- Crop a photo effectively.
- Create and modify a border.
- Stroke a selection.
- Resize and print a photo.
- Save, close, and then reopen a photo.
- Save a photo for the Web.
- Use Mini Bridge.
- Use Photoshop Help.

▶ Plan Ahead

General Project Guidelines

When editing a photo, the actions you perform and decisions you make will affect the appearance and characteristics of the finished product. As you edit a photo, such as the one shown in Figure 1–1a, you should follow these general guidelines:

1. **Find an appropriate image or photo.** Keep in mind the purpose and the graphic needs of the project when choosing an image or photo. Decide ahead of time on the file type and decide if the image will be used on the Web. An eye-catching graphic image should convey a universal theme. The photo should grab the attention of viewers and draw them into the picture, whether in print or on the Web.

2. **Determine how to edit the photo to highlight the theme.** As you edit, use standard design principles, and keep in mind your subject, your audience, the required size and shape of the graphic, color decisions, the rule of thirds, the golden rectangle, and other design principles. Decide which parts of the photo portray your message and which parts are visual clutter. Crop the photo as needed.

3. **Identify finishing touches that will further enhance the photo.** The overall appearance of a photo significantly affects its ability to communicate clearly. You might want to add text or a border.

4. **Prepare for publication.** Resize the photo as needed to fit the allotted space. Save the photo on a storage medium, such as a hard drive, USB flash drive, or CD. Print the photo or publish it to the Web.

When necessary, more specific details concerning the above guidelines are presented at appropriate points in the chapter. The chapter also will identify the actions performed and decisions made regarding these guidelines during the creation of the edited photo shown in Figure 1–1b on the previous page.

BTW

Screen Resolution
If your computer has a high-resolution monitor with a screen resolution of 1280 × 800 or higher, lowering that resolution to 1024 × 768 may cause some images to be distorted because of a difference in the aspect ratio. If you want to keep your high-resolution setting, be aware that the location of on-screen tools might vary slightly from the book.

Starting Photoshop

If you are using a computer to step through the project in this chapter, and you want your screen to match the figures in this book, you should change your screen's resolution to 1024 × 768. For information about how to change a screen's resolution, read Appendix C.

To Open a Photo

The following steps open the Cyclist file from a CD located in [ ] might differ.

1
- Insert the CD containing the Data Files for Students that accompanies this book into your CD drive. After a few seconds, if Windows displays a dialog box, click its Close button.

- Click File on the menu bar to display the File menu (Figure 1–10).

Q&A What if I do not have the CD?

You will need the Data Files for Students to complete the activities and exercises in this book. See your instructor for information on how to acquire the necessary files.

Q&A Can I use a shortcut key to open a file?

Yes, the shortcut keys are displayed on the menu. In this textbook, the shortcut keys also are displayed at the end of each series of steps in the Other Ways box.

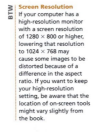

Figure 1–10

2
- Click Open on the File menu to display the Open dialog box.

- Click the Look in box arrow (Open dialog box) to display a list of the available storage locations on your system (Figure 1–11).

Q&A Are there other ways to navigate in the Open dialog box?

Yes, the Go To Last Folder Visited button and Up One Level button help you move through the folders on your computer. The navigation pane also displays links to common storage locations.

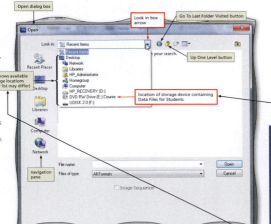

Figure 1–11

BTW

Screen Shots
Callouts in screenshots give students information they need, when they need to know it. The Series has always used plenty of callouts to ensure that students don't get lost. Now, color distinguishes the content in the callouts to make them more meaningful.

Navigational callouts in red show students where to click.

Explanatory callouts summarize what is happening on screen.

Optimization is the process of changing the photo to make it most effective for its purpose. The Save for Web & Devices command allows you to preview optimized images in different file formats, and with different file attributes, for precise optimization. You can view multiple versions of a photo simultaneously and modify settings as you preview the image.

Using the Save for Web & Devices Command

To optimize the cyclist photo for use on the Web, you need to make decisions about the file size and how long it might take to load on a Web page. These kinds of decisions must take into consideration the audience and the nature of the Web page. For example, Web pages geared for college campuses probably could assume a faster download time than those that target a wide range of home users. An e-commerce site that needs high-quality photography to sell its product will make certain choices in color and resolution.

The hardware and software of Web users also is taken into consideration. For instance, if a Web photo contains more colors than the user's monitor can display, most browsers will **dither**, or approximate, the colors that it cannot display, by blending colors that it can. Dithering might not be appropriate for some Web pages, because it increases the file size and therefore causes the page to load more slowly.

Many other appearance settings play a role in the quality of Web graphics, some of which are subjective in nature. As you become more experienced in Photoshop, you will learn how to make choices about dithering, colors, texture, image size, and other settings.

To Preview Using the Save for Web & Devices Dialog Box

The followings steps use the Save for Web & Devices command to display previews for four possible Web formats.

1
- With the Cyclist Resized photo open, click File on the menu bar to display the File menu and then click Save for Web & Devices to display the Save for Web & Devices dialog box.

- Click the 4-Up tab to display four versions of the photo.

- Click the upper-right preview, if necessary, to choose a high-quality, version of the photo (Figure 1–66).

Why are there four frames?

Photoshop displays four previews — the original photo and three others that are converted to different resolutions to optimize download times on the Web.

Figure 1–66

Saturation icon (shown in Figure 3–60 on page PS 183) on the Adjustments panel.

- Click the Clip to Layer button on the Adjustments panel status bar to adjust only the layer.

Figure 3–63

- Drag the Hue slider to +5. Drag the Saturation slider to −5. Drag the Lightness slider to −10 (Figure 3–63).

 Experiment

- Drag the sliders to view the affect of hue and saturation settings to the layer. When you are done experimenting, drag the sliders to the settings listed in the step.

2
- Click the 'Return to adjustment list' button to display all of the adjustment icons and settings on the Adjustments panel.

Brightness and Contrast

Brightness refers to color luminance or intensity of a light source, perceived as lightness or darkness in an image. Photoshop measures brightness on a sliding scale from −150 to +150. Negative numbers move the brightness toward black. Positive numbers compress the highlights and expand the shadows. For example, the layer might be an image photographed on a cloudy day; conversely, the image might appear overexposed by having been too close to a photographer's flash. Either way, editing the brightness might enhance the image.

Contrast is the difference between the lightest and darkest tones in an image, involving mainly the midtones. When you increase contrast, the middle-to-dark areas become darker, and the middle-to-light areas become lighter. High-contrast images contain few color variations between the lightest and darkest parts of the image; low-contrast images contain more tonal gradations.

To Adjust the Brightness and Contrast

Sometimes it is easier to create a layer adjustment from the Layers panel. The following steps edit the brightness and contrast of the Background layer using the 'Create new fill or adjustment layer' button on the Layers panel.

Other Ways
1. Select layer, press CTRL+U, complete adjustments, right-click layer, click Create Clipping Mask

BTW

Layer Selection
Sometimes a menu or panel will cover the Layers panel, or a layer might be scrolled out of sight. You always can identify which layer you are working with by looking at the document window tab as shown in Figure 3–64 on the next page. The name of the current layer appears in parentheses.

Textbook Walk-Through

Other Ways boxes that follow many of the step sequences explain the other ways to complete the task presented.

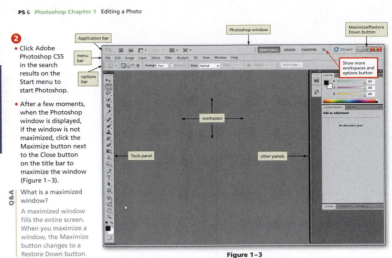

2
- Click Adobe Photoshop CS5 in the search results on the Start menu to start Photoshop.
- After a few moments, when the Photoshop window is displayed, if the window is not maximized, click the Maximize button next to the Close button on the title bar to maximize the window (Figure 1–3).

Q&A What is a maximized window?

A maximized window fills the entire screen. When you maximize a window, the Maximize button changes to a Restore Down button.

Figure 1–3

Other Ways
1. Double-click Photoshop icon on desktop, if one is present
2. Click Adobe Photoshop CS5 on Start menu

Customizing the Photoshop Workspace

The screen in Figure 1–3 shows how the Photoshop workspace looks the first time you start Photoshop after installation on most computers. Photoshop does not open a blank or default photo automatically; rather, the Application bar, a menu bar, and the options bar [...] oss the top of the screen with a gray work area below the options bar. The Tools [...] splayed on the left; other panels are displayed on the right. The gray work area [...] s are referred to collectively as the **workspace**.

[...] ou work in Photoshop, the panels, the selected tool, and the options bar [...] ight change. Therefore, if you want your screen to match the figures in this [...] should restore the default workspace, select the default tool, and reset the [...] ar. For more information about how to change other advanced Photoshop [...] ee Appendix C.

[...] ause of a default preference setting, each time you start Photoshop, the [...] p workspace is displayed the same way it was the last time you used [...] p. If the panels are relocated, then they will appear in their new locations [...] ime you start Photoshop. You can create and save your own workspaces, or [...] shop's saved workspaces that show a group of panels used for certain tasks. [...] le, the Painting workspace displays the Brush presets panel and the Swatches [...] ong others — all of which you would need when painting. You will learn more [...] els later in this chapter. Similarly, if values on the options bar are changed or a [...] tool is selected, they will remain changed the next time you start Photoshop. If [...] to return the workspace to its default settings, follow these steps each time you [...] toshop.

Photoshop Chapter 1

Chapter Summary

In this chapter, you gained a broad knowledge of Photoshop. First, you learned how to start Photoshop. You were introduced to the Photoshop workspace. You learned how to open a photo and zoom in and out. You learned about design issues related to the placement of visual points of interest. You then learned how to crop a photo to eliminate extraneous background. After you added a blended border, you resized the image.

Once you saved the photo, you learned how to print it. You used the Save for Web & Devices command to optimize and save a Web version. You learned how to use Adobe Mini Bridge to view files and Adobe Help to research specific help topics. Finally, you learned how to quit Photoshop.

The items listed below include all the new Photoshop skills you have learned in this chapter:

1. Start Photoshop (PS 5)
2. Select the Essentials Workspace (PS 7)
3. Reset the Tools Panel (PS 8)
4. Reset the Options Bar (PS 8)
5. Open a Photo (PS 10)
6. Save a Photo in the PSD Format (PS 19)
7. Use the Zoom Tool (PS 23)
8. Open the Navigator Panel (PS 25)
9. Use the Navigator Panel (PS 26)
10. Collapse the Navigator Panel (PS 26)
11. Use the Hand Tool (PS 27)
12. Change the Magnification (PS 27)
13. Change the Screen Mode (PS 28)
14. Display Rulers (PS 30)
15. Crop a Photo (PS 33)
16. Position the Rule of Thirds Overlay (PS 34)
17. Create a Selection (PS 35)
18. Stroke a Selection (PS 36)
19. Modify a Selection (PS 38)
20. Switch Foreground and Background Colors (PS 40)
21. Deselect (PS 41)
22. Save a Photo with the Same File Name (PS 42)
23. Close a Photo (PS 42)
24. Open a Recent File (PS 43)
25. Resize the Image (PS 44)
26. Save a Photo with a Different Name (PS 46)
27. Print a Photo (PS 47)
28. Preview Using the Save for Web & Devices Dialog Box (PS 48)
29. Choose a Download Speed (PS 49)
30. Preview the Photo on the Web (PS 51)
31. Save the Photo as a Web Page (PS 52)
32. Use Mini Bridge to View Files (PS 54)
33. Collapse the Panel (PS 57)
34. Access Photoshop Help (PS 58)
35. Use the Help Search Box (PS 59)
36. Quit Photoshop (PS 60)

Chapter Summary includes a concluding paragraph, followed by a listing of the tasks completed within a chapter together with the pages on which the step-by-step, screen-by-screen explanations appear.

Every chapter features a **Learn It Online** section that is comprised of six exercises. These exercises include True/False, Multiple Choice, Short Answer, Flash Cards, Practice Test, and Learning Games.

Apply Your Knowledge usually requires students to open and manipulate a file from the Data Files that parallels the activities learned in the chapter.

STUDENT ASSIGNMENTS

Learn It Online

Test your knowledge of chapter content and key terms.

Instructions: To complete the Learn It Online exercises, start your browser, click the Address bar, and then enter the Web address `scsite.com/psCS5/learn`. When the Photoshop CS5 Learn It Online page is displayed, click the link for the exercise you want to complete and then read the instructions.

Chapter Reinforcement TF, MC, and SA
A series of true/false, multiple choice, and short answer questions that test your knowledge of the chapter content.

Flash Cards
An interactive learning environment where you identify chapter key terms associated with displayed definitions.

Practice Test
A series of multiple choice questions that tests your knowledge of chapter content and key terms.

Who Wants To Be a Computer Genius?
An interactive game that challenges your knowledge of chapter content in the style of a television quiz show.

Wheel of Terms
An interactive game that challenges your knowledge of chapter key terms in the style of the television show *Wheel of Fortune*.

Crossword Puzzle Challenge
A crossword puzzle that challenges your knowledge of key terms presented in the chapter.

Apply Your Knowledge

Reinforce the skills and apply the concepts you learned in this chapter.

Editing a Photo in the Photoshop Workspace
Instructions: Start Photoshop and perform the customization steps found on pages PS 6 through PS 9. Open the Apply 1-1 Water Park file in the Chapter 01 folder from the Data Files for Students. You can access the Data Files for Students on the CD that accompanies this book. See the inside back cover of this book for instructions on downloading the Data Files for Students, or contact your instructor for information about accessing the required files.

First, you will save the photo in its own folder. Then you will crop the photo, add a white border, and save the edited photo, as shown in Figure 1–85. Next, you will resize the photo for printing and print one copy. Finally, you will reopen your edited photo, and then you will optimize it for the Web, save it, and close it.

Perform the following tasks:
1. On the File menu, click Save As. When Photoshop displays the Save As dialog box, navigate to your USB flash drive and then click the Create New Folder button. Type Apply 1-1 as the folder name and then press the ENTER key. Double-click the folder to open it. In the File name box, type Apply 1-1 Water Park Edited. Click the Format button and choose the PSD file format. Click the Save button to save the file.

Textbook Walk-Through

Extend Your Knowledge projects at the end of each chapter allow students to extend and expand on the skills learned within the chapter. Students use critical thinking to experiment with new skills to complete each project.

STUDENT ASSIGNMENTS

Extend Your Knowledge

Extend the skills you learned in this chapter and experiment with new skills. You may need to use Help to complete the assignment.

Separating Objects from the Background

Instructions: Start Photoshop and perform the customization steps found on pages PS 6 through PS 9. Open the Extend 2-1 Flowers file in the Chapter 02 folder from the Data Files for Students and save it, in the PSD format, as Extend 2-1 Flowers Edited. You can access the Data Files for Students on the CD that accompanies this book; see the inside back cover of this book for instructions on downloading the Data Files for Students, or contact your instructor for information about accessing the required files.

The original flower image displays the flowers in their natural settings, with various colors in the background. After moving the frame and making a copy, you will select the flowers while preventing background colors from straying into the selection. Finally, you will position each flower in front of a frame as shown in Figure 2–74.

Figure 2–74

STUDENT ASSIGNMENTS

Make It Right

Analyze a project and correct all errors and/or improve the design.

Changing a Photo's Focus and Optimizing It for the Web

Instructions: Start Photoshop and perform the customization steps found on pages PS 6 through PS 9. Open the Make It Right 1-1 Young Stars file in the Chapter 01 folder from the Data Files for Students and save it as Make It Right 1-1 Young Stars Edited in the PSD file format. You can access the Data Files for Students on the CD that accompanies this book. See the inside back cover of this book for instructions on downloading the Data Files for Students, or contact your instructor for information about accessing the required files.

Members of your Astronomy Club have selected the Young Stars photo (Figure 1 – 87) for the club's Web site. You are to edit the photo to more clearly focus on the cluster of stars and its trailing dust blanket, and then optimize the photo for the Web.

View the photo in different screen modes and at different magnifications.

Keeping the rule of thirds and the golden rectangle 5:8 ratio concepts in mind, crop the photo to change its focal point and resave it. Then save the photo for the Web as Make-It-Right-1-1-Young-Stars-for-Web using the optimal settings for a GIF file with maximum colors and 250 pixels in width.

Figure 1– 87

Make It Right projects call on students to analyze a file, discover errors in it, and fix them using the skills they learned in the chapter.

In the Lab

Design and/or create a project using the guidelines, concepts, and skills presented in this chapter. Labs are listed in order of increasing difficulty.

Lab 1: Cropping a Photo and Adding a Feathered Border

Problem: A nature magazine has accepted the submission of your photo of an American bald eagle, but they would like you to crop the photo more, add a feathered border, and resize it. Also, the editor would like the final version saved in the TIFF format. The edited photo is displayed in Figure 1–88. See the inside back cover of this book for instructions on downloading the Data Files for Students, or contact your instructor for information about accessing the required files.

Figure 1–88

In the Lab assignments require students to utilize the chapter concepts and techniques to solve problems on a computer.

Instructions: Start Photoshop. Perform the customization steps found on pages PS 6 through PS 9. Open the file, Lab 1-3 Tram, from the Chapter 01 folder of the Data Files for Students. Save the file in the PSD format with the name Lab 1-3 Tram Edited, in a new folder named Lab 1-3. (*Hint:* Use the Create New Folder button in the toolbar of the Save As dialog box.) Resize the photo to 500 pixels wide. Zoom to 50% magnification. Search Photoshop Help for help related to optimization. Read about optimizing for the Web. Print a copy of the help topic and then close the Photoshop Help window.

Use the Save for Web & Devices dialog box to view the 4-Up tab. Choose the best looking preview. Select the connection speed of your Internet connection. Save the HTML and Images in the Lab 1-3 folder using the name, Lab-1-3-Tram-for-Web. Use Mini Bridge to check your file structure and see your photos. Collapse the Mini Bridge panel. For extra credit, upload the HTML file and the accompanying Image folder to a Web server. See your instructor for ways to submit this assignment.

Cases and Places

Apply your creative thinking and problem-solving skills to design and implement a solution.

Note: To complete these assignments, you may be required to use the Data Files for Students. See the inside back cover of this book for instructions on downloading the Data Files for Students, or contact your instructor for information about accessing the required files.

1: Cropping a Photo for a Picture Directory

Academic

As a member of your high school reunion committee, it is your task to assemble the class photo directory. You are to edit a high school student photo and prepare it for print in the reunion directory. The photo needs to fit in a space 1.75 inches high and 1.33 inches wide. Each photo needs to have approximately the same amount of space above the headshot: .25 inches. After starting Photoshop and resetting the workspace, select the photo, Case 1-1 Student, from the Chapter 01 folder of the Data Files for Students. Save the photo on your USB flash drive storage device as Case 1-1 Student Edited, using the PSD format. Resize the photo to match the requirements. Use the rulers to help you crop the photo to leave .25 inches above the top of the student's head. Save the photo again with the file name Case 1-1 Student for Print and print a copy for your instructor.

2: Creating a Photo for a Social Networking Site

Personal

You would like to place a photo of your recent tubing adventure on your social networking site. The photo you have is of two people. You need to crop out the other person who is tubing. After starting Photoshop and resetting the workspace, select the photo, Case 1-2 Tubing, from the Chapter 01 folder of the Data Files for Students. Save the photo on your USB flash drive storage device as Case 1-2 Tubing Edited, using the PSD format. Crop the photo to remove one of the inner tubes, keeping in mind the rule of thirds, the golden rectangle, and the direction of the action. Save the photo again and print a copy for your instructor.

Found within the Cases and Places exercises, the **Personal** activities call on students to create an open-ended project that relates to their personal lives.

1 | Editing a Photo

Objectives

You will have mastered the material in this chapter when you can:

- Start Photoshop and customize the Photoshop workspace
- Open a photo
- Identify parts of the Photoshop workspace
- Explain file types
- Save a photo for both print and the Web
- View a photo using the Zoom Tool, Navigator panel, Hand Tool, and screen modes
- Display rulers

- Crop a photo using the Rule of Thirds overlay
- Create a blended border by stroking a selection
- Open a recent file
- Resize a photo
- Print a photo
- View files in Mini Bridge
- Access Photoshop Help
- Close a file
- Quit Photoshop

1 | Editing a Photo

What Is Photoshop CS5?

Photoshop CS5 is a popular image editing software program produced by Adobe Systems Incorporated. **Image editing software** refers to computer programs that allow you to create and modify **digital images**, or pictures in electronic form. One type of digital image is a digital **photograph** or **photo**, which is a picture taken with a camera and stored as a digitized file. The photo then is converted into a print, a slide, or used in another file. Other types of digital images include scanned images or electronic forms of original artwork created from scratch. Digital images are used in graphic applications, advertising, print publishing, and on the Web. Personal uses include private photos, online photo sharing, scrapbooking, blogging, and social networking, among others. Image editing software, such as Photoshop, can be used for basic adjustments such as rotating, cropping, or resizing, as well as for more advanced manipulations, such as airbrushing, retouching, photo repair, changing the contrast of an image, balancing, or combining elements of different images. Because Photoshop allows you to save multilayered, composite images and then return later to extract parts of those images, it works well for repurposing a wide variety of graphic-related files.

Photoshop CS5 is part of the **Adobe Creative Suite 5** and comes packaged with most of the suite versions. It also is sold and used independently as a stand-alone application. Photoshop CS5 is available for both the PC and Macintosh computer platforms. Photoshop CS5 Extended includes all of the features of Photoshop CS5 and some new features for working with 3D imagery, motion-based content, and advanced image analysis. The chapters in this book use Photoshop CS5 on the PC platform, running the Windows 7 operating system.

To illustrate the features of Photoshop CS5, this book presents a series of chapters that use Photoshop to edit photos similar to those you will encounter in academic and business environments, as well as photos for personal use.

Project Planning Guidelines

The process of editing a photo requires careful analysis and planning. As a starting point, choose a photo that correctly expresses your desired subject or theme. Once the theme is determined, analyze the intended audience. Define a plan for editing that enhances the photo, eliminates visual clutter, improves color and contrast, and corrects defects. Always work on a duplicate of an original image. Finally, determine the file format and print style that will be most successful at delivering the message. Details of these guidelines are provided in Appendix A. In addition, each chapter in this book provides practical applications of these planning considerations.

Project — Rack Card Graphic

A **rack card** is a popular form of advertising, typically measuring 4 × 9 inches and printed in color on both sides. Organizations print rack cards on sturdy paper so the publications can last longer and stand up in a rack. Interested parties, such as students, tourists, clients, or the public can see the rack card easily. Rack cards commonly use graphics to attract attention.

The project in this chapter uses Photoshop to enhance a photograph of a cyclist to be used on a rack card produced by a university to show prospective students some leisure-time activities on campus. Figure 1–1a displays the original photo. Figure 1–1b displays the edited photo. The enhancements will emphasize the cyclist by positioning the scene to make the layout appear more visually appealing and to crop some of the background. A complimentary border will make the photo stand out. Finally, you will resize the photo to fit on a rack card and then optimize it for the university's Web site.

(a) Original photo

(b) Edited photo

Figure 1–1

Overview

As you read this chapter, you will learn how to edit the photo shown in Figure 1–1a on the previous page by performing these general tasks:

- Customize the workspace.
- Display and navigate a photo at various magnifications.
- Crop a photo effectively.
- Create and modify a border.
- Stroke a selection.
- Resize and print a photo.
- Save, close, and then reopen a photo.
- Save a photo for the Web.
- Use Mini Bridge.
- Use Photoshop Help.

Plan Ahead

General Project Guidelines

When editing a photo, the actions you perform and decisions you make will affect the appearance and characteristics of the finished product. As you edit a photo, such as the one shown in Figure 1–1a, you should follow these general guidelines:

1. **Find an appropriate image or photo.** Keep in mind the purpose and the graphic needs of the project when choosing an image or photo. Decide ahead of time on the file type and decide if the image will be used on the Web. An eye-catching graphic image should convey a universal theme. The photo should grab the attention of viewers and draw them into the picture, whether in print or on the Web.

2. **Determine how to edit the photo to highlight the theme.** As you edit, use standard design principles, and keep in mind your subject, your audience, the required size and shape of the graphic, color decisions, the rule of thirds, the golden rectangle, and other design principles. Decide which parts of the photo portray your message and which parts are visual clutter. Crop the photo as needed.

3. **Identify finishing touches that will further enhance the photo.** The overall appearance of a photo significantly affects its ability to communicate clearly. You might want to add text or a border.

4. **Prepare for publication.** Resize the photo as needed to fit the allotted space. Save the photo on a storage medium, such as a hard drive, USB flash drive, or CD. Print the photo or publish it to the Web.

When necessary, more specific details concerning the above guidelines are presented at appropriate points in the chapter. The chapter also will identify the actions performed and decisions made regarding these guidelines during the creation of the edited photo shown in Figure 1–1b on the previous page.

BTW

Screen Resolution
If your computer has a high-resolution monitor with a screen resolution of 1280 × 800 or higher, lowering that resolution to 1024 × 768 may cause some images to be distorted because of a difference in the aspect ratio. If you want to keep your high-resolution setting, be aware that the location of on-screen tools might vary slightly from the book.

Starting Photoshop

If you are using a computer to step through the project in this chapter, and you want your screen to match the figures in this book, you should change your screen's resolution to 1024 × 768. For information about how to change a screen's resolution, read Appendix C.

To Start Photoshop

The following steps, which assume Windows 7 is running, start Photoshop, based on a typical installation. You may need to ask your instructor how to start Photoshop for your computer.

1

• Click the Start button on the Windows 7 taskbar to display the Start menu.

• Type **Photoshop CS5** as the search text in the 'Search programs and files' text box, and watch the search results appear on the Start menu (Figure 1–2).

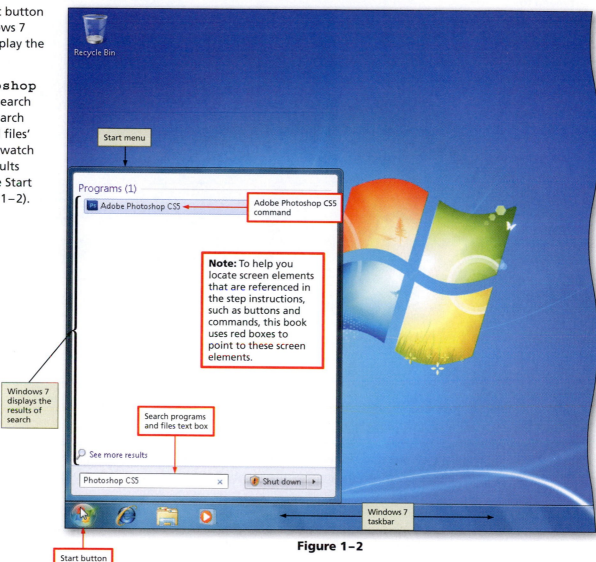

Start menu

Programs (1)

[Ps] Adobe Photoshop CS5 ← Adobe Photoshop CS5 command

Note: To help you locate screen elements that are referenced in the step instructions, such as buttons and commands, this book uses red boxes to point to these screen elements.

Windows 7 displays the results of search

Search programs and files text box

See more results

Photoshop CS5   Shut down ▶

Windows 7 taskbar

Start button

Figure 1–2

Q&A | Why do I have documents and files in my list of results?

Any documents containing the words, Photoshop CS5, and any files that have been opened with Photoshop CS5 may appear in your list.

2
- Click Adobe Photoshop CS5 in the search results on the Start menu to start Photoshop.

- After a few moments, when the Photoshop window is displayed, if the window is not maximized, click the Maximize button next to the Close button on the title bar to maximize the window (Figure 1–3).

Q&A

What is a maximized window?

A maximized window fills the entire screen. When you maximize a window, the Maximize button changes to a Restore Down button.

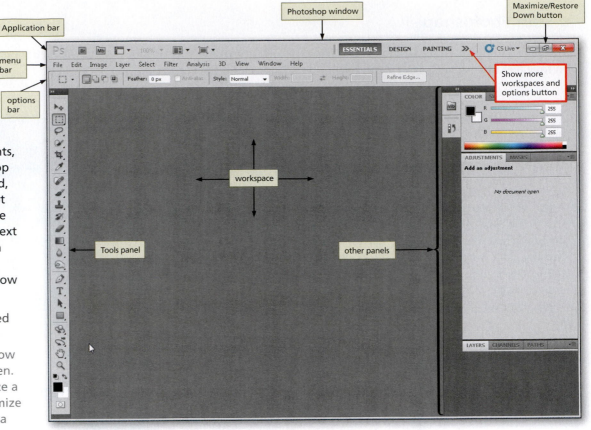

Figure 1–3

Other Ways

1. Double-click Photoshop icon on desktop, if one is present
2. Click Adobe Photoshop CS5 on Start menu

BTW

Adobe Suite Workspaces
The workspaces of the various applications in Adobe Creative Suite 5 share the same appearance to make it easy to move between applications. The toolbars, panels, and workspace are located in the same positions. Many shortcut keys are the same. Common menu terminology reduces the learning curve.

Customizing the Photoshop Workspace

The screen in Figure 1–3 shows how the Photoshop workspace looks the first time you start Photoshop after installation on most computers. Photoshop does not open a blank or default photo automatically; rather, the Application bar, a menu bar, and the options bar appear across the top of the screen with a gray work area below the options bar. The Tools panel is displayed on the left; other panels are displayed on the right. The gray work area and panels are referred to collectively as the **workspace**.

As you work in Photoshop, the panels, the selected tool, and the options bar settings might change. Therefore, if you want your screen to match the figures in this book, you should restore the default workspace, select the default tool, and reset the options bar. For more information about how to change other advanced Photoshop settings, see Appendix C.

Because of a default preference setting, each time you start Photoshop, the Photoshop workspace is displayed the same way it was the last time you used Photoshop. If the panels are relocated, then they will appear in their new locations the next time you start Photoshop. You can create and save your own workspaces, or use Photoshop's saved workspaces that show a group of panels used for certain tasks. For example, the Painting workspace displays the Brush presets panel and the Swatches panel, among others — all of which you would need when painting. You will learn more about panels later in this chapter. Similarly, if values on the options bar are changed or a different tool is selected, they will remain changed the next time you start Photoshop. If you wish to return the workspace to its default settings, follow these steps each time you start Photoshop.

To Select the Essentials Workspace

The default workspace, called Essentials, displays commonly used panels. The following steps select the Essentials workspace.

1
- Click the 'Show more workspaces and options' button on the Application bar to display the names of saved workspaces (Figure 1–4).

🔍 **Experiment**

- Click each of the workspaces that are displayed in the list to view the different panel configurations. When you are finished, click the 'Show more workspaces and options' button again to display the list.

Figure 1–4

2
- If necessary, click Essentials to select the default workspace panels.

- Click the 'Show more workspaces and options' button again to display the list (Figure 1–5).

Q&A What does the New Workspace command do?

The New Workspace command displays a dialog box where you can create a new workspace based on the currently displayed panels. You also can add the current keyboard shortcuts and menus to the new workspace.

Figure 1–5

3
- Click Reset Essentials to restore the workspace to its default settings and reposition any panels that may have been moved (Figure 1–6).

Q&A My screen did not change. Did I do something wrong?

If Photoshop is a new installation on your system, you might notice few changes on your screen.

Other Ways

1. On Window menu, point to Workspace, click Essentials (Default)

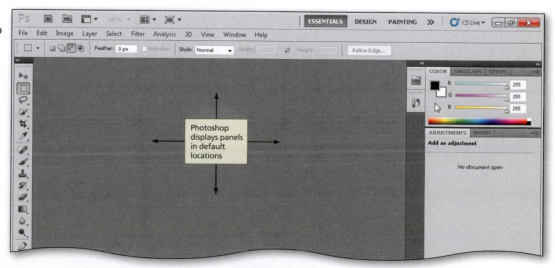

Figure 1–6

To Reset the Tools Panel

The following step resets the Tools panel to its default setting. When you select a tool on the Tools panel, the options bar reflects the settings of that tool.

- If necessary, click the second button from the top on the Tools panel to select it (Figure 1–7).

- If the tools in the Tools panel appear in two columns, click the double arrow at the top of the Tools panel.

Q&A What appears when I point to the button?

When you point to many objects in the Photoshop workspace, such as a tool or button, Photoshop displays a tool tip. A **tool tip** is a short, on-screen note associated with the object to which you are pointing, which helps you identify the button. This button's name is the Rectangular Marquee Tool.

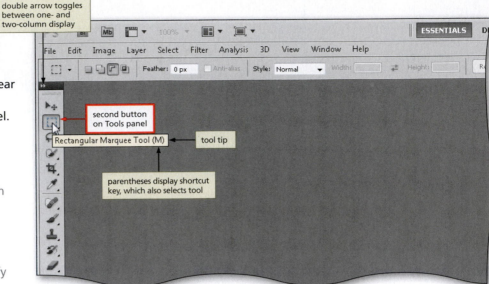

Figure 1–7

Other Ways
1. Press M

To Reset the Options Bar

As you work through the chapters, editing and creating photos, you will find that the options bar is **context sensitive**, which means it changes as you select different tools. In addition, the options and settings are retained for the next time you use Photoshop. To match the figures in this book, you should reset the options bar each time you start Photoshop using a context menu. A **context menu**, or **shortcut menu**, appears when you right-click some objects in the Photoshop workspace. The menu displays commands representing the active tool, selection, or panel.

The following steps reset all tool settings in the options bar using a context menu.

- Right-click the Rectangular Marquee Tool icon on the options bar to display its context menu (Figure 1–8).

Q&A Why is my icon elliptical?

It is possible that a previous user has used the Elliptical Marquee Tool. Press SHIFT+M to return to the Rectangular Marquee Tool.

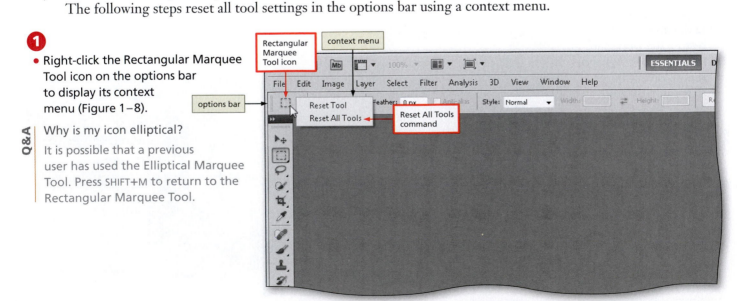

Figure 1–8

2
- Click Reset All Tools to display a confirmation dialog box (Figure 1–9).

3
- Click the OK button (confirmation dialog box) to restore the tools to their default settings.

Figure 1–9

Opening a Photo

To open a photo in Photoshop, it must be stored as a digital file on your computer system or on an external storage device. To **open** a photo, you bring a copy of the file from the storage location to the screen where you can **edit** or make changes to the photo. The changes do not become permanent, however, until you **save** or store the changed file on a storage device. The photos used in this book are stored on a CD located in the back of the book. Your instructor may designate a different location for the photos.

Find an appropriate image or photo.
Sometimes a person or business gives you a specific photo for use in a project. Other times, you are assigned a theme and asked to find or take the photo. An eye-catching graphic image should convey a universal theme or visually convey a message that is not expressed easily with words. Keep the audience in mind as you choose a photo. Photos generally fall into one of four categories:

- In advertising, a photo might show a product, service, result, model, or benefit.

- In a public service setting, a photo might represent a topic of interest, nature, signage, buildings, or a photo of historical importance.

- In industry, a photo might display a process, product, work organization, employee, facility, layout, equipment, safety, result, or culture.

- For personal or journalistic use, a photo might be a portrait, scenery, action shot, or event.

The images used in rack cards must fit into a small space. A picture on a rack card might contain text printed over the picture or a border to attract attention. A graphic designed for a rack card should be of high quality, use strong color, and must deliver a message in the clearest, most attractive, and most effective way possible.

BTW

Context Menus
Photoshop uses the term, context menu, for any short menu that appears when you right-click. Other applications may call it a shortcut menu. The two terms are synonymous.

To Open a Photo

The following steps open the Cyclist file from a CD located in drive E. The drive letter of your CD drive might differ.

• Insert the CD containing the Data Files for Students that accompanies this book into your CD drive. After a few seconds, if Windows displays a dialog box, click its Close button.

• Click File on the menu bar to display the File menu (Figure 1–10).

Q&A What if I do not have the CD?

You will need the Data Files for Students to complete the activities and exercises in this book. See your instructor for information on how to acquire the necessary files.

Q&A Can I use a shortcut key to open a file?

Yes, the shortcut keys are displayed on the menu. In this textbook, the shortcut keys also are displayed at the end of each series of steps in the Other Ways box.

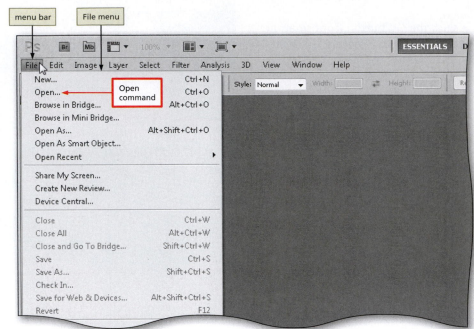

Figure 1–10

2

• Click Open on the File menu to display the Open dialog box.

• Click the Look in box arrow (Open dialog box) to display a list of the available storage locations on your system (Figure 1–11).

Q&A Are there other ways to navigate in the Open dialog box?

Yes, the Go To Last Folder Visited button and Up One Level button help you move through the folders on your computer. The navigation pane also displays links to common storage locations.

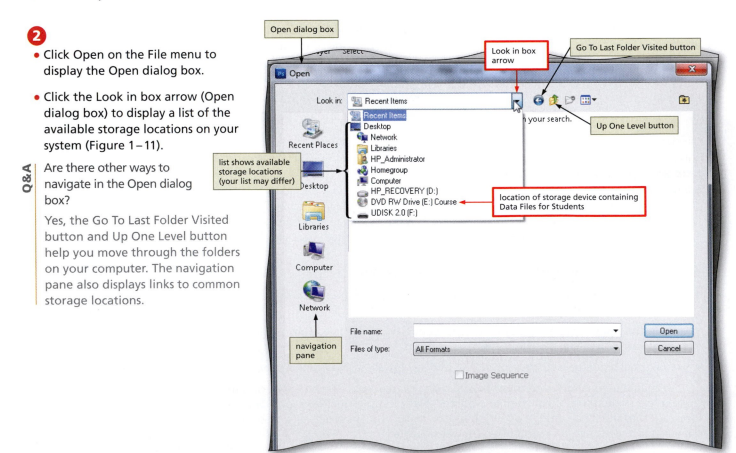

Figure 1–11

3

- Click DVD RW Drive (E:) Course, or the drive associated with your CD, to display its contents (Figure 1–12).

Q&A Why is the third button at the top of the Open dialog box disabled?

That button is the Create New Folder button. It is disabled because the CD is read-only.

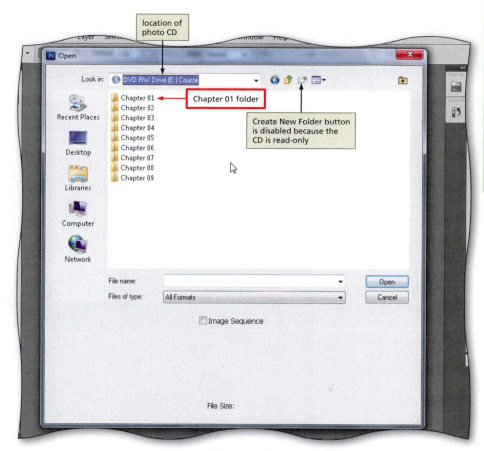

Figure 1–12

4

- Double-click the Chapter 01 folder and then click the file, Cyclist, to select the file to be opened (Figure 1–13).

Q&A Why does my file list look different?

Your list will vary. Also, the files in Figure 1–13 are displayed in List view. Click the View Menu button to verify your view.

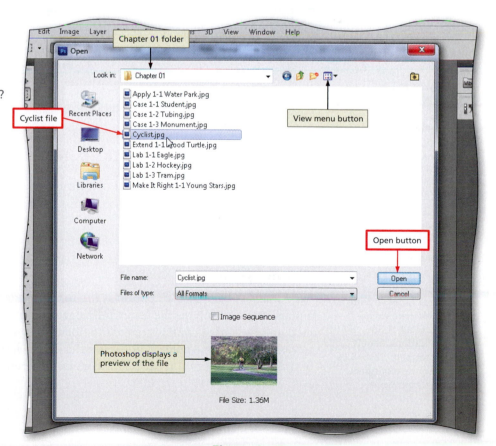

Figure 1–13

5
- Click the Open button to open the selected file and display the open photo in the Photoshop workspace (Figure 1–14).

Q&A

Can I edit a printed photo?

Most of the images you will use in this book already are stored in digital format; however, when you have a print copy of a picture, rather than a digital file stored on your system, it sometimes is necessary to scan the picture using a scanner. A **scanner** is a device used to convert a hard copy into a digital form for storage, retrieval, or other electronic purposes. Photoshop allows you to bring a copy from the scanner directly into the workspace.

Figure 1–14

Other Ways

1. Press CTRL+O, select file, click Open

2. In Windows, right-click file, click Open with, click Adobe Photoshop CS5

The Photoshop Workspace

The Photoshop workspace consists of a variety of components to make your work more efficient and to make your photo documents look more professional. The following sections discuss these components.

The Application Bar

The Application bar appears at the top of the workspace (Figure 1–15). The Application bar contains the Launch Bridge button, the Launch Mini Bridge button, and commonly used controls related to document and workspace manipulation. On the right side of the Application bar are the CS Live button and common window clip controls. Your Application bar might contain different controls depending on the chosen saved workspace.

BTW

Panels vs. Palettes
In previous versions of the Adobe Creative Suite, the panels were called palettes. In all of the CS5 applications, panels can be grouped, stacked, or docked in the workspace, just as palettes were.

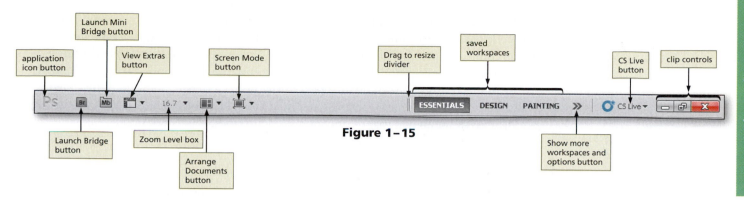

Figure 1–15

The Menu Bar

The menu bar appears at the top of the screen just below the Application bar (Figure 1–16). The **menu bar** is a toolbar that displays the Photoshop menu names. Each **menu** contains a list of commands you can use to perform tasks such as opening, saving, printing, and editing photos. To display a menu, such as the View menu, click the View menu name on the menu bar. If you point to a command on a menu that has an arrow on its right edge, as shown in Figure 1–16, a **submenu**, or secondary menu, displays another list of commands.

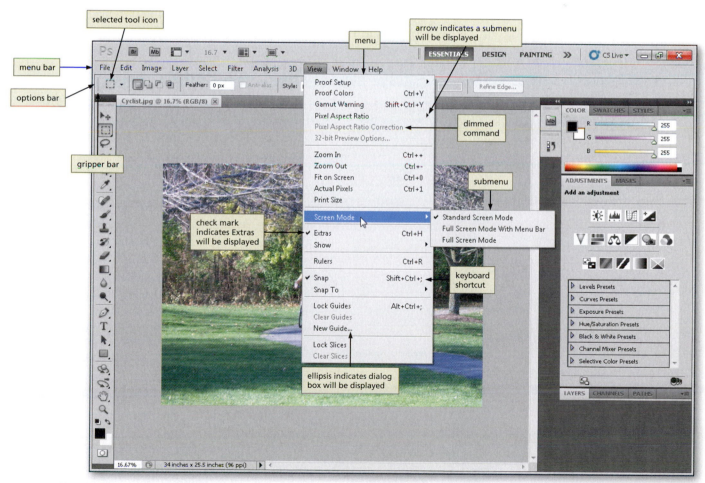

Figure 1–16

When Photoshop first is installed, all of the menu commands within a menu appear when you click the menu name. To hide seldom-used menu commands, you can click the Menus command on the Edit menu and follow the on-screen instructions. A **hidden command** does not immediately appear on a menu. If menu commands have been hidden, a Show All Menu Items command will appear at the bottom of the menu list. Click the Show All Menu Items command, or press and hold the CTRL key when you click the menu name to display all menu commands, including hidden ones.

The Options Bar

The options bar (Figure 1–16 on the previous page) appears below the menu bar. Sometimes called the Control panel, the options bar contains buttons and boxes that allow you to perform tasks more quickly than when using the menu bar and related menus. Most buttons on the options bar display words or images to help you remember their functions. When you point to a button or box on the options bar, a tool tip is displayed below the mouse pointer. The options bar changes to reflect the tool currently selected on the Tools panel. For example, a tool related to text might display a font box on the options bar, whereas a tool related to painting will display a brush button. The selected tool always appears as an icon on the left side of the options bar. As each tool is discussed throughout this book, the associated options bar will be explained in more detail.

You can **float**, or move, the options bar in the workspace by dragging the gray **gripper bar** on the left side of the options bar. You can **dock** or reattach the options bar below the menu bar by resetting the workspace. To hide or show the options bar, click Options on the Window menu.

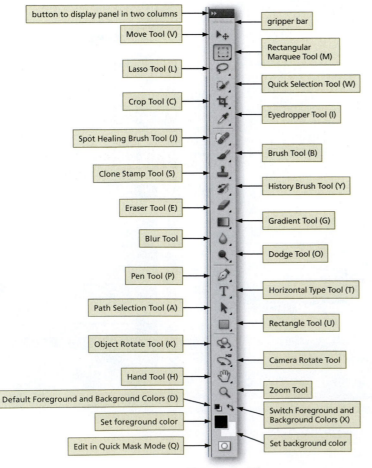

Figure 1–17

The Tools Panel

On the left side of the workspace is the Photoshop Tools panel. The Tools panel is a group of **tools**, or buttons, organized into a toolbar. Like the options bar, you can float, dock, hide, or show the Tools panel. Each tool on the Tools panel displays a **tool icon**. When you point to the tool icon, a tool tip displays the name of the tool including its shortcut key. You can expand some tools to show hidden tools beneath them. Expandable tools display a small triangle in the lower-right corner of the tool icon. Click and hold the tool button or right-click to see or select one of its hidden tools from the context menu. The default tool names and their corresponding shortcut keys are listed in Figure 1–17.

When you click a tool on the Tools panel to use it, Photoshop selects the button and changes the options bar as necessary. When using a tool from the Tools panel, the mouse pointer changes to reflect the selected tool.

The Tools panel is organized by purpose. At the very top of the panel is a button to display the panel in two columns, followed underneath by the gripper bar. Below that, the selection tools appear, then the crop and slice tools, followed by retouching, painting, drawing and type, annotation, measuring, and navigation tools. At the bottom of the Tools panel are buttons to set colors and create a quick mask. As each tool is introduced throughout this book, its function and options bar characteristics will be explained further.

The Document Window

The **document window** is the light gray area within the workspace that displays the active file or image. The document window contains a title bar, display area, scroll bars, and status bar (Figure 1–18).

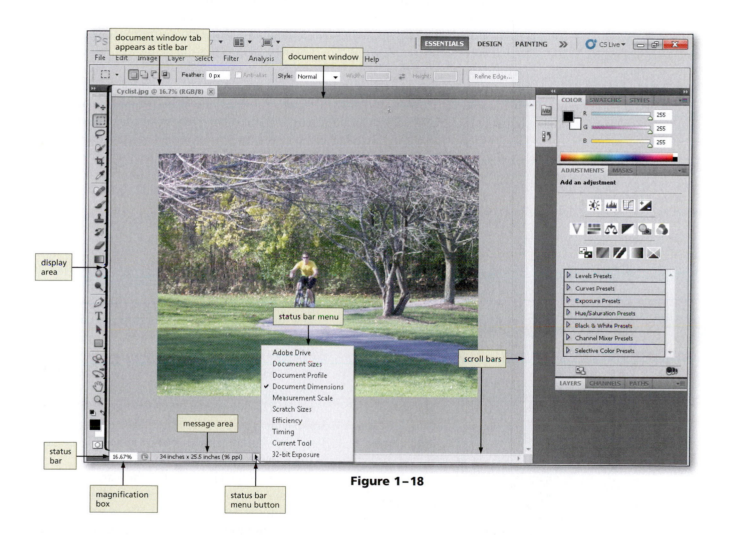

Figure 1–18

Title Bar Photoshop displays a **title bar**, or **document window tab**, at the top of the document window that shows the name of the file, the magnification, the color mode, and a Close button. If you have multiple files open, each has its own document window tab. You can move the document window by dragging the document window tab, or dock it again by dragging the title bar close to the options bar. When floating, the title bar expands across the top of the document window and displays Minimize, Restore Down, and Close buttons.

Display Area The **display area** (Figure 1–18 on the previous page) is the portion of the document window that displays the photo or image. You perform most tool tasks and edit the photo in the display area.

Scroll Bars **Scroll bars** appear on the right and bottom of the document window. When the photo is bigger than the document window, the scroll bars become active and display scroll arrows and scroll boxes to move the image up, down, left, and right.

Status Bar Across the bottom of the document window, Photoshop displays the **status bar**. The status bar contains a magnification box. **Magnification** refers to the percentage of enlargement or reduction on the screen. For example, a 50% indication in the magnification box means the entire photo is displayed at 50 percent of its actual size. Changing the magnification does not change the size of the photo physically; it merely displays it on the screen at a different size. You can type a new percentage in the magnification box to display a different view of the photo.

Next to the magnification box is the **message area**. Messages can display information about the file size, the current tool, or the document dimensions. When you first start Photoshop, the message area displays information about the document size in storage.

On the right side of the status bar is the status bar menu button that, when clicked, displays a status bar menu. You use the status bar menu to change the message area or to change to other versions of the document.

Your installation of Photoshop might display rulers at the top and left of the document window. You will learn about rulers later in this chapter.

BTW

Status Bar
The status bar may display different messages, depending upon your previous settings, the previous kind of file you had open, and your installation. If you want your status bar to match the figures in this chapter, click the status bar menu and then click Document Dimensions.

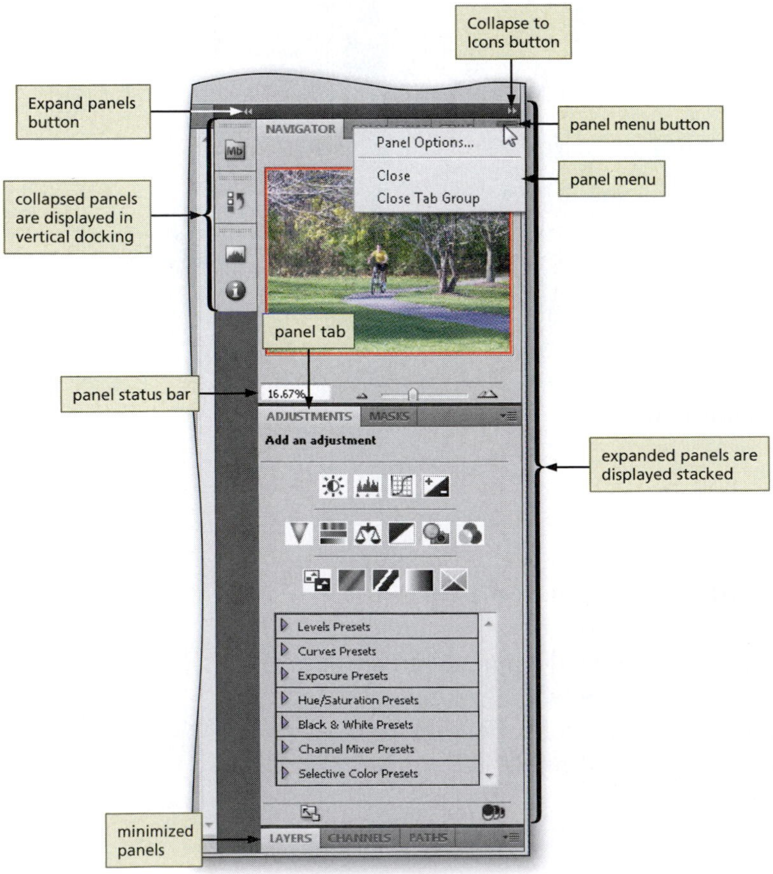

Figure 1–19

Panels

A **panel** is a collection of graphically displayed choices and commands, such as those involving colors, brushes, actions, or layers (Figure 1–19). Panels help you monitor and modify your work. Each panel displays a panel tab with the name of the panel and a panel menu button. When you click the panel menu button, also called the panel menu icon, Photoshop displays a context-sensitive menu that allows you to make changes to the panel. Some panels have a status bar across the bottom. A panel can display buttons, boxes, sliders, scroll bars, or drop-down lists.

Several panels appear in the Essentials workspace. Some panels are expanded to display their contents, and are grouped by general purpose. A **panel group** or **tab group** displays several panels horizontally. The panel group is docked vertically on the right side of the workspace. Two other panels are displayed as icons or buttons in a vertical docking between the document window and the expanded panels. Panels are **collapsed** when they appear as a button or **expanded** when they display their contents. Panels are **minimized** when they display only their tab. To collapse or expand a panel, click the double arrow in the panel title bar. To minimize a panel, double-click its tab. To close a panel, click Close on the panel menu. To redisplay the panel, click the panel name on the Window menu or use a panel shortcut key.

You can arrange and reposition panels either individually or in groups. To move them individually, drag their tabs; to move a group, drag the area to the right of the tabs. To float a panel in the workspace, drag its tab outside of the vertical docking. You can create a **stack** of floating panels by dragging a panel tab to a location below another floating panel and docking it.

Sometimes you might want to hide all the panels to display more of the document window. To hide all panels, press the TAB key. Press the TAB key again to display the panels.

Photoshop comes with 26 panels, described in Table 1–1. As each panel is introduced throughout this book, its function and characteristics will be explained further.

Table 1–1 Photoshop Panels	
Panel Name	**Purpose**
3D	to show the 3D layer components, settings, and options of the associated 3D file — available in Photoshop Extended only
Actions	to record, play, edit, and delete individual actions
Adjustments	to create nondestructive adjustment layers with color and tonal adjustments
Animation	to create a sequence of images or frames, displayed as motion over time
Brush	to select preset brushes and design custom brushes
Brush Presets	to create, load, save, and manage preset brush tips
Channels	to create and manage channels
Character	to provide options for formatting characters
Clone Source	to set up and manipulate sample sources for the Clone Stamp tools or Healing Brush tools
Color	to display the color values for the current foreground and background colors
Histogram	to view tonal and color information about an image
History	to jump to any recent state of the image created during the current working session
Info	to display color values and document status information
Layer Comps	to display multiple compositions of a page layout
Layers	to show and hide layers, create new layers, and work with groups of layers
Masks	to create precise, editable pixel- and vector-based masks
Mini Bridge	to assist in navigating folders and files, and to access other modules in the suite
Measurement Log	to record measurement data about a measured object — available in Photoshop Extended only
Navigator	to change the view or magnification of the photo using a thumbnail display
Notes	to insert, edit, and delete notes attached to files
Paragraph	to change the formatting of columns and paragraphs
Paths	to manipulate each saved path, the current work path, and the current vector mask
Styles	to view and select preset styles
Swatches	to select and store colors that you need to use often
Tools	to select tools
Tool Presets	to save and reuse tool settings

BTW

File Extensions
The default setting for file extensions in Photoshop is to use a lowercase three-letter extension. If you want to change the extension, do the following: Press SHIFT+CTRL+S to access the Save As dialog box. In the File name text box, type the file name, period, and extension within quotation marks. Click the Save button.

BTW

Saving Photos
When you save a photo on a storage device, it also remains in main memory and is displayed on the screen.

File Types

A **file type** refers to the internal characteristics of digital files; it designates the operational or structural characteristics of a file. Each digital file, graphic or otherwise, is stored with specific kinds of formatting related to how the file appears on the screen, how it prints, and the software it uses to do so. Computer systems use the file type to help users open the file with the appropriate software. A **file extension**, in most computer systems, is a three- or four-letter suffix after the file name that distinguishes the file type. For example, Cyclist.jpg refers to a file named Cyclist with the extension and file type JPG. A period separates the file name and its extension. When you are exploring files on your system, you might see the file extensions as part of the file name, or you might see a column of information about file types.

Graphic files are created using many different file types and extensions. The type of file sometimes is determined by the hardware or software used to create the file. Other times, the user has a choice in applying a file type and makes the decision based on file size, the intended purpose of the file — such as whether the file is to be used on the Web — or the desired color mode. A few common graphic file types are listed in Table 1–2.

BTW

File Name Characters
A file name can have a maximum of 260 characters, including spaces. The only invalid characters are the backslash (\), slash (/), colon (:), asterisk (*), question mark (?), quotation mark ("), less than symbol (<), greater than symbol (>), and vertical bar (|).

Table 1–2 Graphic File Types

File Extension	File Type	Description
BMP	Bitmap	BMP is a standard Windows image format used on DOS and Windows-compatible computers. BMP format supports many different color modes.
EPS	Encapsulated PostScript	EPS files can contain both bitmap and vector graphics. Most graphics, illustrations, and page-layout programs support the EPS format, which can be used to transfer PostScript artwork between applications.
GIF	Graphics Interchange Format	GIF commonly is used to display graphics and images on Web pages. It is a compressed format designed to minimize file size and electronic transfer time.
JPG or JPEG	Joint Photographic Experts Group	JPG files commonly are used to display photographs on Web pages. JPG format supports many different color modes. JPG retains all color information in an RGB image, unlike GIF format. Most digital cameras produce JPG files.
PDF	Portable Document Format	PDF is a flexible file format based on the PostScript imaging model that is cross-platform and cross-application. PDF files accurately display and preserve fonts, page layouts, and graphics. PDF files can contain electronic document search and navigation features such as hyperlinks.
PNG	Portable Network Graphics	PNG graphics display images without jagged edges, while keeping the file size small. The PNG format is used for clip art, Web graphics, and when graphics need to display transparent backgrounds rather than white.
PSD	Photoshop Document	PSD format is the default file format in Photoshop and the only format that supports all Photoshop features. Other Adobe applications can import PSD files directly and preserve many Photoshop features due to the tight integration among Adobe products.
RAW	Photoshop Raw	RAW format is a flexible file format used for transferring images between applications and computer platforms. There are no pixel or file size restrictions in this format. Documents saved in the Photoshop Raw format cannot contain layers.
TIF or TIFF	Tagged Image File Format	TIF is a flexible bitmap image format supported by almost all paint, image-editing, and page-layout applications. This format often is used for files that are to be exchanged between applications or computer platforms. Most desktop scanners can produce TIF images.

Saving a Photo

As you make changes to a file in Photoshop, the computer stores it in memory. If you turn off the computer or if you lose electrical power, the file in memory is lost. If you plan to use the photo later, you must save it on a storage device such as a USB flash drive or on your hard drive.

While you are editing, to preserve the most features such as layers, effects, masks, and styles, Photoshop recommends that you save photos in the **PSD format**. PSD, which stands for Photoshop Document Format, is the default file format for files created from scratch in Photoshop, and supports files up to two gigabytes (GB) in size. The PSD format also maximizes portability among other Adobe versions and applications.

To Save a Photo in the PSD Format

The following steps save the photo on a USB flash drive using the file name, Cyclist Edited. In addition to saving in the PSD format, you will save the photo with a new file name and in a new location, so that the original photo is preserved in case you need to start again. Even though you have yet to edit the photo, it is a good practice to save a copy of the file on your personal storage device early in the process.

1

- With a USB flash drive connected to one of the computer's USB ports, click File on the menu bar to display the File menu (Figure 1–20).

Q&A Do I have to save to a USB flash drive?

No. You can save to any device or folder. A **folder** is a specific location on a storage medium. You can save to the default folder or a different folder.

Q&A What if my USB flash drive has a different name or letter?

It is very likely that your USB flash drive will have a different name and drive letter and be connected to a different port. Verify that the device in your Computer list is correct.

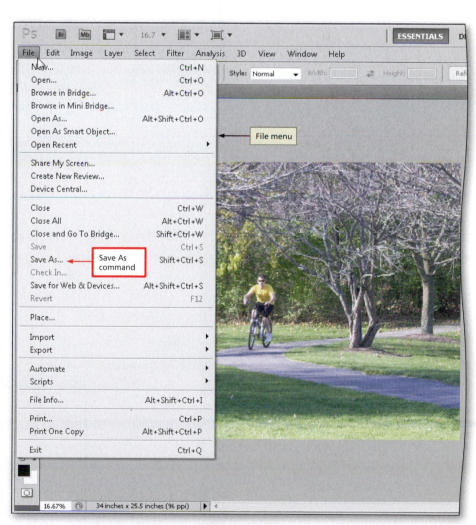

Figure 1–20

2

- Click Save As to display the Save As dialog box.

- Type **Cyclist Edited** in the File name text box (Save As dialog box) to change the file name. Do not press the ENTER key after typing the file name.

- Click the Save in box arrow to display the list of available drives (Figure 1–21).

Q&A Do I have to use that file name?

It is good practice to identify the relationship of this photo to the original by using at least part of the original file name with some notation about its status.

Q&A Why is my list of drives arranged and named differently?

The size of the Save As dialog box and your computer's configuration determine how the list is displayed and how the drives are named.

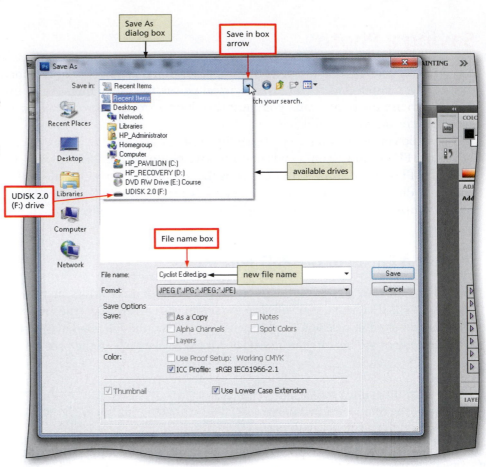

Figure 1–21

3

- Click UDISK 2.0 (F:), or the name of your USB flash drive, in the list of available storage devices to select that drive as the new save location.

- Click the Format button (Save As dialog box) to display the list of available file formats (Figure 1–22).

Q&A Should I make a special folder for my photos?

You might want to create a folder for each chapter in this book. If so, click the Create New Folder button in the Save As dialog box. When the new folder is displayed, type a chapter name such as **Chapter 01** and then press the ENTER key. Double-click the new folder to open it.

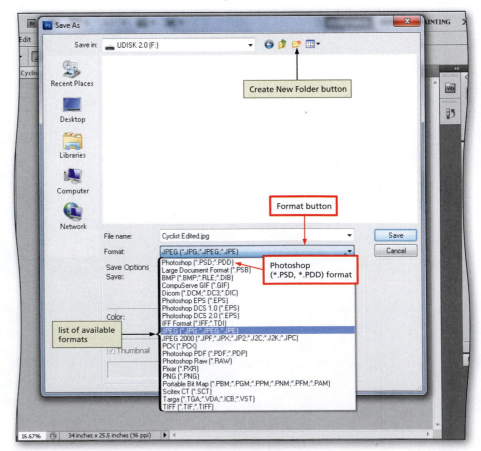

Figure 1–22

4
- Click Photoshop (*.PSD, *.PDD) to select it (Figure 1–23).

Q&A What is PDD?

The **PDD format** is used with images created by Photo Deluxe and other software packages. Some older digital cameras produce files with a PDD extension as well.

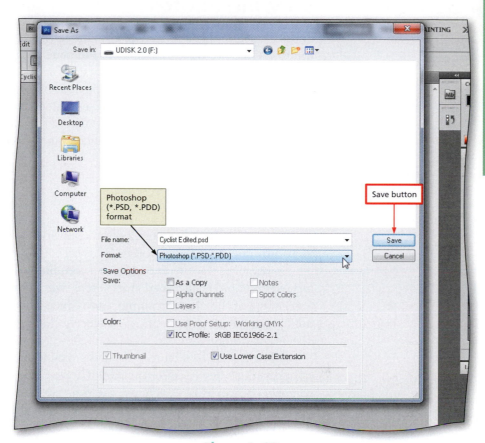

Figure 1–23

5
- Click the Save button (Save As dialog box) to save the document on the selected drive with the new file name (Figure 1–24).

Q&A How do I know that the project is saved?

While Photoshop is saving your file, it briefly displays a Working in Background mouse pointer. In addition, your USB drive might have a light that flashes during the save process. The new file name appears on the document window tab.

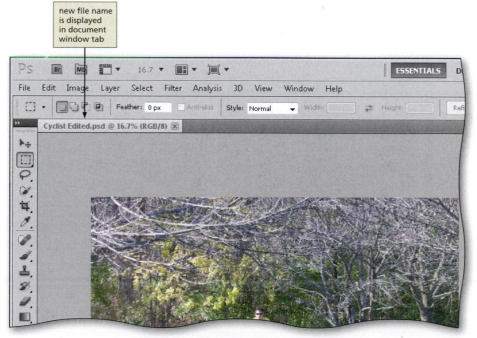

Figure 1–24

Other Ways

1. Press SHIFT+CTRL+S, choose settings, click Save button

Viewing Photos

Photoshop allows you to view photos in many different ways, by adjusting the document window and by using different tools and panels. Using good navigation techniques to view images can help you edit the details of a photo or check for problems. For example, you might want to zoom in on a specific portion of the photo or move to a different location in a large photo. You might want to use a ruler to measure certain portions of the photo. Or you might want to view the image without the distraction of the panels and menu. Zooming, navigating, scrolling, and changing the screen mode are some ways to view the document window and its photo.

Zooming

To make careful edits in a photo, you sometimes need to change the magnification, or **zoom**. Zooming allows you to focus on certain parts of the photo, such as a specific person in a crowd scene or details in a complicated picture. A magnification of 100% means the photo is displayed at its actual size. Zooming in enlarges the magnification and percentage of the photo; zooming out reduces the magnification. Note that zooming does not change the size of the photo; it merely changes the appearance of the photo in the document window.

The Zoom Tool button displays a magnifying glass icon on the Tools panel. You also can press the z key to select the Zoom Tool. Choosing one over the other is a matter of personal choice. Most people use the shortcut key. Others sometimes choose the button because of its proximity to the mouse pointer at the time.

When you use the Zoom Tool, each click magnifies the image to the next preset percentage. When positioned in the photo, the Zoom Tool mouse pointer displays a magnifying glass, with either a plus sign, indicating an increase in magnification, or a minus sign, indicating a decrease in magnification. Right-clicking with the Zoom Tool in the photo displays a context menu with options to zoom in or zoom out, among others.

Figure 1–25 displays the Zoom Tool options bar, with buttons to zoom in and out. Other options include check boxes used when working with multiple photos, displaying the actual pixels, fitting the entire photo on the screen, filling the screen, and displaying the photo at its print size.

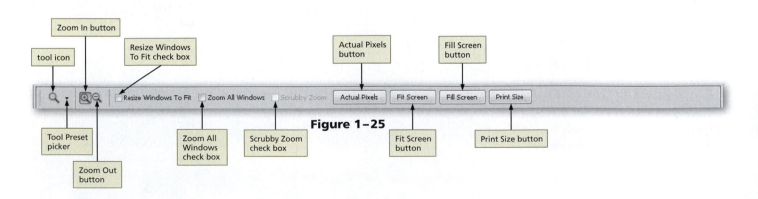

Figure 1–25

To Use the Zoom Tool

The following steps zoom in on the cyclist for careful editing later in the chapter.

1
- Click the Zoom Tool button on the Tools panel to select the Zoom tool.

- Move the mouse pointer into the document window to display the magnifying glass mouse pointer (Figure 1–26).

Q&A

Why does my mouse pointer display a minus sign?

Someone may have previously zoomed out and the setting has carried over. Click the Zoom In button on the options bar.

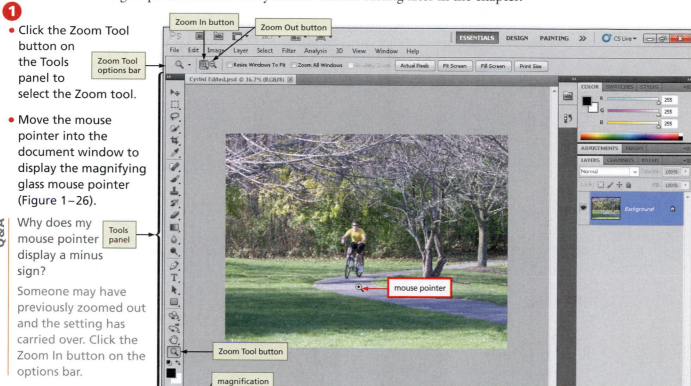

Figure 1–26

2
- Click the cyclist three times to zoom in (Figure 1–27).

🔎 **Experiment**

- On the options bar, click the Zoom Out button and then click the photo. ALT+click the photo to zoom in the opposite direction from the options bar setting. Zoom to 50% magnification.

Other Ways

1. Press Z, click document window
2. Press CTRL+PLUS SIGN (+) or CTRL+MINUS SIGN (–)
3. On View menu, click Zoom In or Zoom Out

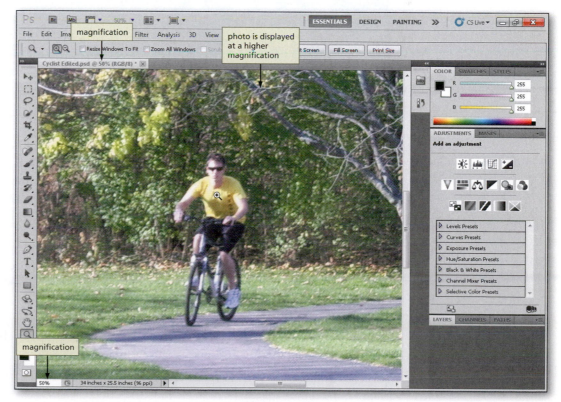

Figure 1–27

The Navigator Panel

Another convenient way to zoom and move around the photo is to use the Navigator panel. The Navigator panel (Figure 1–28) is used to change the view of your document window using a thumbnail display. To display the Navigator panel, choose Navigator from the Window menu.

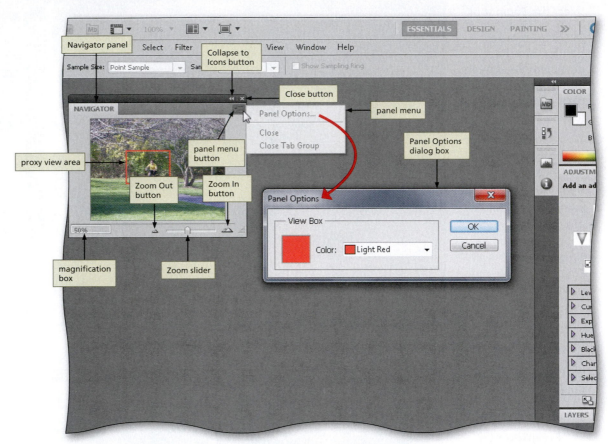

Figure 1–28

The rectangle with the red border in the Navigator panel is called the **proxy view area** or **view box**, which outlines the currently viewable area in the window. Dragging the proxy view area changes the portion of the photo that is displayed in the document window. In the lower portion of the Navigator panel, you can type in the desired magnification, or you can use the slider or buttons to increase or decrease the magnification.

In Figure 1–28, the Navigator panel menu appears when you click the panel menu button. The Panel Options command displays the Panel Options dialog box.

To move the panel, drag the panel tab. To collapse the panel, click the Collapse to Icons button. To close the panel, click the panel's Close button or click Close on the panel menu.

When you are using a different tool on the Tools panel, such as a text tool or brush tool, it is easier to use the Navigator panel to zoom in or out and move around in the photo. That way, you do not have to change to the Zoom tool, perform the zoom, and then change back to your editing tool.

To Open the Navigator Panel

The following steps open the Navigator panel.

1
• Click Window on the menu bar to display the Window menu (Figure 1–29).

Q&A

What do the check marks mean?

Each panel with a check mark already is displayed and expanded in the workspace.

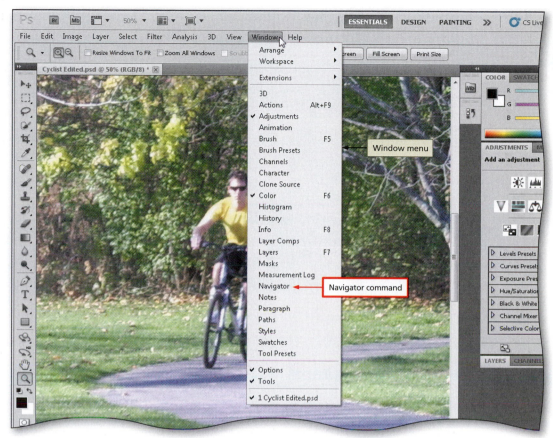

Figure 1–29

2
• Click Navigator on the Window menu to open the Navigator panel (Figure 1–30).

Q&A

Why does the Navigator panel extend into the document window?

Panels that are not part of the current workspace appear in the vertical panel docking. When displayed, they expand to the left.

Figure 1–30

To Use the Navigator Panel

The following step repositions the view of the photo using the proxy view area.

- Drag the proxy view area on the Navigator Panel to display the lower-right portion of the photo (Figure 1–31).

 Experiment

- Drag the proxy view area to display different portions of the photo, and then drag to display the lower-right portion of the photo.

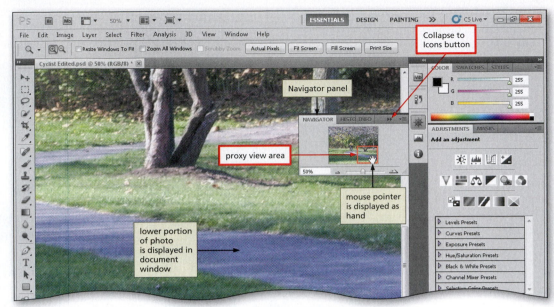

Figure 1–31

To Collapse the Navigator Panel

The following step collapses the Navigator panel.

1

- Click the Collapse to Icons button (shown in Figure 1–31) on the Navigator panel title bar to collapse the Navigator panel (Figure 1–32).

Q&A

How would I close the Navigator panel completely?

Click the panel menu button and then click Close on the panel menu.

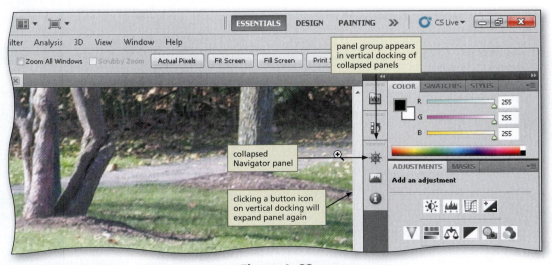

Figure 1–32

The Hand Tool

The Hand tool also can be used to move around in the photo if the photo has been magnified to be larger than the document window. To use the Hand tool, click the Hand Tool (H) button on the Tools panel, and then drag in the display area of the document window.

The Hand Tool options bar (Figure 1–33) displays boxes and buttons to assist you in scrolling and manipulating the document window.

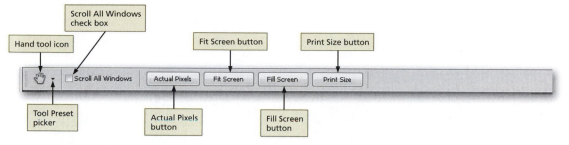

Figure 1–33

To Use the Hand Tool

The following step uses the Hand Tool to view a different part of the photo.

1

• Click the Hand Tool button on the Tools panel to select the Hand Tool.

• Drag in the document window to display the center portion of the photo (Figure 1–34).

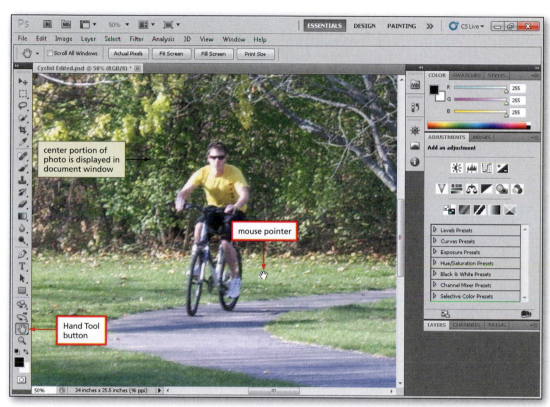

Figure 1–34

Other Ways

1. Press H, drag photo

To Change the Magnification

The following steps use the magnification box on the status bar to change the magnification.

1

• Double-click the magnification box on the status bar to select the current magnification (Figure 1–35).

Figure 1–35

2

• Type 20 and then press the ENTER key to change the magnification (Figure 1–36).

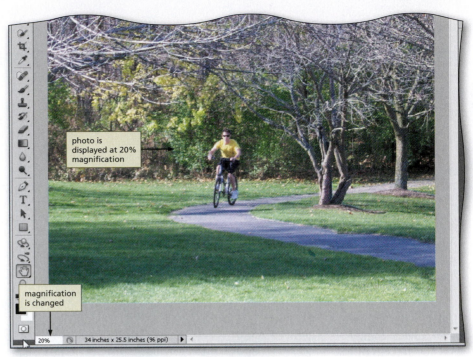

Figure 1–36

Other Ways

1. On Navigator panel, type percentage in magnification box

2. On Application bar, type percentage in magnification box

3. On Application bar, click Zoom Level box arrow, click desired percentage

To Change the Screen Mode

To change the way the panels, bars, and document window appear, Photoshop includes three **screen modes**, or ways to view the document window. **Standard screen mode** displays the Application bar, menu bar, options bar, document window, scroll bars, and visible panels. **Full screen mode** displays only the image and rulers, if they are visible, on a black background. **Full screen mode with menu** enlarges the document window to fill the workspace and combines the Application bar and menu bar with no status bar or scroll bars. A fourth way to view the screen is to hide the panels.

The following steps view the document window in different modes.

1

• On the Application bar, click the Screen Mode button to display its menu (Figure 1–37).

Q&A

Which mode is best?

It depends on what you are trying to accomplish. While editing a single photo, standard screen mode may be the best, especially for beginners. If you are working on multiple files, screen space is at a premium and you might want to use one of the full screen modes.

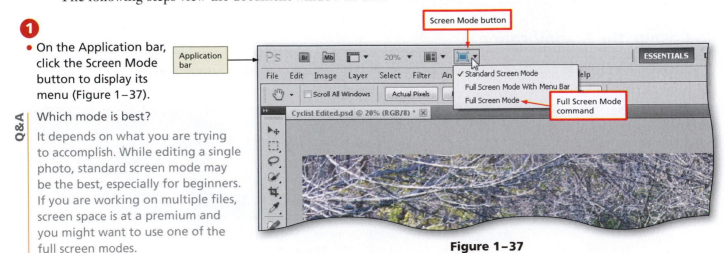

Figure 1–37

2

- Click Full Screen Mode to display the Message dialog box (Figure 1–38).

What does the 'Don't show again' check box do?

If you check this box, Photoshop will not display the Message dialog box the next time you select Full Screen Mode. Until you are familiar with how to manipulate the screen modes, you should not check this box. The message is a good reminder while you are learning.

Figure 1–38

3

- Click the Full Screen button (Message dialog box) to view the document in full screen mode (Figure 1–39).

- Press the F key to exit full screen mode.

 **Experiment**

- Press the TAB key to hide the panels. Press the TAB key again to display the panels.

Figure 1–39

Other Ways
1. On View menu, point to Screen Mode, click desired mode

To Display Rulers

To make careful edits in a photo, sometimes it is necessary to use precise measurements in addition to zooming and navigating. In these cases, it is necessary to change the Photoshop document window to view the rulers. **Rulers** appear on the top and left sides of the document window. Rulers help you position images or elements precisely. As you move your mouse pointer over a photo, markers on the ruler display the mouse pointer's position.

The following steps display the rulers in the document window.

• On the Application bar, click the View Extras button to display its menu (Figure 1–40).

Q&A What are the other extras?

Guides are individual, nonprinting straight lines that you can drag from the rulers. Grids are a checkerboard of nonprinting straights lines that float above the photo. Both guides and grids help you position and align objects in the photo.

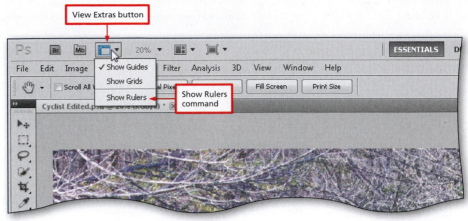

Figure 1–40

• Click Show Rulers to display the rulers in the document window. If the ruler does not display inches, right-click the ruler and then click Inches (Figure 1–41).

Q&A What unit of measurement do the rulers use?

Rulers display inches by default, but you can right-click a ruler to change the increment to pixels, centimeters, or other measurements.

Q&A Is the photo really 34 × 25 inches?

The resolution from photos taken with digital cameras is measured in **megapixels** or millions of pixels. The more megapixels you have, the better the photo resolution; however, it translates to very large print sizes. You will resize the photo later in the chapter.

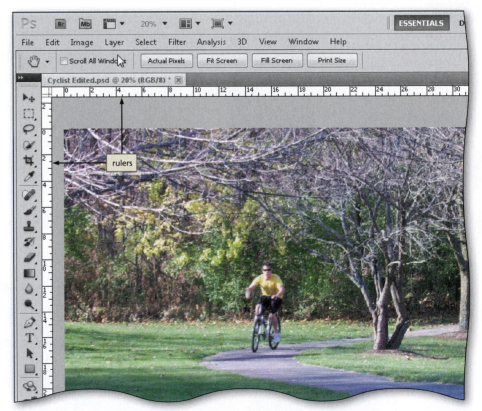

Figure 1–41

Other Ways

1. Press CTRL+R
2. On View menu, click Rulers

Editing the Photo

Editing, or making corrections and changes to a photo, involves a wide variety of tasks such as changing the focus of interest, recoloring portions of the photo, correcting defects, adding new artwork, or changing the file type for specific purposes. Editing also is called **post-processing**, because it includes actions you take after the picture has been processed by the camera or scanner.

Table 1–3 suggests typical categories and types of edits you might perform on photos; there are many others. These edits commonly overlap; and, when performed in combination, they even can create new editing varieties. You will learn more about edits as you work through the chapters in this book.

Table 1–3 Photo Edits	
Category	**Types of Edits**
Transformations	cropping, slicing, changing the aspect, rotating, leveling, mirroring, warping, skewing, distorting, flipping, and changing the perspective
Enhancements and Layering	filtering, layering, cloning, adding borders and artwork, adding text, animating, painting, morphing, ordering, applying styles, masking, creating cutaways, selecting, adding depth perception, anti-aliasing, moving, adding shapes, rasterizing
Color	correcting, contrasting, blending, using modes and systems, using separations, screening, adjusting levels, ruling, trapping, matching, adjusting black and white
Correction	sharpening, fixing red-eye, fixing tears, correcting distortion, retouching, reducing noise, applying a blur, dodging, burning
File Type	camera raw, print, Web, animated images
Resolution	resampling, resizing, collinear editing, interpolating, editing pixel dimensions and document sizes

Editing the Cyclist Edited photo will involve three steps. First, you will crop the photo to remove excessive background. Next, you will add a border and fill it with color. Finally, you will resize the photo to fit the intended use and size requirements.

Determine how to edit the photo to highlight the theme.
You always should perform editing with design principles in mind. Look at your photo carefully. Are there parts that detract from the central figure? Would the theme be illustrated better by only displaying a portion of the photo? If you want to emphasize a single object on a fairly solid background, you might need to crop, or trim, extraneous space around the object. Decide which parts of the photo portray your message and which parts are visual clutter.

- Use the rule of thirds to position visual lines.
- Crop the photo to remove excess border.
- Rotate the photo if necessary.

Plan Ahead

Cropping

The first step in editing the cyclist photo is to **crop**, or cut away, some of the extra grass and visual clutter so the photo focuses on the cyclist. Photographers try to compose and capture images full-frame, which means the object of interest fills the dimensions of the photo. When that is not possible, photographers and graphic artists crop the photo either to create an illusion of full-frame, to fit unusual shapes in layouts, or to make the image more dramatic. From a design point of view, sometimes it is necessary to crop a photo to straighten an image, remove distracting elements, or simplify the subject. The goal of most cropping is to make the most important feature in the original photo stand out. Cropping sometimes is used to convert a digital photo's proportions to those typical for traditional photos.

Most photographers and graphic artists use the **rule of thirds**, also called the principle of thirds, when placing the focus of interest. Imagine that the scene is divided into thirds both vertically and horizontally. The intersections of these imaginary lines suggest four positions for placing the focus of interest. The position you select depends on the subject and its presentation in the photo. For instance, there might be a shadow, path, or visual line you wish to include. In the case of moving objects, you generally should leave space in front of them, into which they theoretically can move. When eyes are involved, it is better to leave space on the side toward which the person or animal is looking, so they do not appear to look directly out of the setting.

Because the cyclist photo will be used on a rack card, the photo's orientation should be **landscape**, or horizontal. In most cases, you should try to crop to a rectangular shape with an approximate short-side to long-side ratio of 5:8. Sometimes called the **golden rectangle**, a 5:8 ratio emulates natural geometric forms such as flowers, leaves, shells, and butterflies. Most digital cameras take pictures with a similar ratio.

The Crop Tool allows you to select the portion of the photo you wish to retain. Photoshop automatically displays handles and a rule of thirds overlay for further adjustments, if necessary. Then, when you press the ENTER key, the rest of the photo is cropped.

The Crop options bar displays boxes and buttons to assist cropping activities (Figure 1–42a). You can specify the exact height and width of the crop, as well as the resampling resolution which you will learn about later in the chapter. The Front Image button allows you to crop using the dimensions of another photo. Once you begin working with the Crop Tool, the options bar changes to include choices about the background display, crop guide overlay, color of the cropped area, and the ability to change the perspective while cropping (Figure 1–42b).

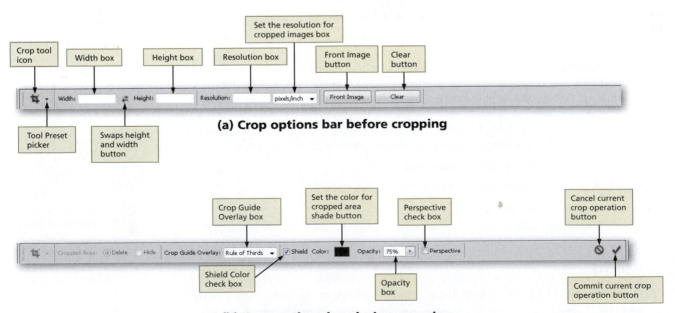

(a) Crop options bar before cropping

(b) Crop options bar during cropping

Figure 1–42

To Crop a Photo

To make the cyclist the focus of the photo, the extra background will be cropped to provide a line of sight to the right, keeping as much of the bike path as possible. The following steps crop the photo of the cyclist.

1

• Click the Crop Tool button on the Tools panel to select the Crop Tool (Figure 1–43).

Q&A Can I force the crop tool to use a 5:8 ratio?

Yes, on the options bar, you can enter 8 in the Width box and 5 in the Height box.

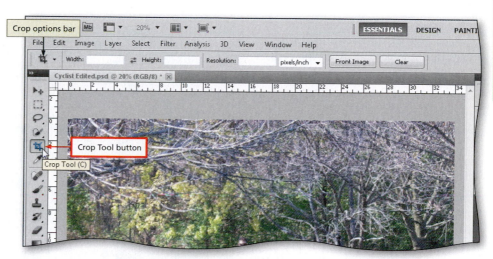

Figure 1–43

2

• Using the rulers as guides, drag a rectangle beginning 10 inches from the left side and 8 inches from the top. Drag down and to the right to include as much of the bike path as possible (Figure 1–44).

Q&A What if I change my mind or make a mistake when cropping?

If you make a mistake while dragging the cropping area and want to start over, you can click the 'Cancel current crop operation' button (Figure 1–42b) or press the ESC key, which cancels the selection. If you already have performed the crop and then change your mind, you have several choices. You can click the Undo command on the Edit menu, or you can press CTRL+Z to undo the last edit.

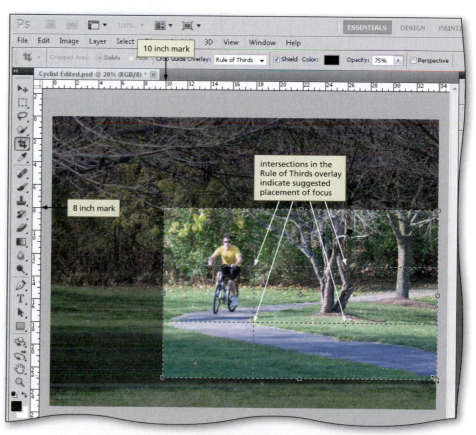

Figure 1–44

Other Ways

1. Press C, drag in photo

2. Select portion of image, on Image menu, click Crop

3. To crop, right-click cropping selection, click Crop on context menu

To Position the Rule of Thirds Overlay

The following steps move the crop selection to position the cyclist at the top-left intersection using the rule of thirds.

1

• Drag the upper-left intersection in the Rule of Thirds overlay to position it in the center of the cyclist (Figure 1–45).

Q&A
Can I turn off the rule of thirds overlay?

Yes, click the Crop Guide Overlay box arrow to display its list, and then click None.

Figure 1–45

**2**

• Press the ENTER key to complete the crop (Figure 1–46).

🔍 **Experiment**

• If you want to practice cropping, drag again. Press the SHIFT key while you crop to a perfect square. After each crop, press CTRL+Z to undo the crop.

Figure 1–46

Other Ways

1. Drag Rule of Thirds grid, click Commit current crop operation button

Break Point: If you wish to take a break, this is a good place to do so. You can quit Photoshop now. To resume at a later time, start Photoshop, open the file called Room Edited, and continue following the steps from this location forward.

Creating a Border

A **border** is a decorative edge on a photo or a portion of a photo. Photoshop provides many ways to create a border, ranging from simple color transformations around the edge of the photo, to predefined decorated layers, to stylized photo frames.

A border helps define the edge of the photo, especially when the photo might be placed on colored paper or on a Web page with a background texture. A border visually separates the photo from the rest of the page, while focusing the viewer's attention. Rounded borders soften the images in a photo. Square borders are more formal. Decorative borders on a static photo can add interest and amusement, but easily can detract from the focus on a busier photo. **Blended borders** are not a solid fill; rather, they blend a fill color from the outer edge toward the middle, sometimes providing a three-dimensional effect. A border that complements the photo in style, color, and juxtaposition is best. In the cyclist photo, you will create a border using selections of 100 black pixels with 50 pixels of overlapping white. A **pixel** is an individual dot of light that is the basic unit used to create digital images.

BTW

Reviewing Your Edits
Each edit or state of the photo is recorded sequentially in the History panel. If you want to step back through the edits or go back to a particular state, such as the previous crop, click the state in the History panel. You will learn more about the History panel in a future chapter.

Identify finishing touches that will further enhance the photo.
Adding a border or decorative frame around a photo sometimes can be an effective way to highlight or make the photo stand out on the page. A border should frame the subject, rather than become the subject. If a border is required by the customer or needed for layout placement, choose a color and width that neither overwhelms nor overlaps any detail in the photo. Using a border color that complements one of the colors already in the photo creates a strong, visually connected image. For more information about graphic design concepts, read Appendix B.

Plan Ahead

To Create a Selection

Specifying or isolating an area of your photo for editing is called making a **selection**. By selecting specific areas, you can edit and apply special effects to portions of your image while leaving the unselected areas untouched.

Selections can be simple shapes such as rectangles or ovals, or unusually shaped areas of a photo, outlining specific objects. Selections can be the entire photo or as small a portion as one pixel. A selection displays a marquee in Photoshop. A **marquee** is a flashing or pulsating border, sometimes called marching ants.

In the case of the Cyclist Edited photo, you will make a selection around the edge of the photo in order to create a border. The following steps select the photo.

1
• On the menu bar, click Select to display the Select menu (Figure 1–47).

Figure 1–47

2

● On the Select menu, click All to display the selection marquee around all of the photo (Figure 1–48).

Q&A

Am I selecting all of the photo itself?

You are identifying the pixels along the edge of the image. Some commands apply to all of the pixels within the selection border, such as copying, deleting, or filling; other commands, such as stroking, apply only to the pixels along the edge of the selection.

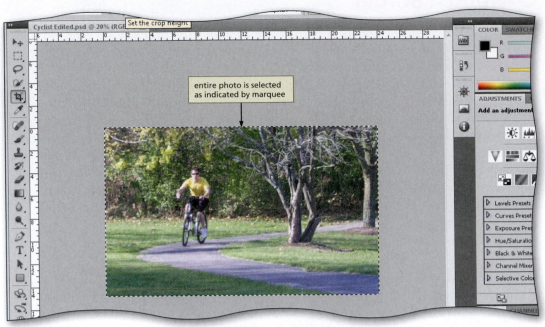

Figure 1–48

Other Ways

1. To select all, press CTRL+A

To Stroke a Selection

A **stroke** is a colored outline. When stroking a selection, you must specify the number of pixels to include in the stroke and the desired color. You also must decide to apply the stroke outside the selection border, inside the selection border, or centered on the selection border. Other stroke settings include blending modes and opacity which you will learn about in a later chapter.

The following steps stroke a selection.

1

● With the photograph still selected, click Edit on the menu bar to display the Edit menu (Figure 1–49).

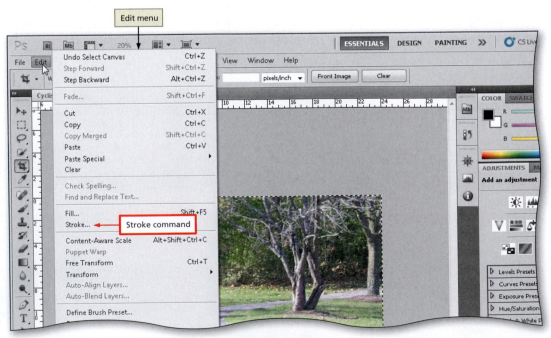

Figure 1–49

2

- Click Stroke to display the Stroke dialog box.

- Type **100** in the Width box.

- Click the Inside option button (Stroke dialog box) to select an inside stroke (Figure 1–50).

Q&A

Do I need to select a color?

No, the default value is the foreground color, black. If someone has changed your foreground color, click the Cancel button, press the D key to choose the default colors and start again with Step 1.

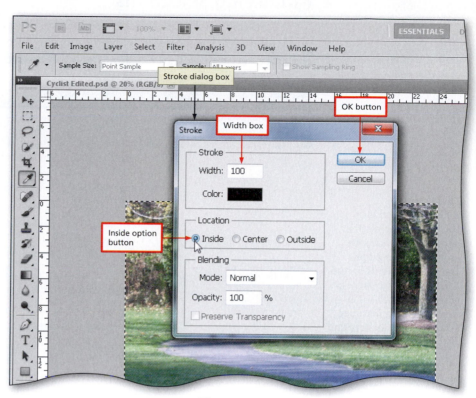

Figure 1–50

3

- Click the OK button to apply the stroke (Figure 1–51).

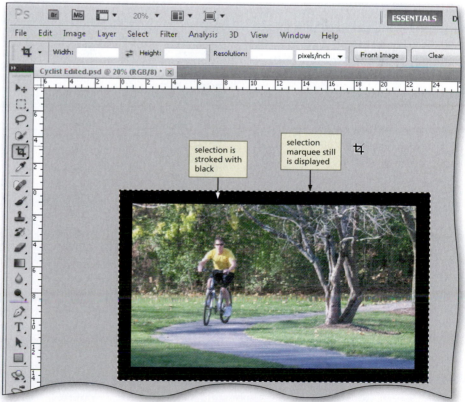

Figure 1–51

Modifying Selections

You can modify the selection border in several different ways. In the cyclist photo, you will modify the selection by increasing the number of pixels along the border so you can add a second color at that location. Table 1–4 displays the modify commands.

Table 1–4 Modify Commands	
Type of Modification	**Result**
Border	This command allows you to select a width of pixels, from 1 to 200, to be split evenly on either side of the existing selection marquee. If the selection is already on the edge, then half of the entered value will be included in the border.
Smooth	Photoshop examines the number of pixels in a radius around the selection. To smooth the selection, if more than half of the pixels already are selected, Photoshop adds the rest within the radius. If less than half are selected, the pixels are removed. The overall effect is to smooth sharp corners and jagged lines, reducing patchiness.
Expand	The border is increased by a number of pixels from 1 to 100. Any portion of the selection border running along the canvas's edge is unaffected.
Contract	The border is decreased by a number of pixels from 1 to 100. Any portion of the selection border running along the canvas's edge is unaffected.
Feather	This command creates a feather edge with a width from 0 to 250 pixels.

BTW

Selections
When you select all, Photoshop displays the photo with a marquee around all four edges. The selection tools on the Tools panel also can help you make selections in the photo. The marquee, lasso, Quick Selection, and Magic Wand tools will be discussed in Chapter 2.

To Modify a Selection

The following steps modify the selection.

1
• On the menu bar, click Select, and then point to Modify to display the Modify submenu (Figure 1–52).

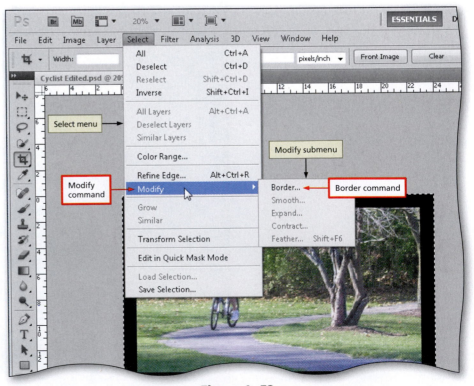

Figure 1–52

2

- Click Border on the Modify submenu to display the Border Selection dialog box.

- Type 2 0 0 in the Width box to create a border on each side of the photo (Figure 1–53).

Q&A Could I use the Contract command to contract the selection?

No, you must specify the border first. The Contract command is **grayed out** so you cannot select it, before choosing the Border command.

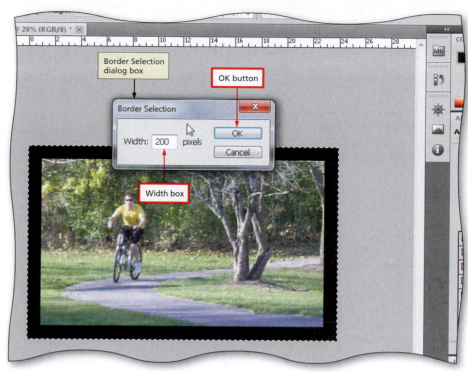

Figure 1–53

3

- Click the OK button in the Border Selection dialog box to define the selection (Figure 1–54).

Q&A Is the border 200 pixels wide?

No. Photoshop adds half of those pixels to either side of the selection marquee. Because the selection was already on the edge of the photo, the selection was moved only 100 pixels.

 Experiment

- To practice smoothing the border, click the Select menu, point to Modify, and then click Smooth. Enter a value in the Sample Radius box and then click the OK button. Notice the rounded rectangle in the border marquee. Press CTRL+Z to undo the Smooth command.

Figure 1–54

To Switch Foreground and Background Colors

On the Tools panel, the default foreground color is black and the default background color is white. Photoshop uses the default foreground color in strokes, files, and brushes — in the previous steps when you stroked, the pixels became black. In order to create a white, overlapping stroke you must make white the foreground color. The following steps switch the foreground and background colors so white is over black.

1
- Click the Switch Foreground and Background Colors button to reverse the colors (Figure 1–55).

white now is displayed as the foreground color

Switch Foreground and Background Colors button

Switch Foreground and Background Colors (X)

Figure 1–55

Other Ways

1. Press X

To Stroke Again

1 Click Edit on the menu bar to display the Edit menu.

2 Click Stroke to display the Stroke dialog box.

3 Type 50 in the Width box.

4 Click the Center option button to select a center stroke.

5 Click the OK button to apply the stroke (Figure 1–56).

selection is stroked with white

selection marquee still is displayed

Figure 1–56

To Deselect

Because the border is complete, you should remove the selection indicator, or **deselect** it, so it no longer appears. The following step removes the selection.

- Click Select on the menu bar and then click Deselect to remove the selection (Figure 1–57).

Q&A

Why does my mouse pointer still display the Crop Tool mouse pointer?

Deselecting does not change the current tool on the Tools panel. Whichever tool you used prior to the deselecting process will display its own mouse pointer.

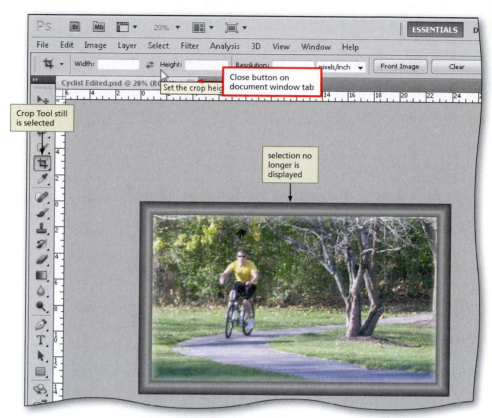

Figure 1–57

<table>
<tr><td colspan="1">**Other Ways**</td></tr>
<tr><td>1. Press CTRL+D</td></tr>
</table>

To Switch Foreground and Background Colors

The following step uses the shortcut key to switch the foreground and background colors back to black over white.

1. Press the X key to switch the foreground and background colors.

Saving a Photo with the Same File Name

Because you have made many edits to the photo, it is a good idea to save the photo again. When you saved the document the first time, you assigned the file name, Cyclist Edited. When you use the following procedure, Photoshop automatically assigns the same file name to the photo, and it is stored in the same location.

To Save a Photo with the Same File Name

The following step saves the Cyclist Edited file with the changes you made.

• Click File on the menu bar and then click Save to save the photo with the same file name.

Other Ways

1. Press CTRL+S

Break Point: If you wish to take a break, this is a good place to do so. You can quit Photoshop now. To resume at a later time, start Photoshop, open the file called Room Edited, and continue following the steps from this location forward.

To Close a Photo

The following step closes the Cyclist Edited document window without quitting Photoshop.

• Click the Close button on the Document window tab (shown in Figure 1–57 on the previous page) to close the document window and the image file (Figure 1–58).

• If Photoshop displays a dialog box asking you to save again, click the No button.

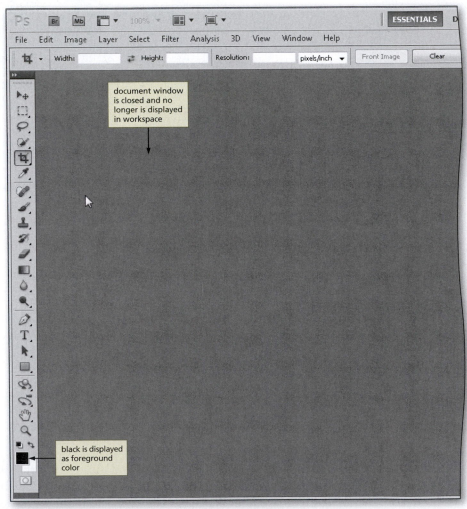

Figure 1–58

Other Ways

1. Press CTRL+W

Opening a Recent File in Photoshop

Once you have created and saved a document, you may need to retrieve it from your storage medium. For example, you might want to edit the photo or print it. Photoshop maintains a list of recently used files in order to give you quick access to them for further editing. Opening a recent file requires that Photoshop is running on your computer.

To Open a Recent File

Earlier in this chapter you saved your edited photo on a USB flash drive using the file name, Cyclist Edited. The following steps open the Cyclist Edited file using the Open Recent list.

- Click File on the menu bar and then point to Open Recent to display the Open Recent submenu (Figure 1–59).

Q&A What does the Clear Recent command do?

If you click the Clear Recent command, your Recent list will be empty. To open a file, you have to click Open on the File menu and then navigate to the location of the file.

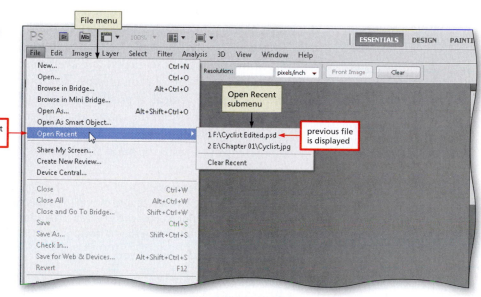

Figure 1–59

2

- Click Cyclist Edited.psd on the Open Recent submenu to open the file.

- If necessary, change the magnification to 25% (Figure 1–60).

Q&A Why is the Crop Tool still selected?

Photoshop tools do not change until you select a new tool. You have been working in the menu system and have yet to choose a new tool in the Tools panel.

Figure 1–60

Changing Image Sizes

Sometimes it is necessary to resize an image to fit within certain space limitations. **Resize** means to scale or change the dimensions of the photo. Zooming in or dragging a corner of the document window to change the size is not the same as actually changing the dimensions of the photo. Resizing in a page layout program, such as Publisher, QuarkXPress, or InDesign, merely stretches the pixels. In Photoshop, resizing means adding to or subtracting from the number of pixels.

Photoshop uses a mathematical process called **interpolation**, or **resampling**, when it changes the number of pixels. The program interpolates or calculates how to add new pixels to the photo to match those already there. Photoshop samples the pixels and reproduces them to determine where and how to enlarge or reduce the photo.

When you resize a photo, you must consider many things, such as the type of file, the width, the height, and the resolution. **Resolution** refers to the number of pixels per inch, printed on a page or displayed on a monitor. Not all photos lend themselves to resizing. Some file types lose quality and sharpness when resized. Fine details cannot be interpolated from low-resolution photos. Resizing works best for small changes where exact dimensions are critical. If possible, it usually is better to take a photo at the highest feasible resolution or rescan the image at a higher resolution rather than resize it later.

In those cases where it is impossible to create the photo at the proper size, Photoshop helps you resize or **scale** your photos for print or online media.

BTW

Resolution
Graphics for print purposes are usually higher resolution than those for use on the Web. Images designed for the Web are limited by the resolution of the computer screen, which usually varies from 72 to 96 pixels per inch.

Plan Ahead

Prepare for publication.
Keep in mind the golden rectangle of well-designed photos and the limitations of your space. Resize the photo. Print a copy and evaluate its visual appeal. If you are going to publish the photo to the Web, determine the following:

- Typical download speed of your audience
- Browser considerations
- Number of colors
- File type

Finally, save the photo with a descriptive name indicating its completion.

To Resize the Image

Because the cyclist photo will be printed on a rack card at a specific size, you will change the width to 3.75 inches. The following steps resize the image to create a custom-sized photo for printing.

1
- Click Image on the menu bar to display the Image menu (Figure 1–61).

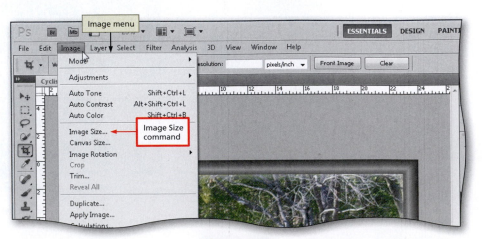

Figure 1–61

2
- Click Image Size to display the Image Size dialog box.

- In the Document Size area, double-click the value in the Width box and then type **3.75** to replace the previous value (Figure 1–62).

Q&A

Why did the height change?

When you change the width, Photoshop automatically adjusts the height to maintain the proportions of the photo. Your exact height might differ slightly depending on how closely you cropped the original photo.

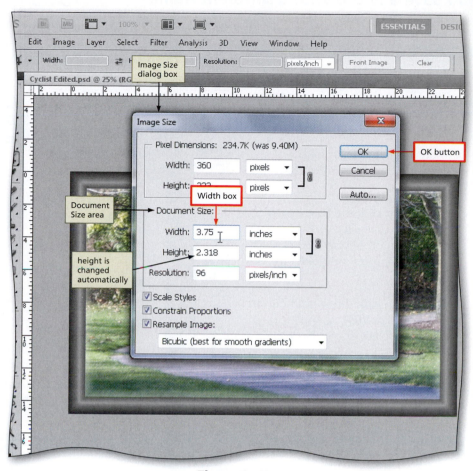

Figure 1–62

3
- Click the OK button (Image Size dialog box) to finish resizing the image.

- Change the magnification to 100% (Figure 1–63).

Figure 1–63

Other Ways

1. Press ALT+CTRL+I, change settings, click OK button (Image Size dialog box)

To Save a Photo with a Different Name

Many graphic designers will save multiple copies of the same photo with various edits. Because this photo has been resized to print properly, you need to save it with a different name. The following step renames the file.

1

• Click File on the menu bar and then click Save As to display the Save As dialog box.

• In the File name text box (Save As dialog box), type **Cyclist Resized**.

• If necessary, click the Save in box arrow and then click UDISK 2.0 (F:), or the location of your USB flash drive and appropriate folder in the list.

• If necessary, click the Format button and then click Photoshop (*.PSD, *.PDD) to select the format type (Figure 1–64).

• Click the Save button (Save As dialog box) to save the image with the new name.

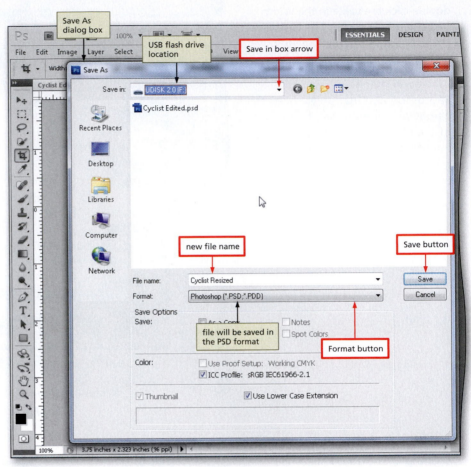

Figure 1–64

Other Ways

1. Press SHIFT+CTRL+S

Printing a Photo

BTW

Printing
When you use the Print One Copy command to print a document, Photoshop prints the photo automatically, using preset options. To print multiple copies, display the Print dialog box by clicking File on the menu bar, clicking Print, and then entering the number of copies you want to print.

The photo now can be printed, saved, taken to a professional print shop, or sent online to a printing service. A printed version of the photo is called a **hard copy** or **printout**. You can print one copy using the Print One Copy command on the File menu, or to display the Print dialog box, you can click Print on the File menu, which offers you more printing options.

The Print One Copy command sends the printout to the default printer. If you are not sure which printer is your default printer, choose the Print command. In the Print dialog box, click the Printer box arrow and choose your current printer. You will learn more about the Print dialog box in a later chapter.

After printing a copy of the photo, you will close the photo. Then, you will return to the version of the photo before resizing to prepare a Web version.

To Print a Photo

The following steps print the photo created in this chapter.

- Ready the printer according to the printer instructions.

- Click File on the menu bar and then click Print to display the Print dialog box.

- If necessary, click the Printer box arrow and then select your printer from the list. Do not change any other settings (Figure 1–65).

Q&A

Does Photoshop have a Print button?

Photoshop's Print commands are available on the menu or by using shortcut keys. There is no Print button on the options bar.

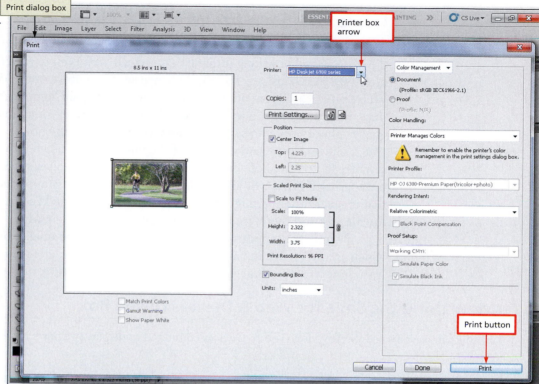

Figure 1–65

- In the Print dialog box, click the Print button to start the printing process. If your system displays a second Print dialog box or a Print Settings dialog box, unique to your printer, click its Print button.

- When the printer stops, retrieve the hard copy of the photo.

Other Ways

1. To print one copy, press ALT+SHIFT+CTRL+P

2. To display Print dialog box, press CTRL+P

Saving a Photo for Use on the Web

When preparing photos for the Web, you often need to compromise between the quality of the display and file size. Web users do not want to wait while large photos load from the Web to their individual computer systems. To solve this problem, Photoshop provides several commands to compress the file size of an image while optimizing its online display quality. Additionally, Photoshop allows you to save the photo in a variety of formats such as **GIF**, which is a compressed graphic format designed to minimize file size and electronic transfer time, or as an **HTML** (Hypertext Markup Language) file, which contains all the necessary information to display your photo in a Web browser.

Therefore, you have two choices in Photoshop CS5 for creating Web images: the Zoomify command and the Save for Web & Devices command. When you **zoomify**, you create a high-resolution image for the Web, complete with a background and tools for navigation, panning, and zooming. To zoomify, click Export on the File menu and then click Zoomify. In the Zoomify Export dialog box, you set various Web and export options. Photoshop creates the HTML code and accompanying files for you to upload to a Web server.

If you do not want the extra HTML files for the background, navigation, and zooming, you can create a single graphic file using the Save for Web & Devices command. The resulting graphic can be used on the Web or on a variety of mobile devices.

Optimization is the process of changing the photo to make it most effective for its purpose. The Save for Web & Devices command allows you to preview optimized images in different file formats, and with different file attributes, for precise optimization. You can view multiple versions of a photo simultaneously and modify settings as you preview the image.

Using the Save for Web & Devices Command

To optimize the cyclist photo for use on the Web, you need to make decisions about the file size and how long it might take to load on a Web page. These kinds of decisions must take into consideration the audience and the nature of the Web page. For example, Web pages geared for college campuses probably could assume a faster download time than those that target a wide range of home users. An e-commerce site that needs high-quality photography to sell its product will make certain choices in color and resolution.

The hardware and software of Web users also is taken into consideration. For instance, if a Web photo contains more colors than the user's monitor can display, most browsers will **dither**, or approximate, the colors that it cannot display, by blending colors that it can. Dithering might not be appropriate for some Web pages, because it increases the file size and therefore causes the page to load more slowly.

Many other appearance settings play a role in the quality of Web graphics, some of which are subjective in nature. As you become more experienced in Photoshop, you will learn how to make choices about dithering, colors, texture, image size, and other settings.

To Preview Using the Save for Web & Devices Dialog Box

The followings steps use the Save for Web & Devices command to display previews for four possible Web formats.

1

- With the Cyclist Resized photo open, click File on the menu bar to display the File menu and then click Save for Web & Devices to display the Save for Web & Devices dialog box.

- Click the 4-Up tab to display four versions of the photo.

- Click the upper-right preview, if necessary, to choose a high-quality, version of the photo (Figure 1–66).

Q&A

Why are there four frames?

Photoshop displays four previews — the original photo and three others that are converted to different resolutions to optimize download times on the Web.

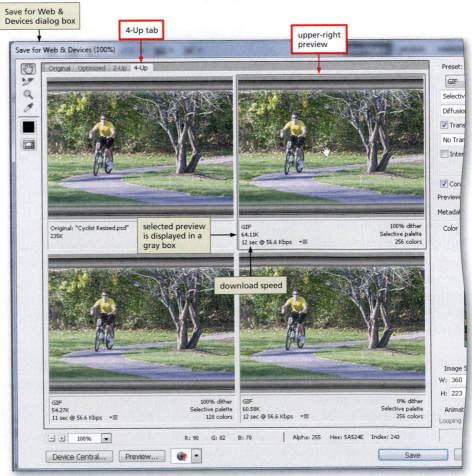

Figure 1–66

Other Ways

1. Press ALT+SHIFT+CTRL+S

To Choose a Download Speed

For even faster downloads when the photo is displayed as a Web graphic, you can choose a download speed that will be similar to that of your target audience. The **annotation area** below each image in the Save for Web & Devices dialog box provides optimization information such as the size of the optimized file and the estimated download time using the selected modem speed.

The following steps change the download speed to 512 kilobytes per second (Kbps).

1

- In the annotation area below the upper-right preview, click the 'Select download speed' button to display the list of connection speeds (Figure 1–67).

Figure 1–67

2

- In the list, click Size/Download Time (512 Kbps Cable/DSL) or another appropriate speed (Figure 1–68).

Q&A

How fast will the picture download?

In Figure 1–66, the speed was 12 seconds at 56.6 Kbps. At 512 Kbps, the photo will download in 2 seconds, as shown in Figure 1–68. Your download times might differ slightly.

Figure 1–68

Experiment

- Click the Select download speed button to display the list of connection speeds and then click various connection speeds to see how the download times are affected. When finished, click Size/Download Time (512 Kbps Cable/DSL) in the list.

Other Ways

1. Right-click annotation area, select download speed

Options in the Save for Web & Devices Dialog Box

On the left side of the Save for Web & Devices dialog box, Photoshop provides several tools to move, zoom, select colors, and slice a portion of the selected preview (Figure 1–69). Along the bottom of the Save for Web & Devices dialog box are buttons to preview the image and perform file functions.

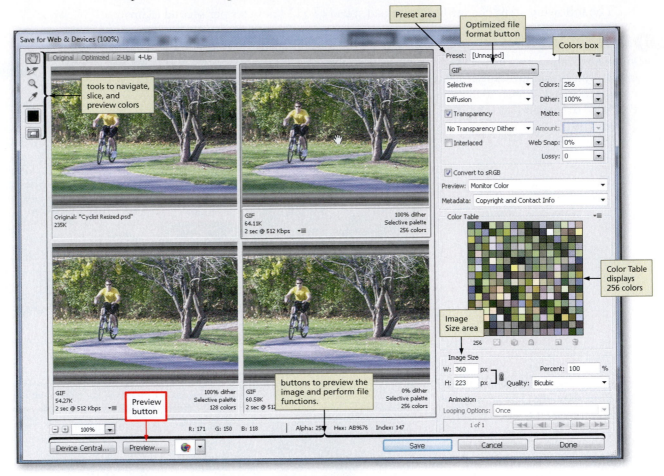

Figure 1–69

BTW

Reviewing the HTML Code
If you want to review the HTML code later, you can either open the file in Photoshop, access the Save for Web & Devices dialog box, and then click the Preview button; or, you can double-click the HTML file to open it in a browser, click View on the browser's menu bar, and then click Source.

If you choose a preview other than the original located on the upper left, the Save for Web & Devices dialog box displays options in the Preset area on the right. The Preset area lets you make changes to the selected preview such as the file type, the number of colors, transparency, dithering, and photo finishes. Fine-tuning these kinds of optimization settings allows you to balance the image quality and file size.

Below the Preset area are the Color Table and Image Size areas. The Color Table area and its buttons and menu display different options based on the choices you made in the Preset area. The colors used in the selected preview can be locked, deleted, set to transparent, or adjusted for standard Web palettes. The Image Size area allows you to make changes to the size of the image similar to those changes you made using the Image Size command earlier in the chapter. Changing the image size affects all four previews. The settings are not permanent until you click the Save button. You will learn more about these settings in a later chapter.

To Preview the Photo on the Web

It is always a good idea to preview a photo before uploading it to the Web to check for errors. When Photoshop displays a Web preview of any photo, it also displays the characteristics of the file and the HTML code used to create the preview. The following steps preview the image in a browser.

1

- Click the Preview button (shown in Figure 1–69) to display the photo in a Web browser.

- If necessary, double-click the browser's title bar to maximize the browser window (Figure 1–70).

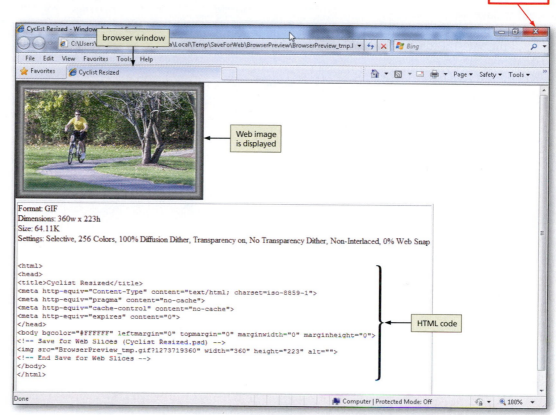

Figure 1–70

Q&A

When I clicked the Preview button, the HTML code was displayed in Notepad. Should it open in a browser?

If Photoshop cannot detect a default browser on your system, you may have to click the box arrow next to the Preview button (Figure 1–69), and then click Edit List to add your browser.

Q&A

How would I use the HTML code?

As a Web designer, you might copy and paste the code into a text editor or Web creation software, replacing BrowserPreview with the name of the file. After saving, the code, the HTML file, and the photo would need to be uploaded to a server.

2

- Click the Close button on the browser's title bar to close the browser window. If necessary, click the Adobe Photoshop CS5 button on the Windows 7 taskbar to return to the Save for Web & Devices dialog box.

To Save the Photo as a Web Page

When you click the Save button in the Save for Web & Devices dialog box, you will name the Web page and create a folder for the files, as performed in the following steps.

- In the Save for Web & Devices dialog box, click the Save button to display the Save Optimized As dialog box.

- Type **Cyclist-for-Web** in the File name text box (Save Optimized As dialog box).

- If necessary, click the Save in box arrow and then click UDISK 2.0 (F:), or the location of your USB flash drive and appropriate folder in the list.

- Click the Create New Folder button (Figure 1–71).

Q&A

Why are the words in the file name hyphenated?

For ease of use, it is standard for Web graphics to have no spaces in their file names.

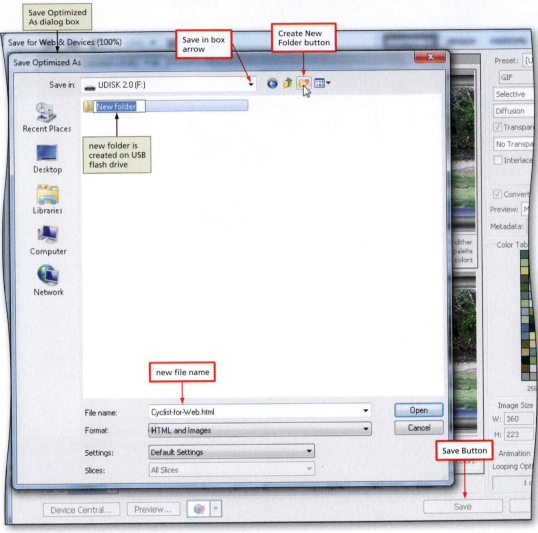

Figure 1–71

- Type **Cyclist Web Page Files** as the new name for the folder and then press the ENTER key (Figure 1–72).

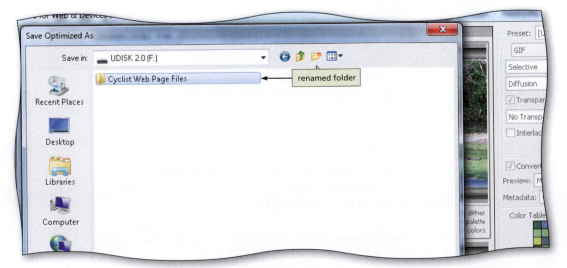

Figure 1–72

3

- Double-click the new folder to open it.

- Click the Format button (Save Optimized As dialog box) to display the saving options (Figure 1–73).

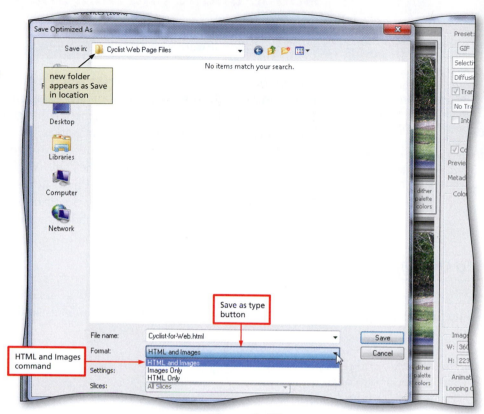

Figure 1–73

4

- Click HTML and Images in the list to direct Photoshop to save the HTML code and the Web version of the photo (Figure 1–74).

Q&A

What are the differences in the three ways to save for the Web?

The Images only option saves the photo itself in a Web-friendly format as a GIF file. The HTML only option saves the coding that creates the Web page, but not the photo. The HTML and Images option saves the Web page and creates an accompanying folder named images to go with the Web page file. Inside the images folder is a GIF version of the photo.

5

- Click the Save button to save the HTML and Image files.

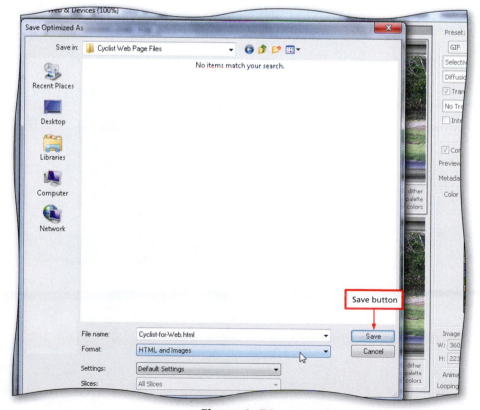

Figure 1–74

Adobe Bridge and Mini Bridge

Opening Files in Adobe Bridge
When working with multiple photos, or organizing your photos, it might be more convenient to use the Bridge tool to open files. In other cases, use the Open command on the Photoshop File menu if you only want to open a single photo for editing.

Adobe Bridge is a file exploration tool similar to Windows Explorer. Bridge can be used with any of the software programs in the Adobe Creative Suite. Using Bridge, you can locate, drag, organize, browse, and standardize color settings across your content for use in print, on the Web and on mobile devices. A useful Bridge tool allows you to attach or assign keywords, or **metadata**, used for searching and categorizing photos. Metadata is divided into three categories: file information, image usage, and image creation data. The Bridge interface is explained in detail in Appendix E.

A subset of Adobe Bridge is the new **Mini Bridge** that helps you navigate folders and files and access other modules in the suite. Mini Bridge provides a search mechanism, and interaction with Web sites such as Photoshop.com and Flickr.com. You can use Mini Bridge to open a file by double-clicking the **thumbnail**, or small picture. You also can view the files in a list, in a grid, or as a slideshow, among other ways.

To Use Mini Bridge to View Files

So far in this chapter, you have saved the edited cyclist photo, a version for printing, and a version for the Web. The following steps open Mini Bridge and view those files as thumbnails and then with details.

1
• Click the Mini Bridge button in the vertical docking to open the Mini Bridge panel (Figure 1–75).

 Experiment
• Point to each of the buttons and settings in the Mini Bridge panel to view the tool tips.

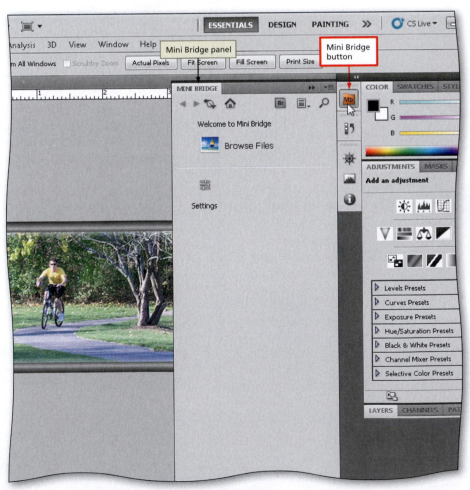

Figure 1–75

2

- Click the Panel View button to display the panel settings (Figure 1–76).

Q&A

What is a pod?

Pod is the term that Adobe uses for content viewing areas or sections within panels.

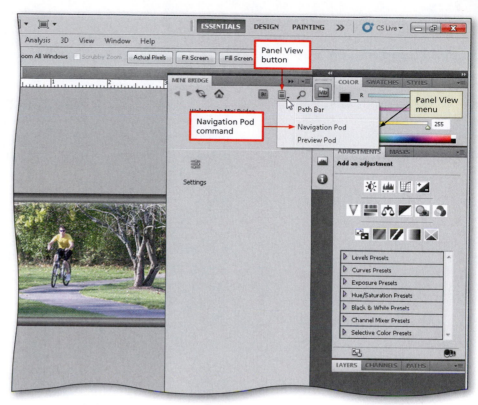

Figure 1–76

3

- Click Navigation Pod to display common and recent locations, as well as the Content area.

- If Photoshop displays a dialog box asking if you want to start Bridge each time you log in, click the No button.

- If necessary, click Recent Folders in the Navigation area, and then click your USB flash drive location to display its contents.

- If you created a Chapter 01 folder, double-click the Chapter 01 folder icon (Figure 1–77).

 Experiment

- Drag the slider at the bottom of the panel to display the thumbnails at different sizes.

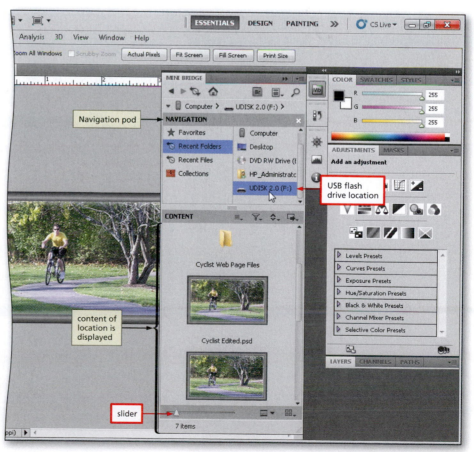

Figure 1–77

4

• In the lower-right corner of the Mini Bridge panel, click the View button to display a menu of other ways to view photos in Mini Bridge (Figure 1–78).

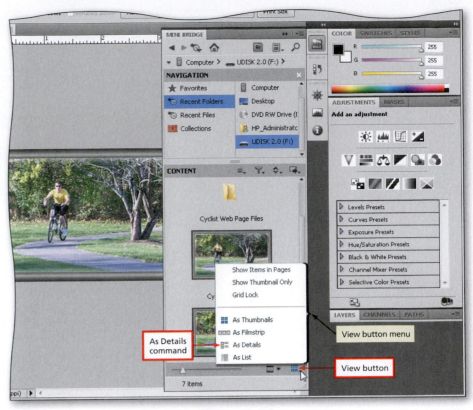

Figure 1–78

5

• Click As Details to show more information about each photo.

• If necessary, drag the slider to see more of the details (Figure 1–79).

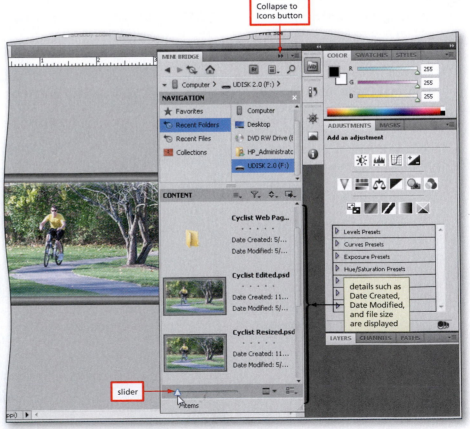

Figure 1–79

Other Ways

1. Click Launch Mini Bridge button on Application bar, adjust settings

Editing a Photo   **Photoshop Chapter 1**   **PS** 57

Photoshop Chapter 1

To Collapse the Panel

The following step collapses the Mini Bridge panel.

- Click the Collapse to Icons button on the Mini Bridge panel title bar to collapse the panel (Figure 1–80).

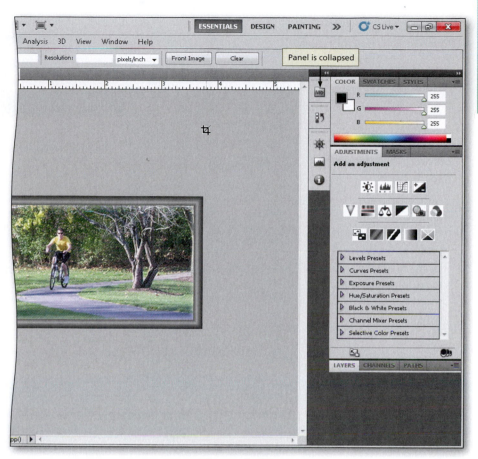

Figure 1–80

Photoshop Help

At anytime while you are using Photoshop, you can get answers to questions using **Photoshop Help**. You activate Photoshop Help either by clicking Help on the menu bar or by pressing the F1 key. The Photoshop Help command connects you, through the Web, to a wealth of assistance, including tutorials with detailed instructions accompanied by illustrations and videos. Used properly, this form of online assistance can increase your productivity and reduce your frustration by minimizing the time you spend learning how to use Photoshop. Additional information about using Photoshop Help is available in Appendix D.

BTW

Community Help
Community Help is an integrated Web environment that includes Photoshop Help and gives you access to community-generated content moderated by Adobe and industry experts. Comments from users help guide you to an answer.

To Access Photoshop Help

The following step accesses Photoshop Help. You must be connected to the Web if you plan to perform this step on a computer.

1

- With Photoshop open on your system, press the F1 key to access Photoshop Help online.

- If necessary, double-click the title bar to maximize the window (Figure 1–81).

Q&A

My help screen is asking me to download an update. Should I do that?

If you are in a lab situation, you should check with your instructor. Updates provide you with the latest help topics, videos, and tutorials, but downloading them takes time and disk space. You must be online to download the updates, and Photoshop might require you to restart your system.

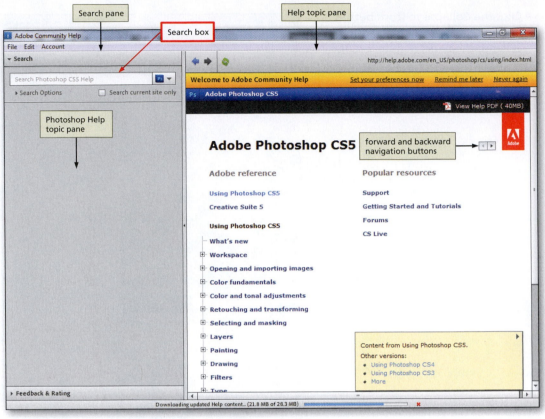

Figure 1–81

Other Ways

1. On Help menu, click Photoshop Help

Using the Search Box in Photoshop Help

The Search box allows you to type words or phrases about which you want additional information and help, such as cropping or printing images. When you press the ENTER key, Photoshop Help responds by displaying a list of topics related to the word or phrase you typed.

To Use the Help Search Box

The following steps use the Search box to obtain information about the Tools panel.

1
- Click to display a check mark in the 'Search current site only' or 'Adobe reference only' check box.

- Click the Search box and then type **Tools** to enter the search topic (Figure 1–82).

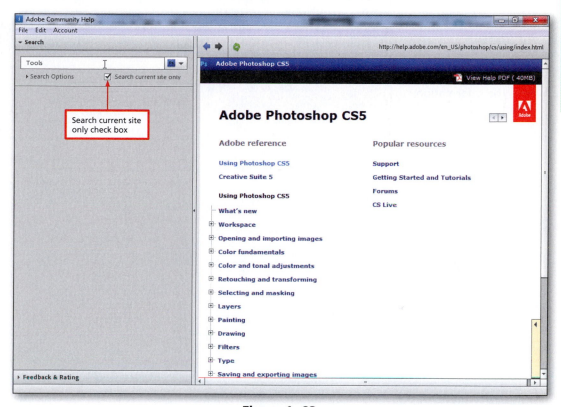

Figure 1–82

2
- Press the ENTER key to display the relevant links.

- Scroll down to display the link named Adobe Photoshop CS5 * Tools (Figure 1–83).

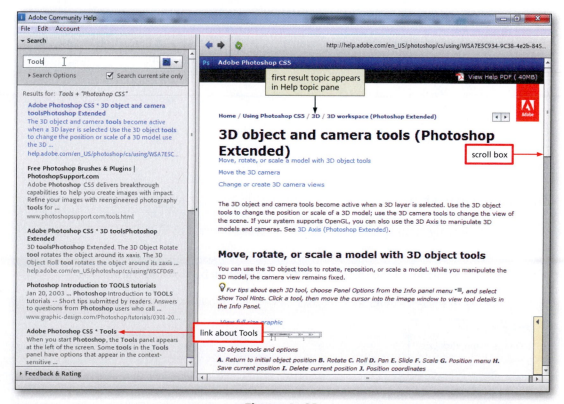

Figure 1–83

- Click the About Photoshop CS5 * Tools link to display the contents (Figure 1–84).

- Scroll as necessary to read the information about tools.

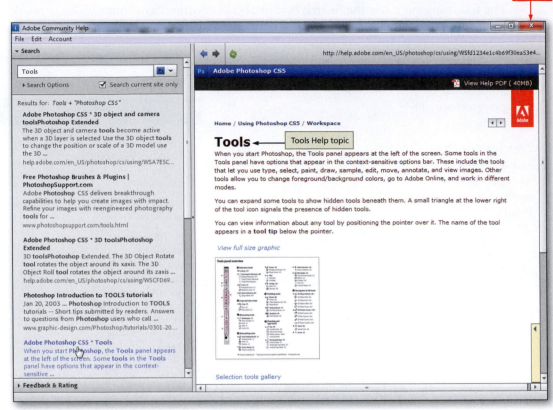

Figure 1–84

 **Experiment**

- Click other links to view more information, or search for other topics using the Search box.

- In the browser title bar, click the Close button to close the window, and then, if necessary, click the Adobe Photoshop CS5 button on the taskbar to return to Photoshop.

Other Ways
1. On Help menu, click Photoshop Help, enter search topic

To Quit Photoshop

The following steps quit Photoshop and return control to Windows.

1

- Click the Close button on the right side of the Application bar to close the window.

- If Photoshop displays a dialog box asking you to save changes, click the No button.

Other Ways
1. On File menu, click Exit
2. Press CTRL+Q

Chapter Summary

In this chapter, you gained a broad knowledge of Photoshop. First, you learned how to start Photoshop. You were introduced to the Photoshop workspace. You learned how to open a photo and zoom in and out. You learned about design issues related to the placement of visual points of interest. You then learned how to crop a photo to eliminate extraneous background. After you added a blended border, you resized the image.

Once you saved the photo, you learned how to print it. You used the Save for Web & Devices command to optimize and save a Web version. You learned how to use Adobe Mini Bridge to view files and Adobe Help to research specific help topics. Finally, you learned how to quit Photoshop.

The items listed below include all the new Photoshop skills you have learned in this chapter:

1. Start Photoshop (PS 5)
2. Select the Essentials Workspace (PS 7)
3. Reset the Tools Panel (PS 8)
4. Reset the Options Bar (PS 8)
5. Open a Photo (PS 10)
6. Save a Photo in the PSD Format (PS 19)
7. Use the Zoom Tool (PS 23)
8. Open the Navigator Panel (PS 25)
9. Use the Navigator Panel (PS 26)
10. Collapse the Navigator Panel (PS 26)
11. Use the Hand Tool (PS 27)
12. Change the Magnification (PS 27)
13. Change the Screen Mode (PS 28)
14. Display Rulers (PS 30)
15. Crop a Photo (PS 33)
16. Position the Rule of Thirds Overlay (PS 34)
17. Create a Selection (PS 35)
18. Stroke a Selection (PS 36)
19. Modify a Selection (PS 38)
20. Switch Foreground and Background Colors (PS 40)
21. Deselect (PS 41)
22. Save a Photo with the Same File Name (PS 42)
23. Close a Photo (PS 42)
24. Open a Recent File (PS 43)
25. Resize the Image (PS 44)
26. Save a Photo with a Different Name (PS 46)
27. Print a Photo (PS 47)
28. Preview Using the Save for Web & Devices Dialog Box (PS 48)
29. Choose a Download Speed (PS 49)
30. Preview the Photo on the Web (PS 51)
31. Save the Photo as a Web Page (PS 52)
32. Use Mini Bridge to View Files (PS 54)
33. Collapse the Panel (PS 57)
34. Access Photoshop Help (PS 58)
35. Use the Help Search Box (PS 59)
36. Quit Photoshop (PS 60)

Learn It Online

Test your knowledge of chapter content and key terms.

Instructions: To complete the Learn It Online exercises, start your browser, click the Address bar, and then enter the Web address `scsite.com/psCS5/learn`. When the Photoshop CS5 Learn It Online page is displayed, click the link for the exercise you want to complete and then read the instructions.

Chapter Reinforcement TF, MC, and SA
A series of true/false, multiple choice, and short answer questions that test your knowledge of the chapter content.

Flash Cards
An interactive learning environment where you identify chapter key terms associated with displayed definitions.

Practice Test
A series of multiple choice questions that tests your knowledge of chapter content and key terms.

Who Wants To Be a Computer Genius?
An interactive game that challenges your knowledge of chapter content in the style of a television quiz show.

Wheel of Terms
An interactive game that challenges your knowledge of chapter key terms in the style of the television show *Wheel of Fortune*.

Crossword Puzzle Challenge
A crossword puzzle that challenges your knowledge of key terms presented in the chapter.

Apply Your Knowledge

Reinforce the skills and apply the concepts you learned in this chapter.

Editing a Photo in the Photoshop Workspace
Instructions: Start Photoshop and perform the customization steps found on pages PS 6 through PS 9. Open the Apply 1-1 Water Park file in the Chapter 01 folder from the Data Files for Students. You can access the Data Files for Students on the CD that accompanies this book. See the inside back cover of this book for instructions on downloading the Data Files for Students, or contact your instructor for information about accessing the required files.

First, you will save the photo in its own folder. Then you will crop the photo, add a white border, and save the edited photo, as shown in Figure 1–85. Next, you will resize the photo for printing and print one copy. Finally, you will reopen your edited photo, and then you will optimize it for the Web, save it, and close it.

Perform the following tasks:
1. On the File menu, click Save As. When Photoshop displays the Save As dialog box, navigate to your USB flash drive and then click the Create New Folder button. Type Apply 1-1 as the folder name and then press the ENTER key. Double-click the folder to open it. In the File name box, type Apply 1-1 Water Park Edited. Click the Format button and choose the PSD file format. Click the Save button to save the file.

Continued >

Figure 1 – 85

2. Use the Zoom Tool to zoom the photo to 50% magnification, if necessary.

3. Use the Hand Tool to reposition the photo in the workspace to view different areas of the zoomed photo.

4. Use the Navigator panel to zoom out to 16.67%.

Apply Your Knowledge *continued*

5. Use the Crop Tool to crop the photo, retaining the top patio of the water slide and the child on the right slide as shown in Figure 1–85 on the previous page. Include more water than sky. Use the Rule of Thirds guide to position the child in the lower-right intersection. (*Hint:* If your cropping selection does not look correct, you can press the ESC key to clear the selection before you press the ENTER key. Immediately after cropping the photo, you can click Undo on the Edit menu to undo the crop action.)

6. To create the border:

   a. Press the X key to reverse the foreground and background colors.

   b. Press CTRL+A to select all of the photo.

   c. Use the Select menu to modify the border to 100 pixels.

   d. Press SHIFT+F5 to display the Fill dialog box and then fill the border with white.

   e. Press CTRL+D to clear your selection when finished creating the border.

7. Press CTRL+S to save the Apply 1-1 Water Park Edited photo with the same file name in the same location.

8. Use the Image menu to resize the photo width to 5 inches wide to create a custom-sized photo for printing.

9. Save the resized file as Apply 1-1 Water Park for Print.

10. Print the photo and then close the file. If Photoshop displays a dialog box about saving again, click the No button.

11. Open the Apply 1-1 Water Park for Print file using the recent list.

12. Save the photo for the Web, displaying it in the 4-Up tab and zoomed to fit on the screen. Select the preview that looks the best for your download speed.

13. Preview the optimized photo in your browser, and print the browser page. Close the browser.

14. Save the photo with the name, Apply-1-1-Water-Park-for-Web, using the HTML and Images file type.

15. Close the Apply 1-1 Water Park for Print file without saving it and close Photoshop.

Extend Your Knowledge

Extend the skills you learned in this chapter and experiment with new skills. You may need to use Help to complete the assignment.

Exploring Border Width and Fill Options

Instructions: Start Photoshop and perform the customization steps found on pages PS 6 through PS 9. Open the Extend 1-1 Wood Turtle file in the Chapter 01 folder from the Data Files for Students and save it as Extend 1-1 Wood Turtle Edited in the PSD file format. You can access the Data Files for Students on the CD that accompanies this book. See the inside back cover of this book for instructions on downloading the Data Files for Students, or contact your instructor for information about accessing the required files.

The wood turtle photo (Figure 1–86) is to be added to a middle school science handout about amphibians and reptiles. Before the photo is inserted in the handout document, you must add a complementary border to the photo. The only requirement is that the border not be black or white.

complementary border color

Figure 1– 86

Before you save the photo with a border, you need to explore different border widths and fill options to find the right combination. As you experiment with border options, you can press the CTRL+ALT+Z keys to quickly step back through the current editing history, returning the photo to a previous state.

Perform the following tasks:

1. Select the entire photo.

2. Specify a border width.

3. Review Table 1–4 on page PS 38. Use the commands on the Modify submenu to set the border fill contents, blending, and opacity options of your choice and apply them to the photo. Make a note of your width and fill settings for future reference.

4. After viewing the resulting border, press the CTRL+ALT+Z keys enough times to step back to the photo's original unedited state.

5. Repeat Steps 1–4 several times to experiment with different border widths and fills, then apply the border that best complements the photo and save the changes to the photo.

6. Close the photo and quit Photoshop.

Make It Right

Analyze a project and correct all errors and/or improve the design.

Changing a Photo's Focus and Optimizing It for the Web

Instructions: Start Photoshop and perform the customization steps found on pages PS 6 through PS 9. Open the Make It Right 1-1 Young Stars file in the Chapter 01 folder from the Data Files for Students and save it as Make It Right 1-1 Young Stars Edited in the PSD file format. You can access the Data Files for Students on the CD that accompanies this book. See the inside back cover of this book for instructions on downloading the Data Files for Students, or contact your instructor for information about accessing the required files.

Members of your Astronomy Club have selected the Young Stars photo (Figure 1–87) for the club's Web site. You are to edit the photo to more clearly focus on the cluster of stars and its trailing dust blanket, and then optimize the photo for the Web.

View the photo in different screen modes and at different magnifications.

Keeping the rule of thirds and the golden rectangle 5:8 ratio concepts in mind, crop the photo to change its focal point and resave it. Then save the photo for the Web as Make-It-Right-1-1-Young-Stars-for-Web using the optimal settings for a GIF file with maximum colors and 250 pixels in width.

Figure 1–87

In the Lab

Design and/or create a project using the guidelines, concepts, and skills presented in this chapter. Labs are listed in order of increasing difficulty.

Lab 1: Cropping a Photo and Adding a Feathered Border

Problem: A nature magazine has accepted the submission of your photo of an American bald eagle, but they would like you to crop the photo more, add a feathered border, and resize it. Also, the editor would like the final version saved in the TIFF format. The edited photo is displayed in Figure 1–88. See the inside back cover of this book for instructions on downloading the Data Files for Students, or contact your instructor for information about accessing the required files.

Figure 1–88

Continued >

In the Lab *continued*

Instructions:

1. Start Photoshop.

2. Click the 'Show more workspaces and options' button on the Application bar and then click Essentials to choose the workspace. Click the button again and then click Reset Essentials to restore the workspace to its default settings.

3. Select the second button on the Tools panel to reset the Tools panel.

4. Right-click the Rectangular Marquee Tool icon on the options bar and then click Reset all Tools to reset the options bar.

5. If black is not over white at the bottom of the Tools panel, click the Switch Foreground and Background Colors button.

6. Open the file, Lab 1-1 Eagle, from the Chapter 01 folder of the Data Files for Students or from a location specified by your instructor.

7. Click Save As on the File menu, and then type the new file name, Lab 1-1 Eagle Edited. Click the Format button and choose TIFF (*.TIF;*.TIFF) format. Click the Save button. If a TIFF Options dialog box is displayed, click the OK button.

8. Use the magnification box to zoom the photo to 50% magnification, if necessary.

9. If the rulers do not appear, press CTRL+R to view the rulers.

10. Select the Crop Tool. Position the mouse pointer at the top of the photo and 2 inches from the left side of the photo as measured on the ruler. Drag down and to the right to include all of the rock that the eagle is standing on.

11. Position the Rule of Thirds overlay so the eagle stands along the right inner line, with his shoulders along the top inner line.

12. Press the ENTER key. If your crop does not seem correct, click the Undo command on the Edit menu and repeat Steps 10 and 11.

13. Save the photo again.

14. Press CTRL+A to select all of the photo. Click Select on the menu bar, point to Modify to display the Modify submenu, and then click Border to display the Border dialog box. Type 100 in the Width box and then click the OK button.

15. Go the Modify submenu again, and click Feather. Type 50 in the Feather Radius box, and then click the OK button to create a second marquee with feathered edges.

16. If white is not the foreground color, press the x key to switch the foreground and background colors. Click Edit on the menu bar and then click Stroke. Type 50 in the Width box. Click the Inside option button in the Location area. Type 75 in the Opacity box. Click the OK button to stroke the selection.

17. Click the Image Size command on the Image menu. When the Image Size dialog box is displayed in the Document Size area, type 4.25 in the Width box. Click the OK button to resize the image.

18. Press CTRL+S to save the file again.

19. Use the Print One Copy command on the File menu to print a copy of the photo.

20. Close your file and quit Photoshop.

21. Send the photo as an e-mail attachment to your instructor, or follow your instructor's directions for submitting the lab assignment.

In the Lab

Lab 2: Creating a Smoothed Border

Problem: The local hockey team is preparing a flyer to advertise its next game. The marketing department would like you to take one of the pictures from the last game and crop it to show just the face-off players and the official. Because the flyer will be printed on white paper, you should create a white border so the photo blends into the background and adds to the ice rink effect. The edited photo is displayed in Figure 1–89. See the inside back cover of this book for instructions on downloading the Data Files for Students, or contact your instructor for information about accessing the required files.

Figure 1–89

Instructions:

1. Start Photoshop. Perform the customization steps found on pages PS 6 through PS 9.

2. Open the file, Lab 1-2 Hockey, from the Chapter 01 folder of the Data Files for Students or from a location specified by your instructor.

3. Use the Save As command on the File menu to save the file on your storage device with the name, Lab 1-2 Hockey Edited, in the PSD format.

4. Click the Zoom Tool button on the Tools panel. Click the official to center the photo in the display. Zoom as necessary so you can make precise edits.

5. Crop the picture to display only the official and the two hockey players ready for the face-off. Use the golden rectangle ratio of approximately 5:8. The vertical line of the hockey stick and the visual line of the official should be positioned using the rule of thirds.

6. Save the photo again with the same name.

7. Close the file and open it again using the Recent submenu.

8. Press CTRL+A to select all of the photo.

9. To create the border, do the following:

   a. On the Select menu, point to Modify, and then click Border.

   b. When the Border Selection dialog box is displayed, type 100 in the Width Box. Click the OK button.

Continued >

STUDENT ASSIGNMENTS

c. On the Select menu, open the Modify submenu, and click Smooth.

d. When the Smooth Selection dialog box is displayed, type **50** in the Sample Radius box to smooth the corners. Click the OK button.

e. Press SHIFT+F5 to access the Fill command.

f. When the Fill dialog box is displayed, click the Use box arrow and then click White in the list.

g. Click the Mode box arrow and then click Normal in the list, if necessary.

h. If necessary, type **100** in the Opacity box. Click the OK button.

i. Press CTRL+D to deselect the border.

10. Save the photo again.

11. Use the Print One Copy command on the File menu to print a copy of the photo.

12. Close the document window.

13. Quit Photoshop.

14. Send the photo as an e-mail attachment to your instructor, or follow your instructor's directions for submitting the lab assignment.

In the Lab

Lab 3: Preparing a Photo for the Web

Problem: As an independent consultant in Web site design, you have been hired by the Department of Tourism to prepare a photo of an aerial tram for use on the department's Web site. The edited photo is displayed in Figure 1–90. See the inside back cover of this book for instructions on downloading the Data Files for Students, or contact your instructor for information about accessing the required files.

Figure 1– 90

Instructions: Start Photoshop. Perform the customization steps found on pages PS 6 through PS 9. Open the file, Lab 1-3 Tram, from the Chapter 01 folder of the Data Files for Students. Save the file in the PSD format with the name Lab 1-3 Tram Edited, in a new folder named Lab 1-3. (*Hint:* Use the Create New Folder button in the toolbar of the Save As dialog box.) Resize the photo to 500 pixels wide. Zoom to 50% magnification. Search Photoshop Help for help related to optimization. Read about optimizing for the Web. Print a copy of the help topic and then close the Photoshop Help window.

Use the Save for Web & Devices dialog box to view the 4-Up tab. Choose the best looking preview. Select the connection speed of your Internet connection. Save the HTML and Images in the Lab 1-3 folder using the name, Lab-1-3-Tram-for-Web. Use Mini Bridge to check your file structure and see your photos. Collapse the Mini Bridge panel. For extra credit, upload the HTML file and the accompanying Image folder to a Web server. See your instructor for ways to submit this assignment.

Cases and Places

Apply your creative thinking and problem-solving skills to design and implement a solution.

Note: To complete these assignments, you may be required to use the Data Files for Students. See the inside back cover of this book for instructions on downloading the Data Files for Students, or contact your instructor for information about accessing the required files.

1: Cropping a Photo for a Picture Directory

Academic

As a member of your high school reunion committee, it is your task to assemble the class photo directory. You are to edit a high school student photo and prepare it for print in the reunion directory. The photo needs to fit in a space 1.75 inches high and 1.33 inches wide. Each photo needs to have approximately the same amount of space above the headshot: .25 inches. After starting Photoshop and resetting the workspace, select the photo, Case 1-1 Student, from the Chapter 01 folder of the Data Files for Students. Save the photo on your USB flash drive storage device as Case 1-1 Student Edited, using the PSD format. Resize the photo to match the requirements. Use the rulers to help you crop the photo to leave .25 inches above the top of the student's head. Save the photo again with the file name Case 1-1 Student for Print and print a copy for your instructor.

2: Creating a Photo for a Social Networking Site

Personal

You would like to place a photo of your recent tubing adventure on your social networking site. The photo you have is of two people. You need to crop out the other person who is tubing. After starting Photoshop and resetting the workspace, select the photo, Case 1-2 Tubing, from the Chapter 01 folder of the Data Files for Students. Save the photo on your USB flash drive storage device as Case 1-2 Tubing Edited, using the PSD format. Crop the photo to remove one of the inner tubes, keeping in mind the rule of thirds, the golden rectangle, and the direction of the action. Save the photo again and print a copy for your instructor.

Continued ˃

Cases and Places *continued*

3: Creating a Rack Card Graphic with a Border

Professional

You are an intern with a tour company. They are planning a bus tour that follows the original Lewis and Clark trail and want to produce a rack card advertising the trip. On the back of the rack card, they would like a photo of one of the sites along the trail. The photo named Case 1-3 Monument is located in the Chapter 01 folder of the Data Files for Students. Save the photo on your USB flash drive storage device as Case 1-3 Monument Edited, using the PSD format. Rack cards typically measure 4×9 inches; the photo needs to fit in the upper half. Resize the photo to be 3.75 inches wide. Create a border of 200 pixels. Do not use smoothing. Fill the border with 50% black opacity.

2 | Using Selection Tools and Shortcut Keys

Objectives

You will have mastered the material in this chapter when you can:

- Explain the terms perspective, layout, and storyboard

- Describe selection tools

- Select objects using the marquee tools

- Move a selection

- Make transformation edits

- Use the History panel

- Use the Grow command and Refine Edges to adjust selections

- Employ the lasso tools

- Add and subtract areas from selections

- Use ruler grids and guides

- Select objects using the Quick Selection and Magic Wand tools

- Print to a PDF file

- Create and test new keyboard shortcuts

2 | Using Selection Tools and Shortcut Keys

Introduction

In Chapter 1, you learned about the Photoshop interface as well as navigation and zooming techniques. You cropped and resized a photo, added a border, and saved the photo for both Web and print media. You learned about online Help, along with opening, saving, and printing photos. This chapter continues to emphasize those topics and presents some new ones.

Recall that when you make a selection, you are specifying or isolating an area of your photo for editing. By selecting specific areas, you can edit and apply special effects to portions of your image, while leaving the unselected areas untouched. The new topics covered in this chapter include the marquee tools used to select rectangular or elliptical areas, the lasso tools used to select free-form segments or shapes, and the Quick Selection and Magic Wand tools used to select consistently colored areas. You also will learn how to use the Move Tool and transformation tools to duplicate, move, scale, skew, and warp those selections. Finally, you will print to a PDF file and create a new keyboard shortcut.

Project — Advertisement Graphic

An advertisement, or ad, is a form of communication that promotes a product or service to a potential customer. An advertisement tries to persuade consumers to purchase a product or service. An advertisement typically has a single message directed toward a specific audience.

A graphic designed for advertising, sometimes called an **advertising piece**, needs to catch the customer's eye and entice him or her to purchase the product. A clear graphic with strong contrast, item repetition, and visual lines will tell the story while enhancing any text that might be added later. Chapter 2 illustrates the creation of a department store advertising piece. You will begin with the image in Figure 2 – 1a that shows pieces from a set of dishes. You then will manipulate the image by selecting, editing, and moving the objects to produce a more attractive layout, creating Figure 2 – 1b to use in the advertisement.

Overview

As you read this chapter, you will learn how to create the advertisement graphic shown in Figure 2 – 1b by performing these general tasks:

- Select portions of the photo.
- Copy, move, rotate, and flip selections.
- Use the transformation commands to edit, scale, warp, and skew selections.
- Eliminate white space in and among objects in selected areas.
- Retrace editing steps using the History panel.
- Refine edges of selections.
- Print to a PDF file.
- Create a new shortcut key.

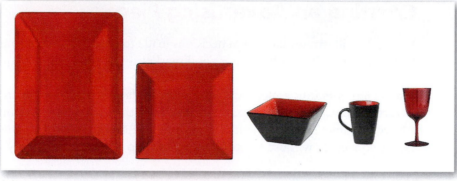

(a) Original Image

(b) Edited Image

Figure 2–1

General Project Guidelines

When editing a photo, the actions you perform and decisions you make will affect the appearance and characteristics of the finished product. As you edit a photo, such as the one shown in Figure 2–1a, you should follow these general guidelines:

1. **Choose the correct tool.** When you need to copy and paste portions of your photo, consider carefully which Photoshop selection tool to use. You want the procedure to be efficient and produce a clear image. Keep in mind the shape, background, purpose, and your expertise with various tools.

2. **Plan your duplications.** Use a storyboard or make a list of the items you plan to duplicate. Then decide whether it will be an exact duplication or a manipulated one, called a transformed copy. The decision depends on the visual effect you want to achieve.

3. **Use grids and guides.** When you are working with exact measurements, closely cropping and moving objects, or if you just want to align things easily, use grids and guides to display nonprinting lines across the document window. Use the Photoshop snapping function to align selections. Visual estimations of size and location are easier to perceive.

4. **Create files in portable formats.** You might have to distribute your artwork in a variety of formats depending on its use. Portability is an important consideration. It usually is safe to begin work in the Photoshop PSD format and then use the Save As command or Print command to convert to the PDF format. PDF files are platform and software independent.

When necessary, more specific details concerning the above guidelines are presented at appropriate points in the chapter. The chapter also will identify the actions performed and decisions made regarding these guidelines during the creation of the edited photo shown in Figure 2–1b.

Creating an Advertising Piece

Figure 2–2 illustrates the design decisions made to create the advertising piece. An attractive layout using multiple objects is a good marketing strategy, visually and subconsciously encouraging the viewer to purchase more than one item. **Layout** refers to placing visual elements into a pleasing and understandable arrangement. In the place setting advertisement, the layout is suggestive of how the product or products might look in a buyer's home. Advertising artists and product designers try to determine how the target consumer will use the product and group objects accordingly in the layout.

diagonal shows line of perspective

horizon line

Figure 2–2

From a design point of view, creating visual diagonal lines creates perspective. **Perspective** is the technique photographers, designers, and artists use to create the illusion of three dimensions on a flat or two-dimensional surface. Perspective is a means of fooling the eye by making it appear as if there is depth or receding space in an image. Adjusting the sizes and juxtaposing the objects creates asymmetrical balance and visual tension between the featured products. The diagonal alignment of the glasses leads the viewer's eye to the background, as does the placement of smaller pieces in front of larger ones.

The **horizon line** in perspective drawing is a virtual horizontal line across the picture. The placement of the horizon line determines from where the viewer seems to be looking, such as down from a high place or up from close to the ground. In the dishes advertisement, the horizon line runs across the middle of the drawing, just below the center.

Using white space, or non-image area, is effective in directing the viewer to notice what is important. The products grouped this way are, in a sense, framed by the white space.

This product layout also helps other members of the design team when it is time to make decisions about type placement. The group of products can be shifted up or down, as one image, to accommodate the layout and text, including the font sizes, placement, title, description, and price information. Recall that the rule of thirds offers a useful means to make effective layouts for images and text.

Designing a preliminary layout sketch, similar to Figure 2–2, to help you make choices about placement, size, perspective, and spacing, is referred to as creating a **storyboard** or **rough**.

BTW

Photoshop Help
The best way to become familiar with Photoshop Help is to use it. Appendix D includes detailed information about Photoshop Help and exercises that will help you gain confidence in using it.

To Start Photoshop

If you are stepping through this project on a computer and you want your screen to match the figures in this book, then you should change your computer's resolution to 1024 × 768 and reset the tools and panels. For more information about how to change the resolution on your computer, and other advanced Photoshop settings, read Appendix C.

The following steps, which assume Windows 7 is running, start Photoshop based on a typical installation. You may need to ask your instructor how to start Photoshop for your system.

1 Click the Start button on the Windows 7 taskbar to display the Start menu and then type `Photoshop CS5` in the 'Search programs and files' box.

2 Click Adobe Photoshop CS5 in the list to start Photoshop.

3 If the Photoshop window is not maximized, click the Maximize button next to the Close button on the Application bar to maximize the window.

To Reset the Workspace

As discussed in Chapter 1, it is helpful to reset the workspace so that the tools and panels appear in their default positions. The following steps select the Essentials workspace.

1 Click the 'Show more workspaces and options' button on the Application bar to display the names of saved workspaces and then click Essentials to select the default workspace panels.

2 Click the 'Show more workspaces and options' button again to display the list and then click Reset Essentials to restore the workspace to its default settings and reposition any panels that may have been moved.

To Reset the Tools and the Options Bar

Recall that the Tools panel and the options bar retain their settings from previous Photoshop sessions. The following steps select the Rectangular Marquee Tool and reset all tool settings in the options bar.

1 If the tools in the Tools panel appear in two columns, click the double arrow at the top of the Tools panel.

2 If necessary, click the Rectangular Marquee Tool button on the Tools panel to select it.

3 Right-click the Rectangular Marquee Tool icon on the options bar to display the context menu and then click Reset All Tools. When Photoshop displays a confirmation dialog box, click the OK button to restore the tools to their default settings.

To Reset the Default Colors

Photoshop retains the foreground and background colors from session to session. Your colors might not display black over white on the Tools panel. The following step resets the default colors.

1 Press the D key to reset the default foreground and background colors.

BTW

Resetting Default Colors
At the bottom of the Tools panel, the Default Foreground and Background Colors button always sets black as the foreground color and white as the background color. You also can press the D key to reset the colors.

To Open a Photo

To open a photo in Photoshop, it must be stored as a digital file on your computer system or on an external storage device. The photos used in this book are stored in the Data Files for Students. You can access the Data Files for Students on the CD that accompanies this book. See the inside back cover of this book for instructions on downloading the Data Files for Students, or contact your instructor for information about accessing the required files.

The following steps open the file, Dishes, from a CD located in drive E.

1 Insert the CD that accompanies this book into your CD drive. After a few seconds, if Windows displays a dialog box, click its Close button.

2 With the Photoshop window open, click File on the menu bar, and then click Open to display the Open dialog box.

3 In the Open dialog box, click the Look in box arrow to display the list of available locations, and then click drive E or the drive associated with your CD.

4 Double-click the Chapter 02 folder to open it, and then double-click the file, Dishes, to open it.

5 When Photoshop displays the image in the document window, if the magnification shown on the status bar is not 25%, double-click the magnification box on the status bar, type 25, and then press the ENTER key to change the magnification (Figure 2–3).

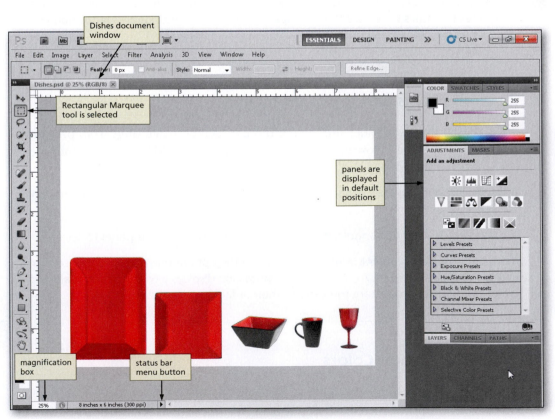

Figure 2–3

To View Rulers

The following steps display the rulers in the document window to facilitate making precise measurements.

1 If the rulers are not shown on the top and left sides of the document window, press CTRL+R to display the rulers in the workspace.

2 If necessary, right-click the horizontal ruler and then click Inches on the context menu to display the rulers in inches.

To Save a Photo

Even though you have yet to edit the photo, it is a good practice to save the file on your personal storage device early in the process. The following steps save the photo with the name Dishes Edited.

1 With your USB flash drive connected to one of the computer's USB ports, click File on the menu bar to display the File menu and then click Save As to display the Save As dialog box.

2 In the File name text box, type **Dishes Edited** to rename the file. Do not press the ENTER key after typing the file name.

3 Click the Save in box arrow and then click UDISK 2.0 (F:), or the location associated with your USB flash drive, in the list, if necessary.

4 Click the Save button in the Save As dialog box to save the file.

> **Break Point:** If you wish to take a break, this is a good place to do so. You can quit Photoshop now. To resume at a later time, start Photoshop, open the file called Dishes Edited, and continue following the steps from this location forward.

The Marquee Tools

The **marquee tools** allow you to draw a marquee that selects a portion of the document window. Marquee tools are useful when the part of an image or photo that you wish to select fits into a rectangular or an elliptical shape. Photoshop has four marquee tools that appear in a context menu when you click the tool and hold down the mouse button, or when you right-click the tool. You can select any of the marquee tools from this context menu. Recall that Photoshop offers the added flexibility of selecting a tool with a single letter shortcut key. Pressing the M key activates the current marquee tool.

The Rectangular Marquee Tool is the default marquee tool that selects a rectangular or square portion of the image or photo. The Elliptical Marquee Tool allows you to select an ellipsis, oval, or circular area.

Dragging with the Rectangular or Elliptical Marquee tools creates a marquee drawn from a corner. If you press the SHIFT key while dragging a marquee, Photoshop constrains the proportions of the shape, creating a perfect square or circle. If you press the ALT key while drawing a selection, Photoshop creates the marquee from the center. Pressing SHIFT+ALT starts from the center and constrains the proportions.

The Single Row Marquee Tool allows you to select a single row of pixels. The Single Column Marquee Tool allows you to select a single column of pixels. A single click in the document window then creates the selection. Because a single row or column of pixels is so small, it is easier to use these two marquee tools at higher magnifications.

BTW

The Tool Preset Picker
Most tools display a Tool Preset picker on the options bar. When you click the button, Photoshop displays a list of settings used during the current Photoshop session or previously saved options bar settings. The list makes it easier to save and reuse tool settings. You can load, edit, and create libraries of tool presets in conjunction with the Tool Presets panel. To choose a tool preset, click the Tool Preset picker in the options bar, and then select a preset from the list.

Table 2 – 1 describes the four marquee tools.

Table 2–1 The Marquee Tools			
Tool	**Purpose**	**Shortcut**	**Button**
Rectangular Marquee	selects a rectangular or square portion of the document window	M SHIFT+M toggles to Elliptical Marquee	
Elliptical Marquee	selects an elliptical, oval, or circular portion of the document window	M SHIFT+M toggles to Rectangular Marquee	
Single Row Marquee	selects a single row of pixels in the document window	(none)	
Single Column Marquee	selects a single column of pixels in the document window	(none)	

Plan Ahead

Choose the correct tool.
When you need to copy, paste, and move portions of your photo, consider carefully which selection tool to use. You want the procedure to be efficient and produce a clear image. Keep in mind the following as you choose a selection tool:

- the shape of the selection

- the background around the selection

- the contrast between the selection and its surroundings

- the proximity of the selection to other objects

- your expertise in using the tool

- the availability of other pointing devices, such as a graphics tablet

- the destination of the paste

The options bar associated with each of the marquee tools contains many buttons and settings to draw effective marquees (Figure 2 – 4). The options bar displays an icon for the chosen marquee on the left, followed by the Tool Preset picker. The Tool Preset picker allows you to save and reuse toolbar settings.

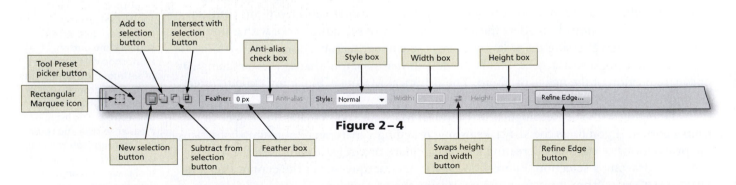

Figure 2–4

The next four buttons to the right adjust the selection. When selected, the New selection button allows you to start a new marquee.

The 'Add to selection' button draws a rectangle or ellipsis and adds it to any current selection. The 'Add to selection' button is useful for selecting the extra corners of an

L-shaped object or for shapes that do not fit within a single rectangle or ellipsis. To activate the 'Add to selection' button, you can click it on the options bar or hold down the SHIFT key while dragging a second selection. When adding to a selection, the mouse pointer changes to a crosshair with a plus sign.

The 'Subtract from selection' button allows you to deselect or remove a portion of an existing selection. The new rectangle or ellipsis is removed from the original selection. It is useful for removing block portions of the background around oddly shaped images, or for deselecting ornamentation in an object. To activate the 'Subtract from selection' button, you can click it on the options bar or hold down the ALT key while dragging a second selection. When subtracting from a selection, the mouse pointer changes to a crosshair with a minus sign.

The 'Intersect with selection' button allows you to draw a second rectangle or ellipsis across a portion of the previously selected area, resulting in a selection border only around the area in which the two selections overlap. To activate the 'Intersect with selection' button, you click it on the options bar, or hold down the SHIFT and ALT keys while dragging a second selection. When creating an intersection, the mouse pointer changes to a crosshair with an X.

To the right of the selection buttons, the options bar displays a Feather box. **Feathering** softens the edges of the selection. In traditional photography, feathering is called **vignetting**, which creates a soft-edged border around an image that blends into the background. Feathering sometimes is used in wedding photos or when a haloed effect is desired. The width of the feather is measured in pixels. When using the Elliptical Marquee Tool, you can further specify blending by selecting the Anti-alias check box. **Anti-aliasing** softens the block-like, staircase look of rounded corners. Figure 2–5 shows a rectangle with no feathering, one with five pixels of feathering, an ellipsis with no anti-aliasing, and one created with a check mark in the Anti-alias check box.

BTW

Anti-Aliasing
Anti-aliasing is available for the Elliptical Marquee Tool, the Lasso Tool, the Polygonal Lasso Tool, the Magnetic Lasso Tool, and the Magic Wand Tool. You must specify this option before using these tools. Once a tool selection is made, you cannot add anti-aliasing.

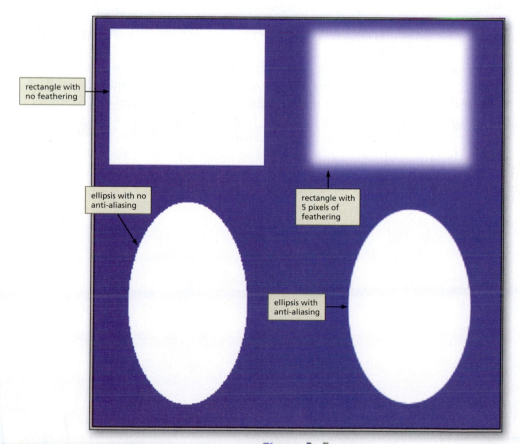

rectangle with no feathering

ellipsis with no anti-aliasing

rectangle with 5 pixels of feathering

ellipsis with anti-aliasing

Figure 2–5

BTW

Marquee Tool Selection
If you are using a different tool, and want to activate the marquee tools, you can click the Rectangular Marquee Tool button on the Tools panel or press the M key to select the tool. Once the tool is selected, pressing SHIFT+M toggles between the Rectangular and Elliptical Marquee tools. You must choose the Single Row and Single Column Marquee tools from the context menu — there are no keyboard shortcuts.

When using the Rectangular Marquee Tool or the Elliptical Marquee Tool, you can click the Style box arrow (Figure 2–4 on page PS 80) to choose how the size of the marquee selection is determined. A Normal style sets the selection marquee proportions by dragging. A Fixed Ratio style sets a height-to-width ratio using decimal values. For example, to draw a marquee twice as wide as it is high, enter **2** for the width and **1** for the height, and then drag in the photo. A Fixed Size style allows you to specify exact pixel values for the marquee's height and width. Photoshop enables the Width box and Height box when you choose a style other than Normal. A button between the two boxes swaps the values, if desired.

Sometimes you need to make subtle changes to a selection marquee. For example, if the border or edge of a selection seems to be jagged or hazy, or if the colors at the edge of a selection bleed slightly across the marquee, you can use the Refine Edge button. When clicked, it opens a dialog box in which you can increase or decrease the radius of the marquee, change the contrast, and smooth the selection border.

Once you have drawn a marquee, you can choose from other options for further manipulation of the selected area. Right-clicking a selection displays a context menu that provides access to many other useful commands such as deselecting, reselecting, or selecting the **inverse**, which means selecting everything in the image outside of the current selection. Right-clicking a selection also enables you to create layers, apply color fills and strokes, and make other changes that you will learn about in future chapters. The Select menu also displays commands to manipulate selections.

If you make a mistake or change your mind when drawing a marquee, you can do one of three things:

1. If you want to start over, and the New selection button is selected on the options bar, you can click somewhere else in the document window to deselect the marquee, and then simply draw a new marquee. Deselecting also is available as a command on the Select menu and on the context menu.

2. If you have already drawn the marquee but wish to move or reposition it, and the New selection button is selected on the options bar, you can drag the selection to the new location.

3. If you want to reposition while you are creating the marquee, do not release the mouse button. Press and hold the SPACEBAR, drag the marquee to the new location, and then release the SPACEBAR. At that point, you can continue dragging to finish drawing the marquee. Repositioning in this manner can be done while using any of the four selection adjustment buttons on the options bar.

BTW

Single Row and Single Column Marquee Tools
To create interesting backgrounds, wallpapers, and color ribbons using the Single Row or Single Column Marquee tools, choose a colorful photo and create a single row or single column marquee. Press CTRL+T to display the bounding box. Then drag the sizing handles until the selection fills the document window.

BTW

Nudging Selections
Instead of dragging to move a selection, you can use the arrow keys on the keyboard to move the selection in small increments in a process called **nudging**.

To Use the Rectangular Marquee Tool

The following step selects the rectangular tray in the Dishes Edited image using the Rectangular Marquee Tool.

1

- With the Rectangular Marquee Tool selected on the Tools panel, drag to draw a rectangle around the tray to create a marquee selection. Do not include the square plate (Figure 2–6).

Experiment

- Practice drawing rectangular and elliptical marquees. Press SHIFT+M to switch between the two. SHIFT+drag to look at the effects. When you are finished, redraw a marquee around the tray.

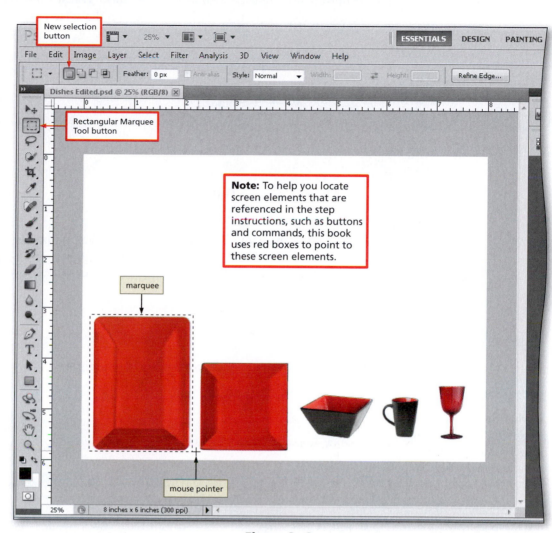

Figure 2–6

The Move Tool

The Move Tool on the Photoshop Tools panel is used to move or make other changes to selections. Activating the Move Tool by clicking the Move Tool button, or by pressing the v key on the keyboard, enables you to move the selection border and its contents by dragging in the document window. When you first use the Move Tool, the mouse pointer displays a black arrowhead with scissors. To move the selection in a straight line, press and hold the SHIFT key while dragging. If you press and hold the ALT key while dragging, you duplicate or move only a copy of the selected area, effectively copying and pasting the selection. While duplicating, the mouse pointer changes to a black arrowhead with a white arrowhead behind it.

When you move selections, you need to be careful about overlapping images. As you will learn in Chapter 3, Photoshop might layer or overlap portions of images when you move them. While that sometimes is preferred when creating collages or composite images, it is undesirable if an important object is obscured. Close tracing while creating selections and careful placement of moved selections will prevent unwanted layering.

Other Ways

1. Press M key or SHIFT+M until Rectangular Marquee Tool is active, drag selection

BTW

Quick Reference
For a table that lists how to complete the tasks covered in this book using the mouse, context menu, and keyboard, see the Quick Reference Summary at the back of this book or visit the Photoshop CS5 Quick Reference Web page (scsite.com/pscs5/qr).

The Move Tool options bar displays tools to help define the scope of the move (Figure 2–7). Later, as you learn about layers, you will use the Auto-Select check box to select layer groupings or single layers. The align and distribute buttons and the Auto-Align Layers button also are used with layers. The Show Transform Controls check box causes Photoshop to display transformation controls on the selection.

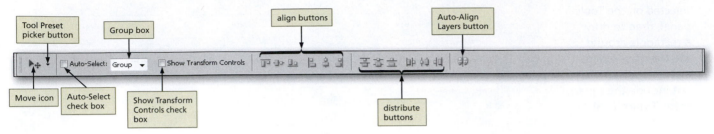

Figure 2–7

As you use the Move Tool throughout this chapter, be careful to position your mouse pointer inside the selection before moving. Do not try to move a selection by dragging its border. If you drag one by mistake, press the ESC key.

To Use the Move Tool

The following steps use the Move Tool to move the tray up and to the right.

1

• With the tray still selected, click the Move Tool button on the Tools panel to activate the Move Tool.

• If necessary, on the options bar, click the Auto-Select check box so it does not display a check mark. If necessary, click the Show Transform Controls check box so it does not display a check mark (Figure 2–8).

Q&A

Are there any other tools nested with the Move Tool?

No, the Move Tool does not have a context menu. Tools with a context menu display a small black triangle in the lower-right corner.

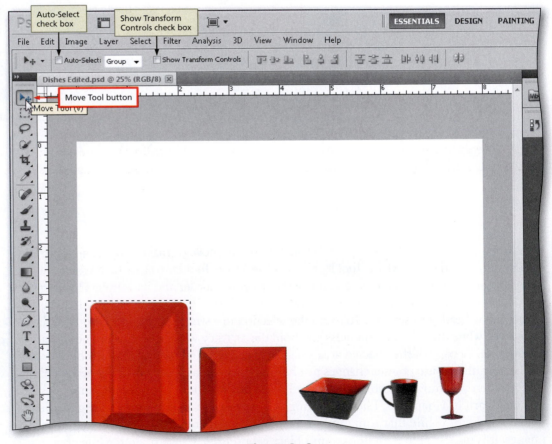

Figure 2–8

2

● Position your mouse pointer over the tray, within the marquee. Drag the selection to a position above the other dishes, near the top margin and approximately centered (Figure 2–9). Do not press any keys.

Q&A

My document window shows a black square. What did I do wrong?

It is possible that the default colors on your system were changed by another user. Press CTRL+Z to undo the move. Press the D key to select the default foreground and background colors. Looking at the bottom of the Tools panel, if black is not showing as being on top, press the X key to exchange the black and white colors.

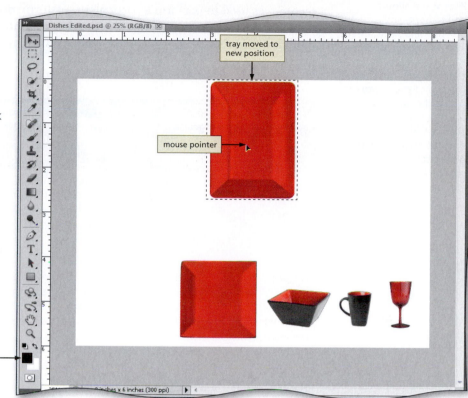

Figure 2–9

Other Ways

1. Press V, drag selection

The Transformation Commands

In Photoshop, the word **transform** refers to making physical changes to a selection. To choose a transformation command, click the Edit menu, point to Transform, and then click the desired transformation. Alternatively, you can click Transform Selection on the context menu that is displayed when you right-click a selection.

When you choose to transform, Photoshop displays a **bounding box**, or border with six sizing handles around the selection (Figure 2–10). A small reference point appears in the center of the selection as a small circle with a crosshair symbol. A **reference point** is a fixed pivot point around which transformations are performed. You can move a reference point by dragging.

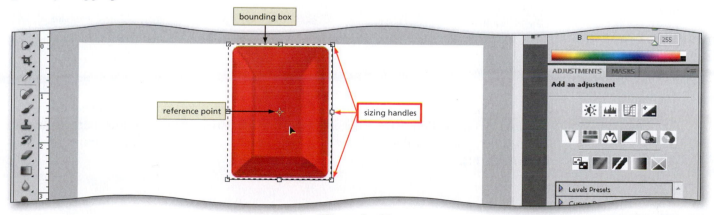

Figure 2–10

Resizing
Photoshop allows you to apply some transformations to entire images or photos, rather than just selections. For example, you can change the size of the photo or rotate the image using the Image menu. You then can enter dimensions or rotation percentages on the submenu and subsequent dialog boxes.

Table 2–2 lists the types of transformations you can perform on a selection, the techniques used to perform a particular transformation, and the result of the transformation. Many of the commands also are on the context menu when you right-click the bounding box. If you choose free transform rather than using the context menu, you must use the mouse techniques to perform the transformation.

Table 2–2 Transformation Commands

Using the Menu	Using the Mouse (Free Transform)	Using the Transform Options Bar	Result
Scale	Drag a sizing handle on the bounding box. SHIFT+drag to scale proportionately. ALT+drag to scale opposite sides at the same time.	To scale numerically, enter percentages in the Width and Height boxes, shown as W and H, on the options bar. Click the Link icon to maintain the aspect ratio.	Selection is displayed at a different size.
Rotate 180° Rotate 90° CW (clockwise) Rotate 90° CCW (counterclockwise)	Move the mouse pointer outside the bounding box border. It becomes a curved, two-headed arrow. Drag in the direction you wish to rotate. SHIFT+drag to constrain the rotation to 15° increments.	In the Set Rotation box, shown as a compass on the options bar, type a positive number for clockwise rotation or a negative number for counterclockwise rotation.	Selection is rotated or revolved around the reference point.
Skew	Right-click selection and then click Skew. Drag a side of the bounding box. ALT+drag to skew both vertically and horizontally.	To skew numerically, enter decimal values in the horizontal skew and vertical skew boxes, shown as H and V on the options bar.	Selection is tilted or slanted either horizontally or vertically.
Distort	Right-click selection and then click Distort. Drag a corner sizing handle to stretch the bounding box.	Enter new numbers in the location, size, rotation, and skew boxes.	Selection is larger on one edge than on the others.
Perspective	Right-click selection and then click Perspective. Drag a corner sizing handle to apply perspective to the bounding box.	Enter new numbers in the size, rotation, and skew boxes.	The selection appears larger on one edge than on the others, giving the larger edge the appearance of being closer to the viewer.
Warp	When the warp mesh is displayed, drag any line or point.	Click the Custom box arrow. Click a custom warp.	Selection is reshaped with bulge, arch, warped corner, or twist.
Flip Horizontal Flip Vertical	Flipping is available only on the menu.	Flipping is available only on the menu.	Selection is turned upside down or mirrored.

Deleting Selections
You can delete a selection by pressing the DELETE key. Photoshop will display a Fill dialog box. Click the OK button. If you delete by accident, press CTRL+Z to bring the selection back.

To display the Transform options bar, create a selection, and then choose Free Transform on the Edit menu, click a sizing handle, or press CTRL+T. Photoshop displays a Transform options bar that contains boxes and buttons to help you with your transformation (Figure 2–11).

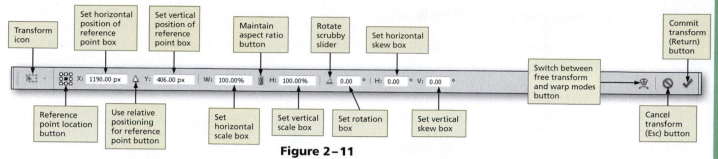

Figure 2–11

On the left side of the Transform options bar, Photoshop displays the 'Reference point location' button. Each of the nine squares on the button corresponds to a point on the bounding box. The default middle square represents the center reference point. To select a different reference point, click a different square on the 'Reference point location' button.

The X and Y boxes allow you to place the reference point at an exact pixel location in the document window by entering horizontal and vertical values. When you enter a value in one of those boxes, Photoshop moves the entire selection. If you click the Use relative positioning for reference point button, located between the X and Y boxes, the movement of the selection is relative to the current location.

The W and H boxes allow you to scale the width and height of the selection. When you click the 'Maintain aspect ratio' button between the W and H boxes, the aspect ratio of the selection is maintained.

To the right of the scale boxes is a Set rotation box. Entering a positive number rotates, or turns, the selection clockwise; a negative number rotates the selection counter-clockwise.

The H and V boxes, to the right of the Set rotation box, set the horizontal and vertical skews of the selection, measured in degrees. A positive number skews the selection to the right; a negative number skews to the left.

A unique feature is the ability to drag labels to change the box values. For example, if you drag the H, Y, W, or other labels, the values in the text boxes change. The interactive labels, called **scrubby sliders**, appear when you position the mouse pointer over the label. When you point to any of the scrubby sliders on the Transform options bar, the mouse pointer changes to a hand with a two-headed arrow, indicating the ability to drag. Dragging to the right increases the value; dragging to the left decreases the value. Holding down the SHIFT key while dragging the scrubby slider accelerates the change by a factor of 10. Many options bars use scrubby sliders.

On the far right of the Transform options bar are three buttons. The first one switches between the Transform options bar and the Warp options bar. After you are finished making transformations, you commit changes, or apply the transformations by pressing the ENTER key or by clicking the 'Commit transform (Return)' button (the second button). Committing the transformation is the same as saving it. If you do not wish to make the transformation, press the ESC key or click the third button, the Cancel transform (Esc) button.

After transforming a selection, you must either commit or cancel the transformation before you can perform any other action in Photoshop.

To Display Transformation Controls

The following step displays the transformation controls, including the bounding box, the reference point and the Transform options bar.

• Press CTRL+T to display the bounding box and the Transform options bar (Figure 2–12).

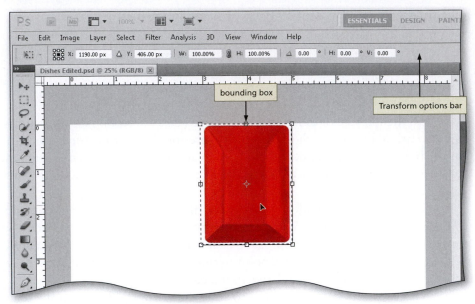

Figure 2–12

To Rotate a Selection

The following steps rotate the tray.

• Move the mouse pointer to the upper-right corner of the tray, just outside of the bounding box.

• When the mouse pointer displays a double-headed curved arrow, drag to the right and down until the tray appears on its side, as shown in Figure 2–13.

Q&A

How do you use the reference point?

The reference point serves as the pivot point during rotation. The default placement is in the center of the selection. If you drag the reference point to another location, any rotation performed on the selection will pivot around that new location.

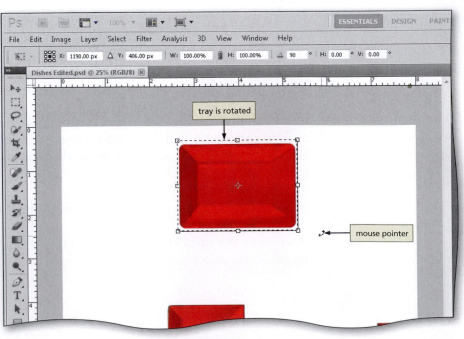

Figure 2–13

 **Experiment**

- On the options bar, drag the Rotate scrubby slider in either direction to watch the selection rotate. When you are done, rotate the tray to match Figure 2–13.

2

- Press the ENTER key to confirm the transformation.

Other Ways		
1. On Edit menu, click Free Transform, drag selection	2. On Edit menu, point to Transform, click desired rotate command	3. On options bar, enter degree rotation in Set Rotation box

To Deselect

The following step removes the selection marquee using the menu.

1   Click Select on the menu bar and then click Deselect to remove the selection marquee.

The Quick Selection Tool

The Quick Selection Tool draws a selection quickly using the mouse. As you drag, Photoshop creates a selection automatically, expanding outward to find and follow the defined edges in the image. The Quick Selection Tool is nested with the Magic Wand Tool on the Tools panel. You can access either tool from the context menu or by pressing the w key; if the Magic Wand Tool has been used previously, press SHIFT+W.

Dragging a quick selection is almost like painting a stroke with a brush. The Quick Selection Tool does not create a rectangular or oval selection; rather, it looks for a contrast in color and aligns the selection border to that contrast. It is most useful for isolated objects or parts of an image that contain a contrasting background. When using the Quick Selection Tool, the mouse pointer changes to a brush tip that displays a circle with a centered cross inside. You can decrease or increase the size of the brush tip by using the LEFT BRACKET ([ ) or RIGHT BRACKET ( ]) keys respectively, or by using the options bar.

The Quick Selection Tool options bar (Figure 2–14) displays the size of the brush and contains some of the same buttons as other selection tools. It also contains an Auto-Enhance check box that reduces roughness in the selection boundary when the box is checked.

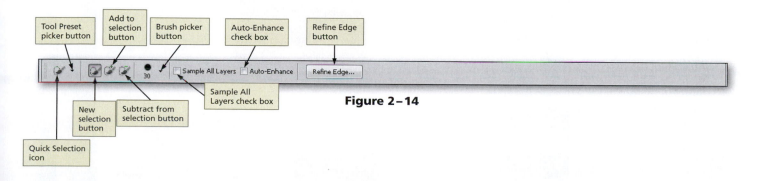

Figure 2–14

To Use the Quick Selection Tool

The following steps use the Quick Selection Tool to select the square plate.

1

- Right-click the Quick Selection Tool button on the Tools panel to display the context menu (Figure 2–15).

Q&A

What should I do if I make a mistake with the Quick Selection Tool?

If you make a mistake and want to start over, you can deselect by pressing CTRL+D, and then begin again.

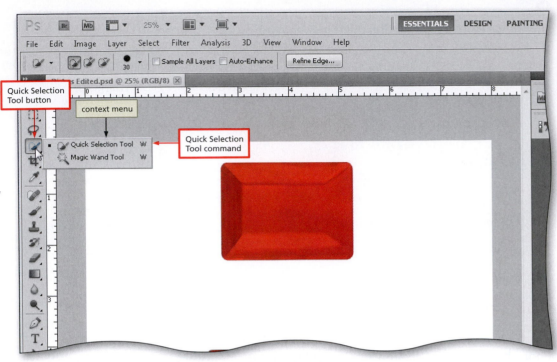

Figure 2–15

2

- If necessary, click Quick Selection Tool to select it.

- On the options bar, click the New selection button, if necessary. Click the Auto-Enhance check box so it displays a check mark, if necessary (Figure 2–16).

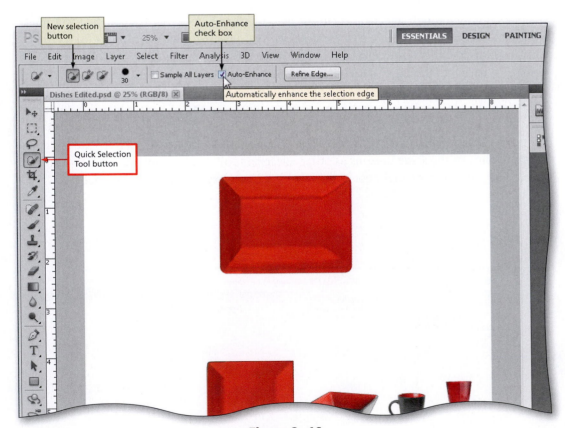

Figure 2–16

3

- Move the mouse pointer to the top-left corner of the square plate, and then slowly drag down and right to select only the plate (Figure 2–17).

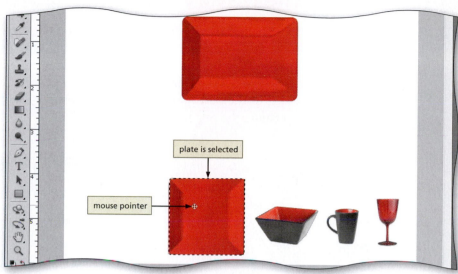

plate is selected

mouse pointer

Figure 2–17

To Move a Selection

The following steps move the plate using the Move Tool. If you make a mistake while moving, press CTRL+Z and then move again. If you accidentally move a sizing handle or the center reference point, press the ESC key to cancel the transformation.

1 On the Tools panel, click the Move Tool button to select it.

2 Drag the selection up to a location in front of the tray (Figure 2–18). Do not press any keys.

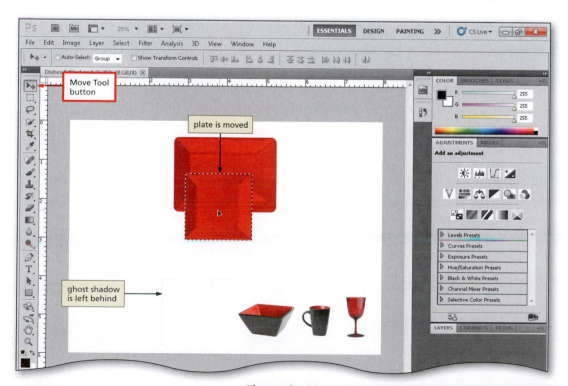

Move Tool button

plate is moved

ghost shadow is left behind

Figure 2–18

The History Panel

The History panel is displayed when you click the History button in the vertical docking of collapsed panels. The History panel records each step, called a **state**, as you edit a photo (Figure 2–19). Photoshop displays the initial state of the document at the top of the panel. Each time you apply a change to an image, the new state of that image is added to the bottom of the panel. Each state lists the name of the tool or command used to change the image.

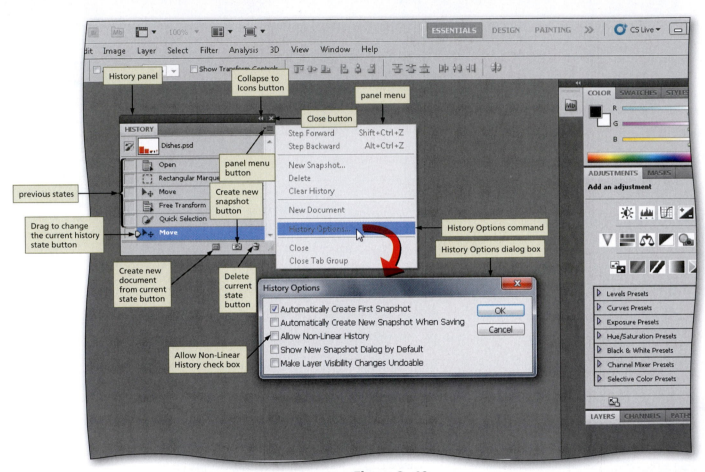

Figure 2–19

The History Panel
The History panel will list a Duplicate state when you use the ALT key to copy a selection. The word, Paste, will appear next to the state when you use the Copy and Paste commands from the keyboard or from the menu. The Copy command alone does not affect how the image looks; it merely sends a copy to the system Clipboard. Therefore, it does not appear as a state.

Like the Navigator panel that you learned about in Chapter 1, the History panel also has a panel menu where you can clear all states, change the history settings, or dock the panel. Buttons on the History panel status bar allow you to create a new document, save the selected state, or delete it. The panel can be collapsed by clicking the History button in the vertical docking or by clicking the Collapse to icons button. To redisplay a collapsed History panel, click the History button in the vertical docking or choose it again from the Window menu.

To Display the History Panel

The following step displays the History panel.

1
• Click the History
button on the vertical
docking of collapsed
panels to expand
the History panel
(Figure 2–20).

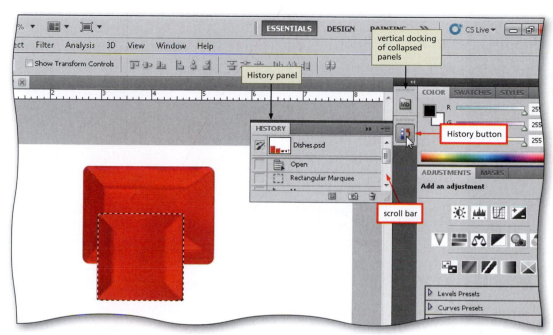

Figure 2–20

Using the History Panel

You can use the History panel in several different ways. When you select one of the states, the image reverts to how it looked when that change first was applied. Some users use the History panel to undo mistakes. Others use it to try out or experiment with different edits. By clicking a state, you can view the state temporarily or start working again from that point. You can step forward and backward through the states in the History panel by pressing CTRL+SHIFT+Z or CTRL+ALT+Z respectively.

Selecting a state and then changing the image in any way eliminates all the states in the History panel that came after it; however, if you select a state and change the image by accident, you can use the Undo command or CTRL+Z to restore the eliminated states. If you select the Allow Non-Linear History check box in the History Options dialog box (Figure 2–20) deleting a state deletes only that state.

You can use the History panel to jump to any recent state of the image created during the current working session by clicking the state. Alternatively, you can give a state a new name called a **snapshot**. Naming a snapshot makes it easy to identify. Snapshots are stored at the top of the History panel and make it easy to compare effects. For example, you can take a snapshot before and after a series of transformations. Then, by clicking between the two snapshots in the History panel, you can see the total effect, or choose the before snapshot and start over. To create a snapshot, right-click the step and then click New Snapshot on the context menu or click the Create new snapshot button on the History panel status bar. Snapshots are not saved with the image; closing an image deletes its snapshots.

Not all steps appear in the History panel. For instance, changes to panels, color settings, actions, and preferences are not displayed in the History panel, because they are not changes to a particular image.

BTW

Moving Among History Panel States
Photoshop uses many function keys to move easily among the states in the History panel. To step forward, press CTRL+SHIFT+Z. To step backward, press CTRL+ALT+Z. You also can use the History panel menu to step forward and backward.

By default, the History panel lists the previous 20 states. You can change the number of remembered states by changing a preference setting (see Appendix C). Photoshop deletes older states automatically to free more memory. Once you close and reopen the document, all states and snapshots from the last working session are cleared from the panel.

To Undo Changes Using the History Panel

Notice that in Figure 2–18 on page PS 91, a ghost shadow appears in the previous location of the plate. That sometimes happens with any of the selection tools, especially when fringe pixels are faded. The following steps undo the Move command.

1
- Scroll down in the History panel to display the last few states.

- Click the Quick Selection state in the History panel to go back one step and undo the move (Figure 2–21). Do not press any keys.

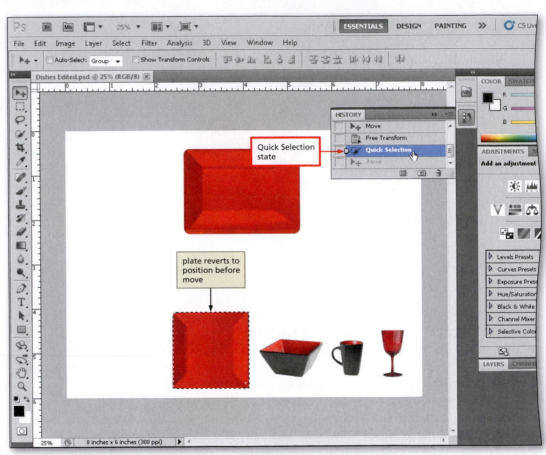

Figure 2–21

Q&A | Could I have pressed CTRL+Z to undo the move?

Yes, if you only need to undo one step, pressing CTRL+Z will work. If you need to go back more than one step, you can press CTRL+ALT+Z or use the History panel.

Q&A | What is the box to the left of each state?

The box sets the source for painting a clone-like image using the Art History Brush Tool.

Other Ways

1. Press CTRL+ALT+Z

To Collapse the History Panel

You can redisplay the History panel whenever you need it; however, the following step collapses the History panel to a button in the vertical docking so you can see more of the document window.

1

• Click the History button to collapse the panel (Figure 2–22).

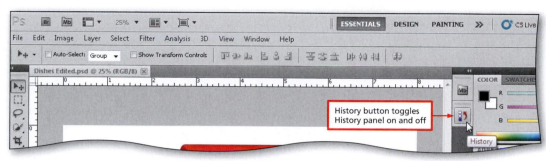

Figure 2–22

Refining Edges

The Refine Edge button located on the options bar of each selection tool displays a dialog box where you can make choices about improving selections with jagged edges, soft transitions, hazy borders, or fine details and improve the quality of a selection's edges. Additionally, it allows you to view the selection on different backgrounds to facilitate editing (Figure 2–23).

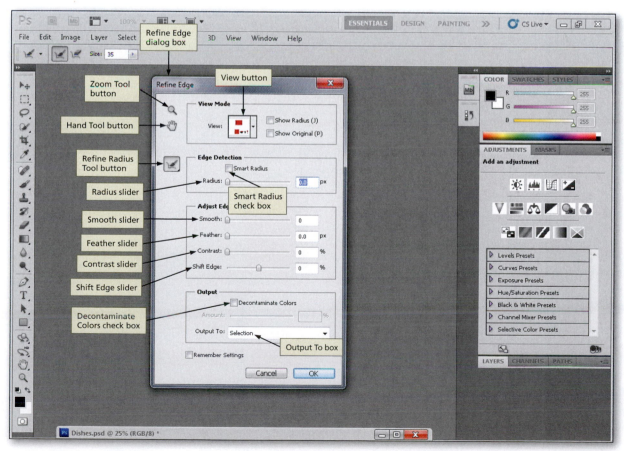

Figure 2–23

Table 2–3 describes some of the controls in the Refine Edge dialog box.

Table 2–3 Controls in the Refine Edge Dialog Box	
Control	**Function**
View Mode area	allows you to choose the background of the selection
Smart Radius check box	adjusts the radius edges automatically
Radius slider	adjusts the size of the selection boundary by pixels
Smooth slider	reduces irregular areas in the selection boundary to create a smoother outline with values from 0 to 100 pixels
Feather slider	softens the edges of the selection for blending into backgrounds using values from 0 to 250 pixels
Contrast slider	sharpens the selection edges to remove any hazy or extraneous pixels, sometimes called fuzzy artifacts or noise; increasing the contrast percentage can remove excessive noise near selection edges caused by a high radius setting
Shift Edge slider	enlarges or shrinks selection border
Decontaminate Colors check box	replaces fringe color fringes
Output To box	sets the output to a mask, layer or new document

The various settings in the Refine Edge dialog box take practice to use intuitively. The more experience you have adjusting the settings, the more comfortable you will feel with the controls. To improve selections for images on a contrasting background, you should first increase the radius and then increase the contrast to sharpen the edges. For grayscale images or selections where the colors of the object and the background are similar, try smoothing first, then feathering. For all selections, you might need to adjust the Shift Edge slider.

To Refine Edges

The following steps refine the edge of the selection to eliminate the ghost shadow.

- On the Tools panel, click the Quick Selection Tool button to return to the Quick Selection Tool.

- On the Quick Selection Tool options bar, click the Refine Edge button to display the Refine Edge dialog box.

- Drag the Contrast slider (Refine Edge dialog box) until the Contrast box displays 35% to increase the contrast.

- Drag the Shift Edge slider until the percentage is +60% to expand the selection (Figure 2–24).

🔍 Experiment

- Drag the Shift Edge slider to various percentages and watch how the selection changes. Return the slider to +60%.

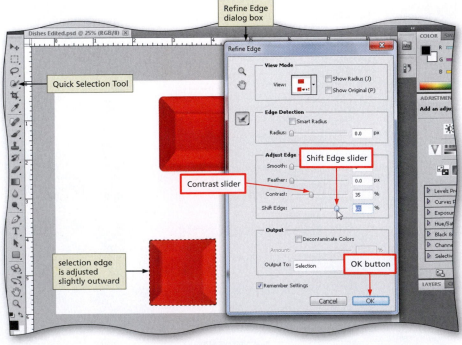

Figure 2–24

2

- Click the OK button (Refine Edge dialog box) to apply the changes and close the dialog box.

Should I have any white area inside the selection marquee?

No. If your selection includes any white areas, select the 'Subtract from selection' button. Drag the white area carefully and slowly to remove it from the selection.

To Move Again

The following steps move the plate again, this time without leaving behind a ghost shadow.

1 Click the Move Tool button on the Tools panel to activate the Move Tool.

2 Drag the selection up and slightly right so the plate is in front of the tray, as shown in Figure 2–25.

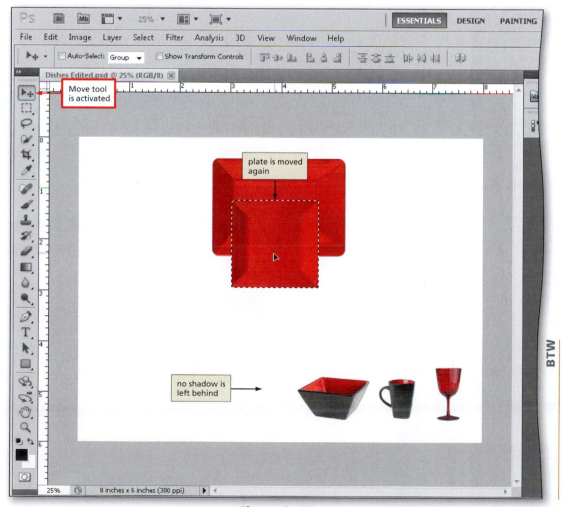

plate is moved again

Move tool is activated

no shadow is left behind

Figure 2–25

BTW

Ghost Shadows
After refining the edges, if you still have a ghost shadow, you can go back a step in the History panel, and then expand the selection even more, using the Refine Edge dialog box. Or, after you finish with the selection, you can use the Eraser tool to erase the shadow.

Plan Ahead

Plan your duplications.

Creating a storyboard, either by hand or by using software, allows you to plan your image and make decisions about copies and placement. Some graphic artists annotate each copy in the storyboard with information about size, shape, location, and the tool they plan to use. For example, when you paste or drag a new copy of an image into a photo, you have two choices. You can keep the copy as an exact duplicate, or you can transform the copy. The choice depends on the visual effect you want to achieve and the customer requirements. Noting those requirements on your storyboard ahead of time will facilitate creating your image.

Use an exact copy to duplicate a logo or a border, or to create a tiled background. Commercial applications may create duplications to represent growth; or several duplications beside each other can emphasize a brand. Sometimes artists will duplicate an item several times when creating a quick sketch or a rough draft. Across photos, exact duplicates maintain consistency and product identification.

Transforming a copy or selection provides additional flexibility and diversity. You might want to create the illusion of multiple, different items to promote sales. Scaling, skewing, warping, and distorting provide interest and differentiation, and sometimes can correct lens errors. Flipping, rotating, or changing the perspective of the copy adds excitement to reproductions and creates the illusion of three dimensions.

Cutting and Pasting
Just as you do in other applications, you can use the Cut, Copy, and Paste commands from the Edit menu or shortcut keys to make changes to selections. Unless you predefine a selection area by dragging a marquee, the Paste command pastes to the center of the document window. Both the commands and the shortcut keys create a new layer when they copy or paste.

To Duplicate the Selection

Recall that pressing and holding the ALT key while dragging with the Move Tool creates a copy, or duplicates, the selection. The following step selects the Move Tool and creates a copy of the selected plate.

1

- With the plate still selected, if necessary, click the Move Tool button to select the Move Tool.

- Press and hold the ALT key while dragging to duplicate and move the selection to a location slightly down and right of the original, as shown in Figure 2–26. The copy will overlap the original.

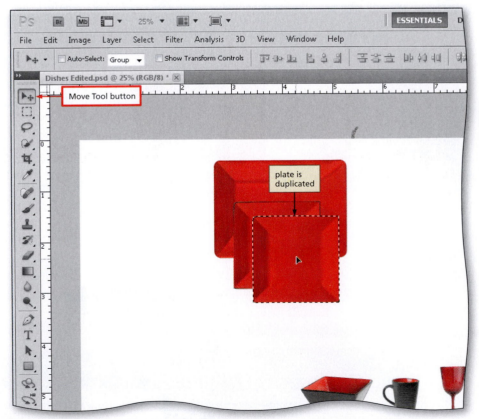

Figure 2–26

Other Ways
1. Press CTRL+C, press CTRL+V, press V, drag selection
2. Press V, ALT+drag selection
3. Select Magic Wand Tool, CTRL+drag selection

To Scale a Selection

As described in Table 2–2 (on page PS 86), when you scale a selection, you resize it by changing its width, height, or both. The following steps scale the duplicated plate.

1

- With the Move Tool button still selected, click the Show Transform Controls check box on the options bar to display the bounding box (Figure 2–27).

Q&A

Could I use CTRL+T to display the bounding box?

Yes, you can use either the check box or those shortcut keys.

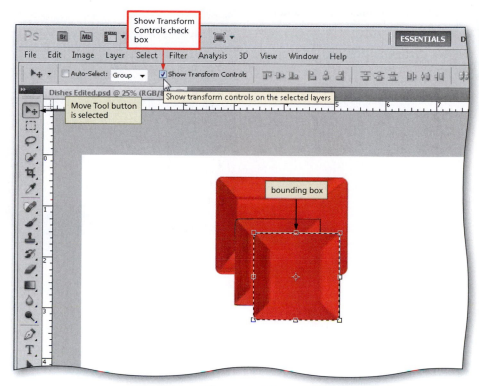

Figure 2–27

2

- SHIFT+drag the upper-right sizing handle toward the center of the plate until it is resized approximately 70 percent of the original (Figure 2–28).

Q&A

How can I estimate 70 percent?

As soon as you begin to scale, the Move options bar changes to the Transform options bar. The values in the W: and H: boxes change as you scale the image. You can drag until they display approximately 70%.

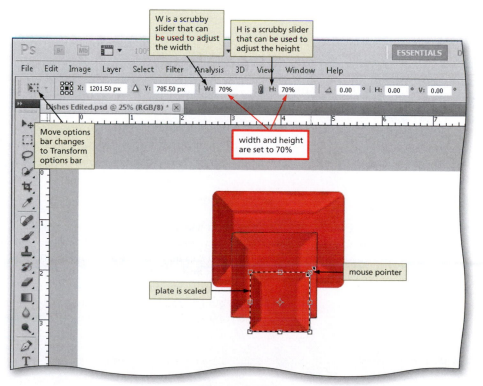

Figure 2–28

3

- Press the ENTER key to commit the change.

- Click the Show Transform Controls check box to remove the bounding box from the selection.

- Press CTRL+D to deselect (Figure 2–29).

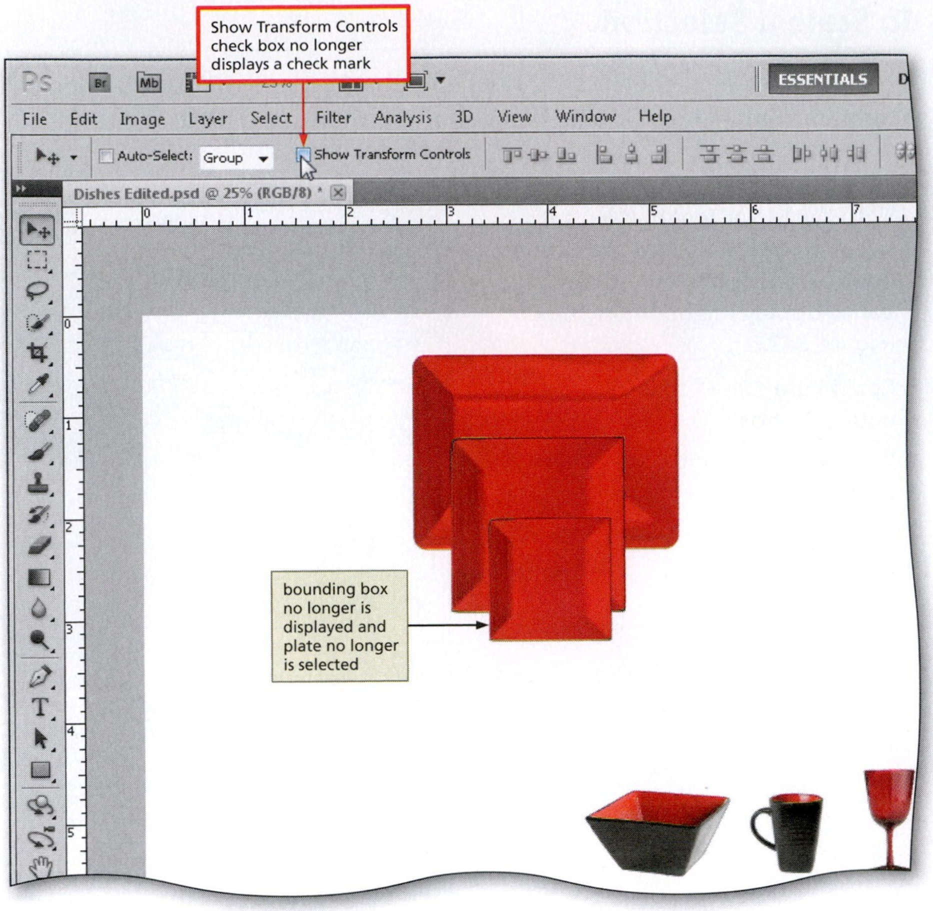

Figure 2–29

Other Ways

1. On Transform options bar, enter new width and height, press ENTER

2. Press CTRL+T, right-click selection, click Scale, drag selection handle

3. On Edit menu point to Transform, click Scale, drag selection handle

Guides and Grids
You can change the color or style of guides and grids. On the Edit menu, point to Preferences, and then click Guides, Grid, & Slices.

Grids and Guides

Photoshop can show a grid of lines superimposed on an image. The **grid** is useful for laying out elements symmetrically or positioning them precisely. The grid can appear as nonprinting lines or dots. A **guide** is a nonprinting ruler line or dashed line that graphic designers use to align objects or mark key measurements. Both grids and guides help position selections precisely. You can change the color, style, and grid dimensions.

Plan Ahead

Use grids and guides.
Showing grids in your document window gives you multiple horizontal and vertical lines with which you can align selections, copies, and new images. Grids also can help you match and adjust sizes and perspective.

Create guides when you have an exact margin, location, or size in mind. Because selections will snap to guides, you easily can create an upper-left corner to use as a boundary when you move and copy. Grids and guides do not print and are turned on and off without difficulty.

Table 2–4 displays various ways to manipulate guides.

Table 2–4 Manipulating Guides	
Action	**Steps**
Change color and style	Double-click guide.
Clear all guides	On the View menu, click Clear Guides.
Convert between horizontal and vertical guide	Select the Move Tool, ALT+CLICK guide.
Create	Drag from ruler into document window; or, on the View menu, click New Guide, and then enter the orientation and position.
Lock in place	On the View menu, click Lock Guides.
Move	Select the Move Tool, and then drag the guide to a new location.
Remove	Select the Move Tool, and then drag the guide to the ruler.
Snap guide to ruler tick	SHIFT+drag the ruler.
Turn on/off display	On the Application bar, click View Extras, and then click Show Guides; or, on the View menu, point to Show, and then click Guides; or press CTRL+SEMICOLON (;).

The term **snapping** refers to the ability of objects to attach, or automatically align with a grid or guide. For example, if you select an object in your image and begin to move it, as you get close to a guide, the object's selection border will attach itself to the guide. It is not a permanent attachment. If you do not wish to leave the object there, simply keep dragging. To turn on or off snapping, click Snap on the View menu.

In a later chapter, you will learn about smart guides that automatically appear when you draw a shape or move a layer. Smart guides further help align shapes, slices, selections, and layers. Appendix C describes how to set guide and grid preferences using the Edit menu.

To Display a Grid

The following steps display the grid.

1
- On the Application bar, click the View Extras button to display its menu (Figure 2–30).

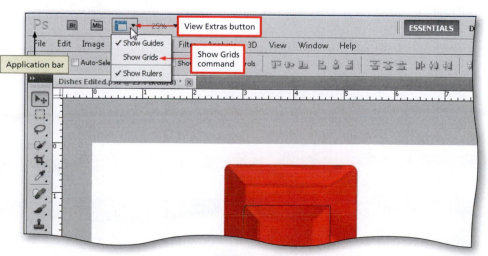

Figure 2–30

- Click the Show Grids command to display the grid (Figure 2–31).

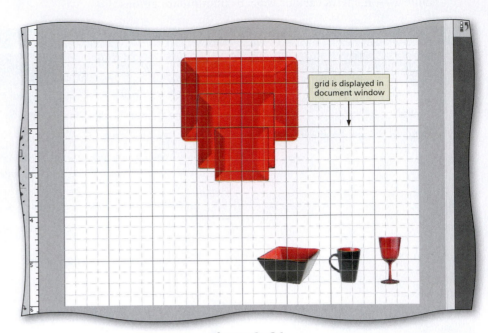

grid is displayed in document window

Figure 2–31

Other Ways

1. Press CTRL+APOSTROPHE (')
2. On View menu, point to Show, click Grid

To Turn Off the Grid Display

The display of a grid is a **toggle**, which means that you turn it off in the same manner that you turned it on; in this case, with the same command. The following step turns off the grid display.

- On the Application bar, click the View Extras button to display its menu.

- Click Show Grids to remove the check mark and remove the grid from the display (Figure 2–32).

grid no longer is displayed

Figure 2–32

To Create a Guide

The following step creates a guide to help place the bowl and cup on the same horizontal plane.

1

- Position the mouse pointer in the horizontal ruler at the top of the document window and then drag down into the image to create a guide at approximately 3.5 inches.

- Release the mouse button (Figure 2–33).

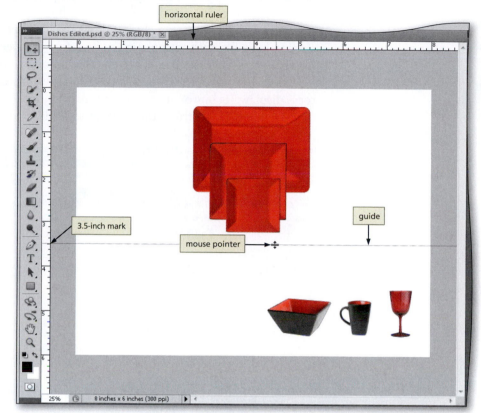

Figure 2–33

Other Ways

1. To show or hide guides, press CTRL+SEMICOLON (;)

2. To create guide, on View menu click New Guide, enter value, click OK

The Lasso Tools

The **lasso tools** draw freehand selection borders around objects. The lasso tools provide more flexibility than the marquee tools with their standardized shapes, and might be more suitable than the Quick Selection Tool when the object has a non-contrasting background. There are three kinds of lasso tools. The first is the default Lasso Tool, which allows you to create a selection by using the mouse to drag around any object in the document window. You select the Lasso Tool button on the Tools panel. You then begin to drag around the desired area. When you release the mouse, Photoshop connects the selection border to the point where you began dragging and completes the loop. The Lasso Tool is useful for a quick, rough selection.

The Polygonal Lasso Tool is similar to the Lasso Tool in that it draws irregular shapes in the image; however, the Polygonal Lasso Tool uses straight line segments. To use the Polygonal Lasso Tool, choose the tool, click in the document window, release the mouse button, and then move the mouse in straight lines, clicking each time you turn a corner. When you get back to the beginning of the polygon, double-click to complete the selection.

The Magnetic Lasso Tool allows you to click close to the edge of the object you wish to select. The Magnetic Lasso Tool tries to find the edge of the object by looking for

BTW

Lasso Tool Selection
If you are using a different tool, and want to activate a lasso tool, you can click the Lasso Tool button on the Tools panel or press the L key to select the Lasso Tool. After selecting the Lasso Tool, pressing SHIFT+L cycles through the three lasso tools.

the closest color change. It then attaches the marquee to the pixel on the edge of the color change. As you move the mouse, the Magnetic Lasso Tool follows that change with a magnetic attraction. The Magnetic Lasso Tool's marquee displays fastening points on the edge of the object. You can create more fastening points by clicking as you move the mouse, to force a change in direction or to adjust the magnetic attraction. When you get all the way around the object, you click at the connection point to complete the loop, or double-click to have Photoshop connect the loop for you. Because the Magnetic Lasso Tool looks for changes in color to define the edges of an object, it might not be as effective to create selections in images with a busy background or images with low contrast. Each of the lasso tools displays its button icon as the mouse pointer.

Table 2–5 describes the three lasso tools.

Table 2–5 The Lasso Tools			
Tool	**Purpose**	**Shortcut**	**Button**
Lasso	used to draw freeform loops, creating a selection border	L SHIFT+L toggles through all three lasso tools	
Polygonal Lasso	used to draw straight lines, creating segments of a selection border	L SHIFT+L toggles through all three lasso tools	
Magnetic Lasso	used to draw a selection border that snaps to the edge of contrasting color areas in the image	L SHIFT+L toggles through all three lasso tools	

Each of the lasso tools displays an options bar similar to the marquee options bar, with buttons to add to, subtract from, and intersect with the selection, as well as the ability to feather the border. The Magnetic Lasso Tool options bar (Figure 2–34) also includes an Anti-alias check box to smooth the borders of a selection and a Contrast box to enter the contrast, or sensitivity of color, that Photoshop evaluates in making the path selection. A higher value detects only edges that contrast sharply with their surroundings; a lower value detects lower-contrast edges. The Width box causes the Magnetic Lasso Tool to detect edges only within the specified distance from the mouse pointer. A Frequency box allows you to specify the rate at which the lasso sets fastening points. A higher value anchors the selection border in place more quickly. A tablet pressure button on the right changes the pen width when using a graphic drawing tablet instead of a mouse.

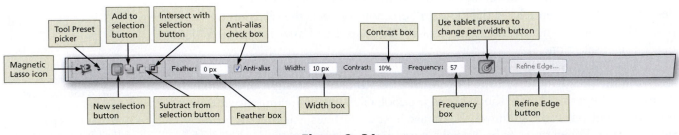

Figure 2–34

To Select Using the Polygonal Lasso Tool

The following steps select the bowl by drawing lines around it with the Polygonal Lasso Tool.

1

• Right-click the Lasso Tool button on the Tools panel to display the context menu (Figure 2–35).

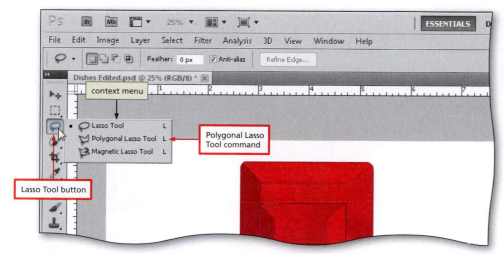

Figure 2–35

2

• Click the Polygonal Lasso Tool to activate the lasso.

• If necessary, on the options bar, click the New selection button to select it (Figure 2–36).

Experiment

• Practice using the Polygonal Lasso Tool to draw a triangle by doing the following: in a blank area of the photo, click to begin; move the mouse pointer to the right and then click to create one side. Move the mouse pointer up and then click to create a second side. Move the mouse pointer to the beginning point and then click to complete the lasso. When you are finished experimenting, press CTRL+D to deselect.

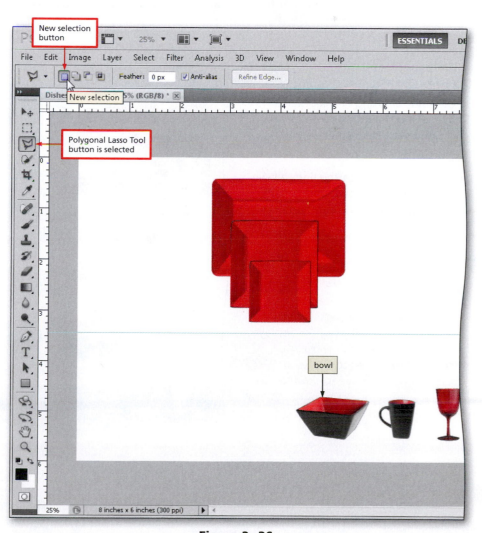

Figure 2–36

3

- Click the upper-left corner of the bowl and then move the mouse pointer to the right to create the first line.

- Click the upper-right corner of the bowl (Figure 2–37).

Q&A Can I reposition the starting point if I make a mistake?

Yes. Press the ESC key and then start again.

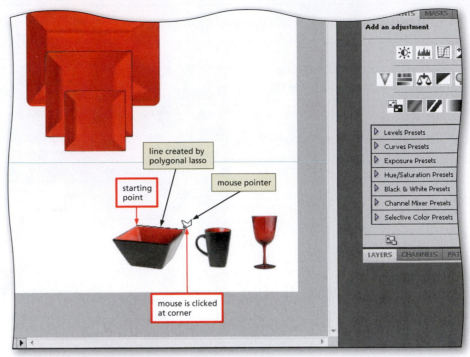

Figure 2–37

4

- Continue creating line segments by moving the mouse pointer and clicking each time you need to change direction.

- When you complete the lines all the way around the bowl, double-click to connect them and complete the selection (Figure 2–38).

Q&A What was the small circle that appeared when I moved close to the beginning of the polygonal lasso?

When the mouse pointer moves close to where you started the polygonal lasso, Photoshop displays a small circle, which means you can click to complete the lasso. Otherwise, you have to double-click.

Figure 2–38

Other Ways

1. Press L or SHIFT+L until Polygonal Lasso Tool is active, click image, move mouse

To Grow the Selection

A quick way to increase the size of a selection without using the Refine Edge dialog box is to use the Grow command on the Select menu. The Grow command will increase, or grow, the selection border to include all adjacent pixels falling within the tolerance range as specified in the options bar of most selection tools. Choosing the Grow command more than once will increase the selection in increments. Similar to refining the edge, the Grow command helps to avoid leaving behind a ghost shadow when you move the selection.

The following steps grow the selection around the bowl, to prevent a ghost shadow.

- Click Select on the menu bar to display the Select menu (Figure 2–39).

Q&A

Will I notice a big difference after I use the Grow command?

You might not see the subtle change in the selection marquee; however, growing the border helps ensure that you will not leave behind a ghost shadow when you move the selection.

2

- Click Grow to increase the selection border.

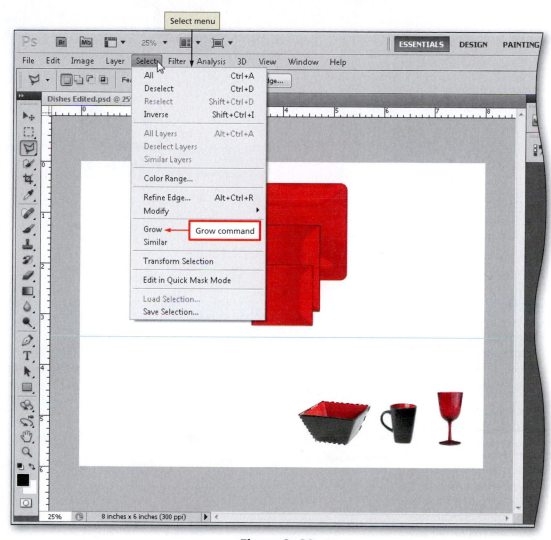

Figure 2–39

To Move and Snap the Bowl

1 Press the V key to activate the Move Tool.

2 Drag the bowl to a location in front of the plate, so the lower-right corner snaps to the guide, as shown in Figure 2–40 on the next page.

3 Press CTRL+D to deselect. If a shadow remains in the original location, you can press ALT+CTRL+Z several times and try again; or, you can ignore the shadow, as it will be cropped out of the image later in the chapter.

BTW

Snapping
To turn on or off the snapping capability, you can press SHIFT+CTRL+SEMICOLON (;).

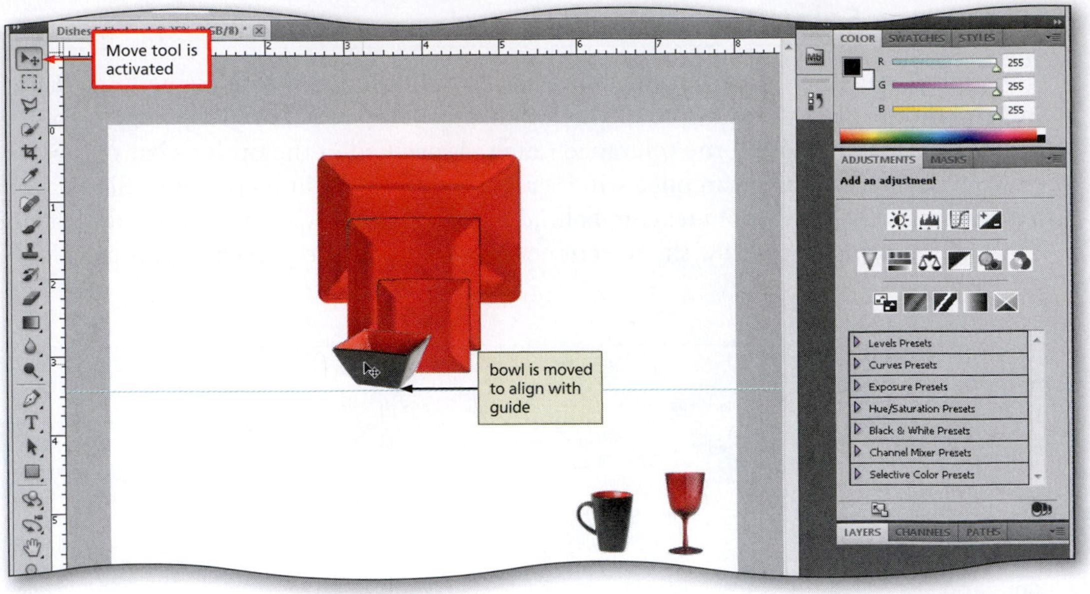

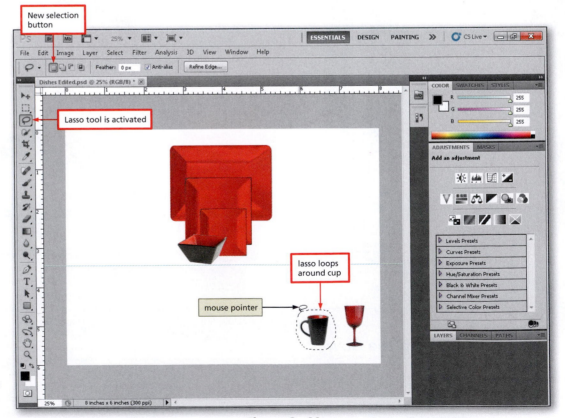

Figure 2–40

To Select Using the Lasso Tool

The following step uses the Lasso Tool to select the cup by dragging around it. As you will notice, the Lasso Tool leaves white space around the cup and inside the handle.

1

• Right-click the current lasso tool button on the Tools panel to display the context menu, and then click Lasso Tool to select it.

• If necessary, on the options bar, click the New selection button.

• Drag around the cup to create a completed lasso and then release the mouse button to connect the beginning and end points (Figure 2–41).

Q&A How will I know if the lasso is complete?

When the lasso ends are connected, the marquee will pulsate. You also can double-click to connect the ends.

Figure 2–41

Other Ways

1. Press L or SHIFT+L until Lasso Tool is active, drag selection

The Magic Wand Tool

The Magic Wand Tool lets you select a consistently colored area with a single click. For example, if you wanted to select the blue sky in an image, clicking with the Magic Wand Tool would automatically select it, no matter what the shape of the blue area. When you use the Magic Wand Tool and click in the image, Photoshop selects every pixel that contains the same or similar colors as the location you clicked. The default setting is to select contiguous pixels only, but Photoshop allows you to change that setting to select all pixels of the same color. The Magic Wand Tool mouse pointer appears as a small line with a starburst, or magic wand, on the end.

The Magic Wand Tool options bar (Figure 2–42) contains the same selection adjustment buttons as the marquee tools, including the ability to create a new selection, add to or subtract from a selection, and intersect selections. The Magic Wand Tool options bar also has a Tolerance box that allows you to enter a value that determines the similarity or difference in the color of the selected pixels. A low value selects the few colors that are very similar to the pixel you click. A higher value selects a broader range of colors. As with the marquee tools, the Anti-alias check box smoothes the jagged edges of a selection by softening the color transition between edge pixels and background pixels. While anti-aliasing is useful when cutting, copying, and pasting selections to create composite images, it might leave behind a trace shadow after cutting or moving a selection.

BTW
The Similar Command
The Similar command increases the selection to include pixels throughout the selection, not just adjacent ones, which fall within the specified tolerance range. Choosing the Similar command more than once will increase the selection in increments.

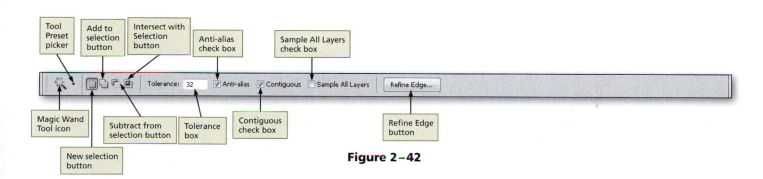

Figure 2–42

When checked, the Contiguous check box selects only adjacent areas using the same colors. Otherwise, Photoshop selects all pixels in the entire image that use the same colors. Finally, the Sample All Layers check box selects colors using data from all visible layers. Otherwise, the Magic Wand Tool selects colors from the active layer only.

Besides using the options bar, the Magic Wand Tool can be used with many shortcut keys. Holding down the SHIFT key while clicking adds to a Magic Wand Tool selection. Holding down the ALT key while clicking subtracts from the selection. Holding down the CTRL key while dragging with the Magic Wand Tool moves the selection.

BTW
Layers
A layer is a portion of the image superimposed, or separated, from other parts of the document. Think of layers as sheets of clear film stacked one on top of the other. In Chapter 3, you will learn how to change the composition of an image by changing the order and attributes of layers.

To Subtract from a Selection Using the Magic Wand Tool

The following steps use the Magic Wand Tool to eliminate the white background in the selection, leaving only the cup inside the marquee.

- With the cup still selected, right-click the Quick Selection Tool button on the Tools panel to display the context menu.

- Click Magic Wand Tool to activate the tool.

- On the options bar, click the 'Subtract from selection' button and then click the Anti-alias check box so it does not display a check mark.

- If necessary, enter 32 in the Tolerance box, and click to display a check mark in the Contiguous check box (Figure 2–43).

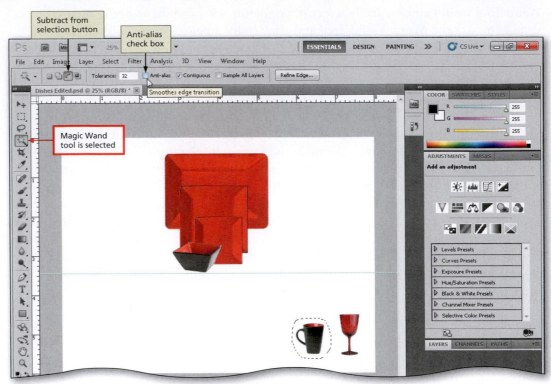

Figure 2–43

- Using the tip of the Magic Wand Tool mouse pointer, click the white space outside the cup, but inside the selection marquee, to remove the white color from the selection (Figure 2–44).

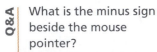

What is the minus sign beside the mouse pointer?

The minus sign appears when you choose to subtract from a selection. A plus sign indicates an addition to the selection, and an X indicates an intersection. Photoshop displays these signs so you do not have to glance up at the options bar to see which button you are using while you drag the selection.

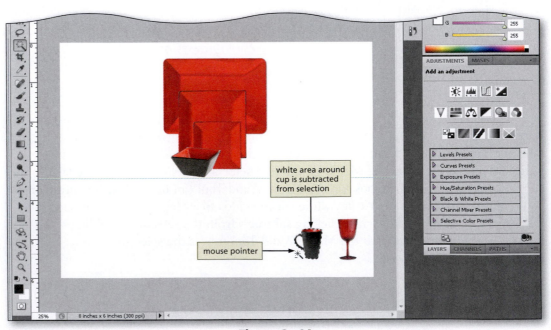

Figure 2–44

3

- Click the white space inside the cup's handle to remove it from the selection (Figure 2–45).

Q&A

What if I make a mistake and click the wrong color?

You can undo the latest edit by pressing CTRL+Z.

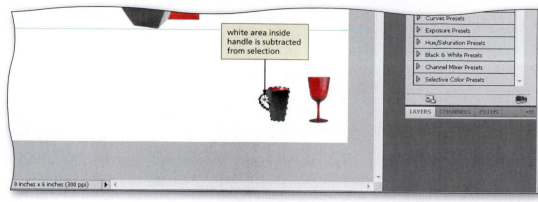

white area inside handle is subtracted from selection

Figure 2–45

Other Ways		
1. To select Magic Wand Tool, press W or SHIFT+W until Magic Wand Tool is active	2. Select Magic Wand Tool, ALT+click selection	3. Select Magic Wand Tool, right-click photo, click Subtract from selection

To Flip a Selection

As described in Table 2–2 on page PS 86, when you flip a selection, Photoshop creates a mirror image with a horizontal flip, or an upside-down version of the selection with a vertical flip. Flipping is available on the Edit menu and its Transform submenu or on the context menu when you right-click. Flip transformations do not have to be committed.

The following steps flip the selection horizontally.

1

- With the cup still selected, click Edit on the menu bar and then point to Transform to display the Transform submenu (Figure 2–46).

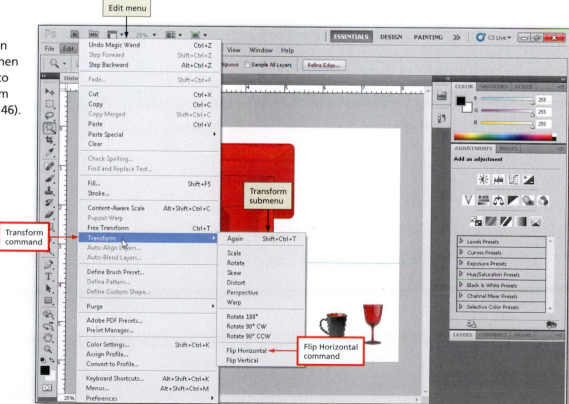

Edit menu

Transform submenu

Transform command

Flip Horizontal command

Figure 2–46

2

- Click Flip Horizontal to flip the selection horizontally (Figure 2–47).

Q&A

What if I make a mistake and flip or rotate the wrong way?

You can undo the latest edit by pressing CTRL+Z.

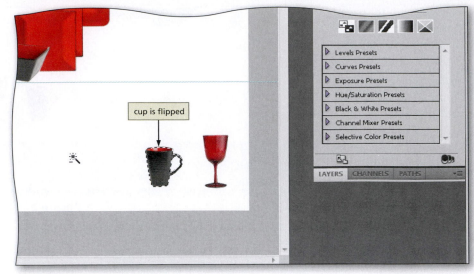

Figure 2–47

Other Ways

1. Press CTRL+T, right-click selection, click desired flip command

To Move the Cup

The following steps move the cup.

1 Press the V key to activate the Move Tool.

2 Drag the cup to a location, right of the bowl. The bottom of the cup should snap to the guide (Figure 2–48).

3 Press CTRL+D to deselect.

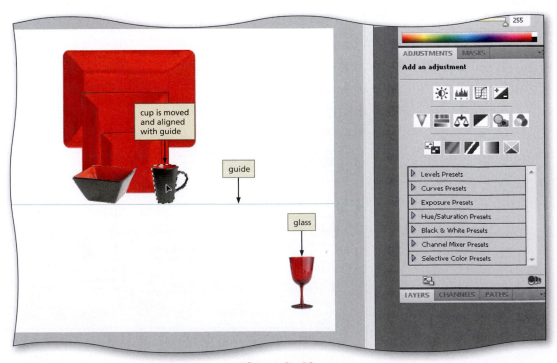

Figure 2–48

To Zoom In

The following steps zoom in on the glass to facilitate editing.

1 Press the z key to activate the Zoom Tool.

2 Click the glass four times to zoom in.

3 If necessary, use the scroll boxes to position the glass in the center of the document window (Figure 2–49).

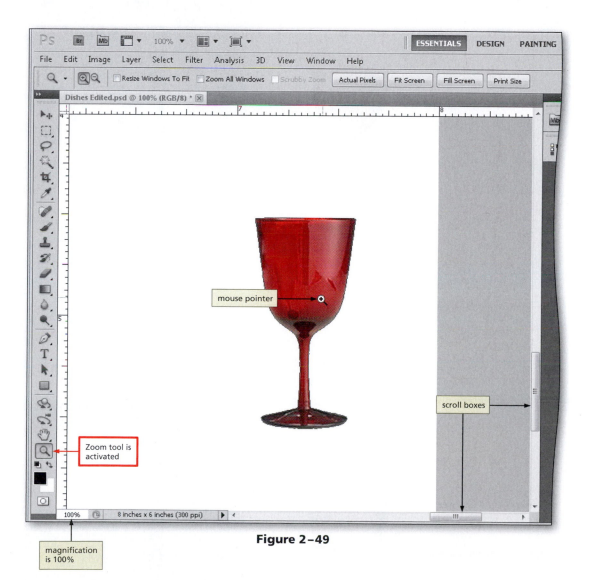

Figure 2–49

To Select Using the Magnetic Lasso Tool

The following steps use the Magnetic Lasso Tool to select the glass. Recall that the magnetic lasso selects by finding the edge of a contrasting color.

1

• Right-click the current lasso tool button and then click Magnetic Lasso Tool to select it from the context menu.

• If necessary, on the options bar, click the New selection button.

• Double-click the Contrast box and type 50 to replace the value (Figure 2–50).

Q&A

What is the effect of changing the value in the Contrast box?

Increasing the contrast helps detect the edges where red meets white, thereby increasing the magnetism of the edge of the glass.

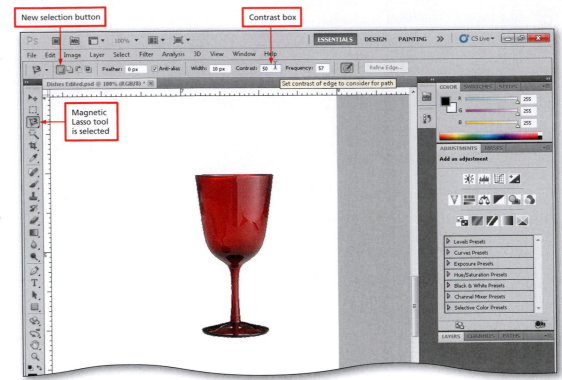

Figure 2–50

2

• Click the upper-left edge of the glass to start the selection.

• Move, rather than drag, the mouse pointer slowly along the left edge of the glass to create the selection marquee (Figure 2–51).

Q&A

How do I correct a mistake?

As you use the Magnetic Lasso Tool, if you make a mistake, press the ESC key and begin again.

Figure 2–51

3
- Continue moving the mouse pointer around the edge of the glass. Click the mouse when turning a corner to create an extra fastening point.

- When you get all the way around the glass, double-click to finish the lasso (Figure 2–52).

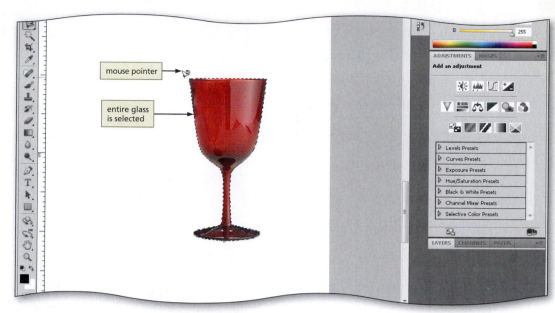

Figure 2–52

To Add to a Selection Using the Quick Selection Tool

The following steps add to the selection to include the rim of the glass.

1
- Press the z key to zoom in. Click the top of the glass several times until the magnification is 300% (Figure 2–53).

Q&A

Why does my selection marquee differ?

The marquee appears as you drag close to the glass. Depending on how close you were to the rim, and how slowly you moved the mouse pointer, your fasteners and resulting marquee might differ.

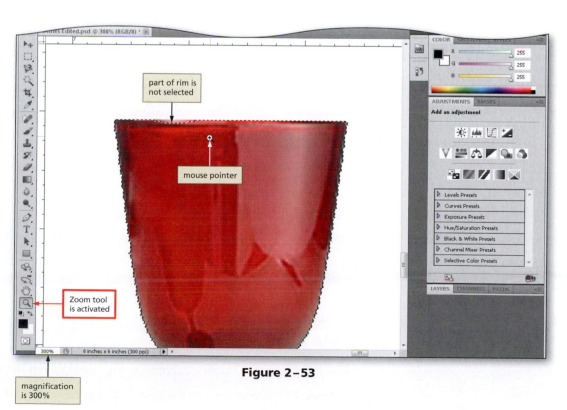

Figure 2–53

2

- Right-click the Magic Wand Tool button to display the context menu, and then click Quick Selection Tool to activate it.

- Click the 'Add to selection' button on the options bar.

- If necessary, use the LEFT BRACKET ([) key or RIGHT BRACKET (]) to either increase or decrease respectively the size of your mouse pointer, so that it more closely matches the figure.

- Drag along the rim in the area that is not inside the selection marquee to add it to the selection (Figure 2–54).

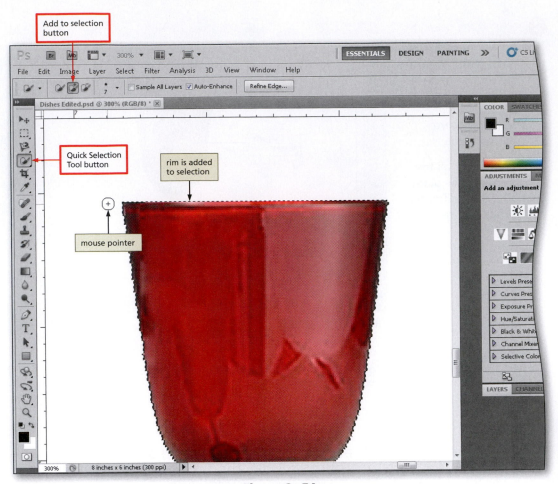

Figure 2–54

Q&A

Should the selection marquee change?

If part of the glass was not previously inside the marquee, dragging with the 'Add to selection' button should move the marquee. The change does not take place until you release the button.

3

- Zoom as necessary to look for other areas that do not fit the selection. Use the 'Add to selection' button or the 'Subtract from selection' button to refine the edge.

To Change the Magnification

The following step changes the magnification to display the entire graphic.

1 Type **25** in the magnification box on the status bar and then press the ENTER key to change the magnification to 25%.

To Create Another Guide

The following step creates a second guide to help align the glass.

1 Drag from the horizontal ruler to a location along the bottom of the tray (Figure 2–55).

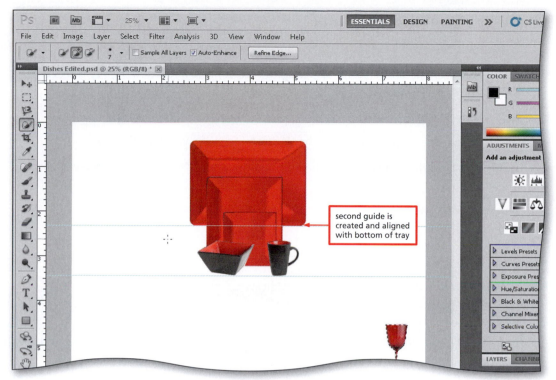

Figure 2–55

To Move a Selection Using Shortcut Keys

The following steps use shortcut keys to zoom and then move the selection.

1 Press the v key to activate the Move Tool.

2 With the glass still selected, drag the glass to a location approximately one inch to the right of the tray, snapping the bottom of the glass to the guide as shown in Figure 2–56.

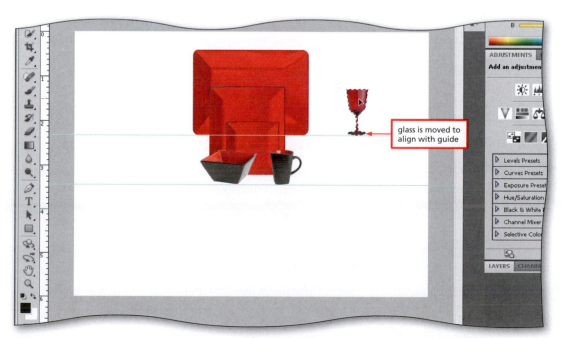

Figure 2–56

To Duplicate and Scale Using the Options Bar

The following steps create a larger copy of the glass.

1 With the Move Tool still selected, ALT+drag the selection to a location slightly down and left of the original glass.

2 Press CTRL+T to display the bounding box and the Transform options bar.

3 On the options bar, type 110% in the W box to scale the width of the glass.

4 Type 110% in the H box to scale the height of the glass. The copy will overlap slightly (Figure 2–57).

5 On the options bar click the 'Commit transform (Return)' button to accept the transformation.

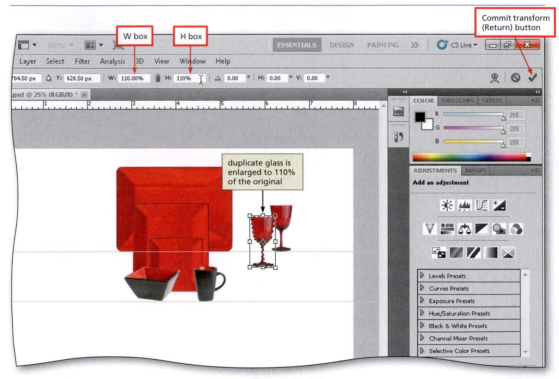

Figure 2–57

To Create and Scale Another Copy

The following steps create another copy of the glass.

1 With the Move Tool still selected, ALT+drag the selection to a location slightly down and left of the original glass. The copy will overlap slightly.

2 Press CTRL+T to display the bounding box and the Transform options bar.

3 On the option bar, type 110% in the W box to scale the width of the glass.

4 Type 110% in the H box to scale the height of the glass (Figure 2–58).

5 On the options bar click the 'Commit transform (Return)' button to accept the transformation.

6 Press CTRL+D to deselect.

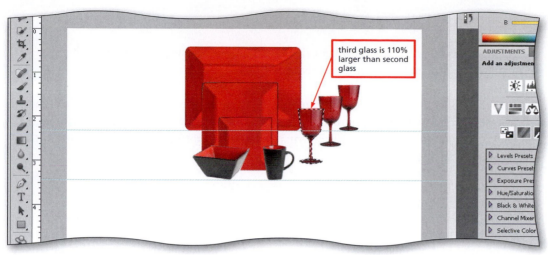

Figure 2–58

To Save Using a Shortcut Key

You will save the image again, with the same file name, using a shortcut key.

1 Press CTRL+S to save the Dishes Edited file with the same name.

To Crop the Advertisement

Finally, you will crop the advertisement to center the dishes, including a minimal amount of border space.

1 Press the C key to activate the Crop Tool.

2 Drag from the top border to create a crop that leaves an even amount of white space on all four sides of the dishes, as shown in Figure 2–59.

3 Press the ENTER key to complete the crop.

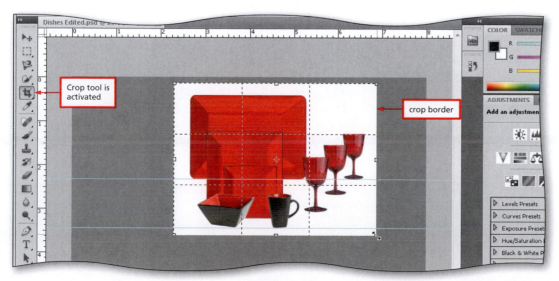

Figure 2–59

Creating PDF Files

The final step is to create a PDF file of the advertising image for document exchange. **PDF** stands for Portable Document Format, a flexible file format based on the cross-platform and cross-application PostScript imaging model. PDF files accurately display and preserve fonts, page layouts, and graphics. There are two ways to create a PDF file in Photoshop. First, you can save the file in the PDF format. Alternatively, you can use the Print command to create the PDF format, allowing you to make some changes to the settings before saving.

**Plan
Ahead**

> **Create files in portable formats.**
> You might have to distribute your artwork in a variety of formats for customers, print shops, Webmasters, and as e-mail attachments. The format you choose depends on how the file will be used, but portability is always a consideration. The document might need to be used with various operating systems, monitor resolutions, computing environments, and servers.
>
> It is a good idea to discuss with your customer the types of formats he or she might need. It usually is safe to begin work in the Photoshop PSD format and then use the Save As command or Print command to convert the files. PDF is a portable format that can be read by anyone with a free reader. The PDF format is platform and software independent. Commonly, PDF files are virus-free and safe as e-mail attachments.

To Save in the PDF Format

The following steps save the graphic in the PDF format for ease in distribution.

1

- Click File on the menu bar and then click Save As to display the Save As dialog box.

- Click the Format button (Save As dialog box) to display the various formats you can use to save Photoshop files (Figure 2–60).

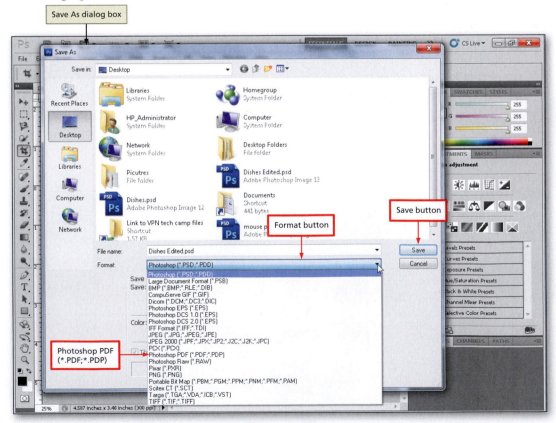

Figure 2–60

• Click Photoshop PDF (*.PDF;*.PDP) in the list to select the PDF format, and then click the Save button (Save As dialog box) to continue the saving process (Figure 2–61).

Figure 2–61

• Click the OK button (Adobe Photoshop CS5 Extended dialog box) to display the Save Adobe PDF dialog box (Figure 2–62).

Q&A

The Save PDF File As dialog box did not appear. What happened?

If you have multiple windows open on your system, the dialog box might be behind some of the other windows. In that case, minimize the other windows until the dialog box appears.

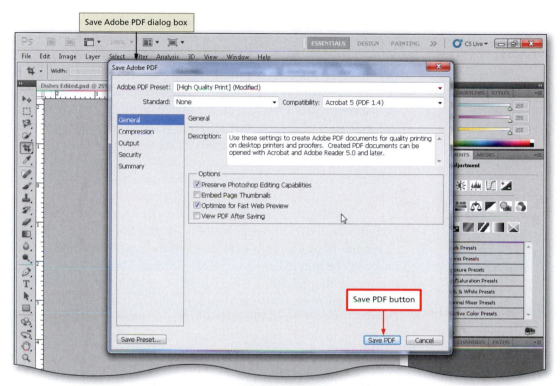

Figure 2–62

• Click the Save PDF button (Save Adobe PDF dialog box) to continue the saving process (Figure 2–63).

Q&A

Will the PDF version have the same name?

Yes. After you save, you will see the name Dishes Edited.pdf in the document window tab because Photoshop can edit PDF files directly. The file also can be viewed with Adobe Acrobat or any PDF reader.

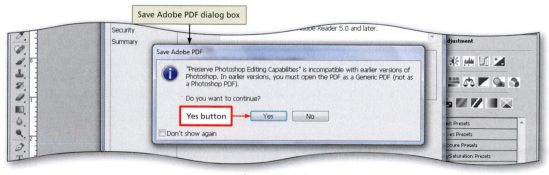

Figure 2–63

• When Photoshop displays the Save Adobe PDF dialog box, click the Yes button to finish saving.

To Close a Photo without Closing Photoshop

Recall that when you are finished editing a photo or file, you should close it to help save system resources. You can close a photo after you have saved it and continue working in Photoshop. The following steps close the Dishes Edited.pdf file.

1 Click the Close button on the document window tab to close the Dishes Edited.pdf file.

2 If Photoshop displays a dialog box, click the No button to ignore the changes since the last time you saved the photo.

Keyboard Shortcuts

Recall that a **keyboard shortcut**, or **shortcut key**, is a way to activate menu or tool commands using the keyboard rather than the mouse. For example, pressing the **L** key on the keyboard immediately selects the current lasso tool without having to move your mouse away from working in the image. Shortcuts with two keystrokes are common as well, such as the use of CTRL+A to select an entire image. Shortcuts are useful when you do not want to take the time to traverse the menu system, or when you are making precise edits and selections with the mouse and do not want to go back to any of the panels to change tools or settings. A Quick Reference Summary describing Photoshop's keyboard shortcuts is included in the back of the book.

While many keyboard shortcuts already exist in Photoshop, there might be times when additional shortcuts would be useful. For instance, the Single Row and Single Column Marquee tools have no shortcut key. If those are tools that you use frequently, adding the Single Row and Single Column Marquee tools to the M keyboard shortcut might be helpful. Photoshop allows users to create, customize, and save keyboard short-cuts in one of three areas: menus, panels, or tools. When you create keyboard shortcuts, you can add them to Photoshop's default settings, save them in a personalized set for retrieval in future editing sessions, or delete them from your system.

Creating a Keyboard Shortcut

To create a new keyboard shortcut, Photoshop provides a dialog box interface, accessible from the Edit menu. Using that dialog box, you can select one of the three shortcut areas. Then you can choose a shortcut key or combination of keys. For menu commands, your shortcut keystrokes must include the CTRL key or a function key. When creating shortcuts for tools, you must use a single alphabetic character. To avoid conflicting duplications, Photoshop immediately warns you if you have chosen a keyboard shortcut that is used somewhere else in the program.

To Create a New Keyboard Shortcut

In the following steps, you will create a shortcut to display the Essentials workspace. While that command is accessible on the Window menu and by using the 'Show more workspaces and options' button on the Applications bar, a shortcut would save time when you need to reset the workspace.

1

- Click Edit on the menu bar to display the Edit menu (Figure 2–64).

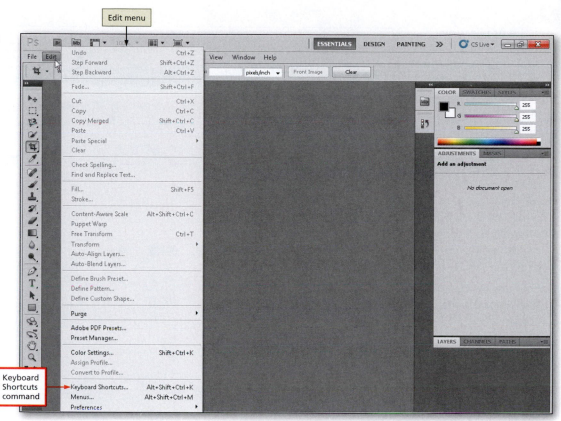

Figure 2–64

2

- Click Keyboard Shortcuts to display the Keyboard Shortcuts and Menus dialog box.

- If necessary, click the Keyboard Shortcuts tab to display its settings.

- If the Set box does not display Photoshop Defaults, click the Set box arrow (Keyboard Shortcuts and Menus dialog box) and then click Photoshop Defaults in the list.

- If the Shortcuts For box does not display Application Menus, click the Shortcuts For box arrow and then click Application Menus in the list (Figure 2–65).

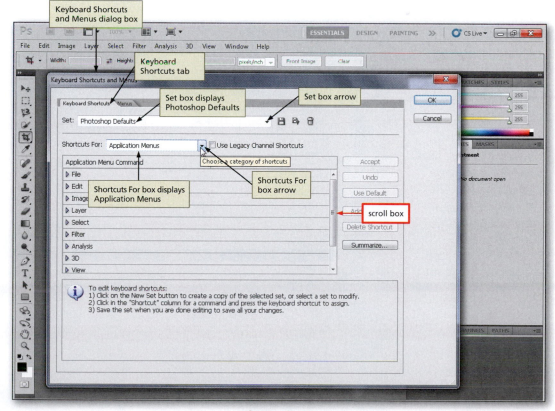

Figure 2–65

3

- In the Application Menu Command list, scroll down and then double-click Window to display the list of Window menu commands.

- Scroll down to display Workspace under the Window menu commands, and then click Essentials (Default) to display a shortcut key box (Figure 2–66).

Q&A

How are the buttons at the top of the dialog box used?

The 'Save all changes to the current set of shortcuts' button allows you to name the set for future retrieval. The 'Create a new set based on the current

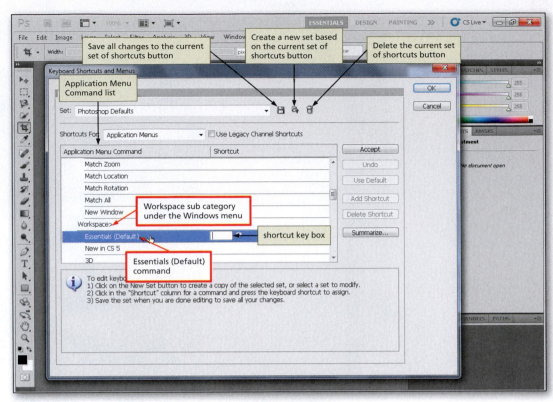

Figure 2–66

set of shortcuts' button creates a copy of the current keyboard shortcut settings. The 'Delete the current set of shortcuts' button deletes the set.

4

- Press the F12 key to enter a new short-cut keystroke for the Essentials (Default) command (Figure 2–67).

Q&A

How can I find out which shortcuts keys still are available?

When you click the Summarize button, Photoshop creates a Web page with all of the keyboard shortcuts in the set. You can save that file on your system.

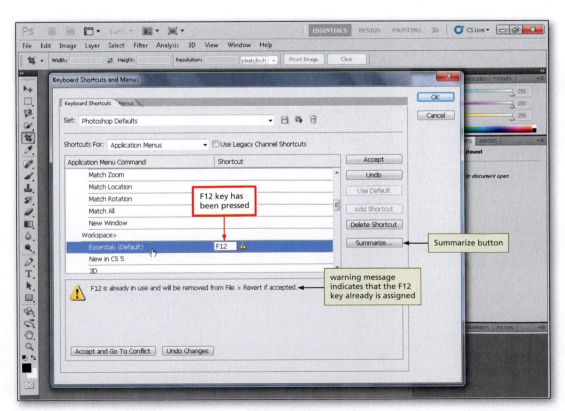

Figure 2–67

5

• Because Photoshop warns you that the F12 key already is being used as a shortcut for a different command, press CTRL+COMMA (,) to enter a new short-cut (Figure 2–68).

6

• Click the Accept button (Keyboard Shortcuts and Menus dialog box) to set the shortcut key.

• Click the OK button to close the dialog box.

Other Ways

1. Press ALT+SHIFT+CTRL+K, edit settings, click OK

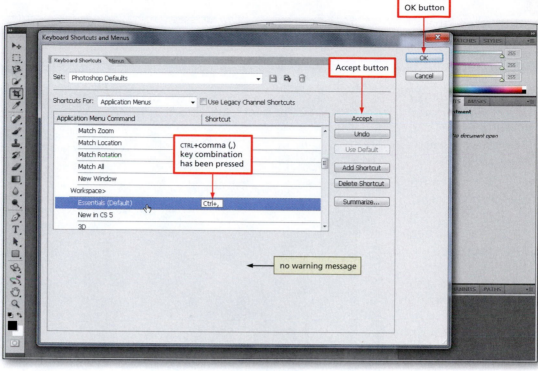

Figure 2–68

To Test a New Keyboard Shortcut

The next steps test the new keyboard shortcut.

1

• Click Design on the Application bar to change to the Design workspace.

• Click Window on the menu bar and point to Workspace to verify the shortcut key assignment (Figure 2–69).

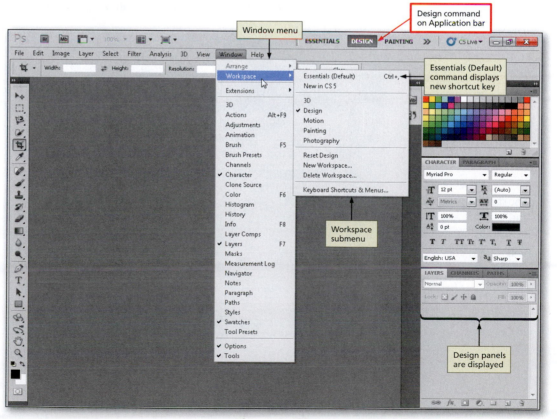

Figure 2–69

2

- Click the workspace away from the Window menu to hide the menu.

- Press CTRL+COMMA (,) to test the shortcut and display the Essentials workspace (Figure 2–70).

Will the new shortcut become permanent?

The new shortcut will be saved on your system in the Photoshop Defaults (modified) set. That set will be in effect the next time you start Photoshop. If you wish to remove it, you can edit that specific shortcut, or delete the set by clicking the Delete the current set of shortcuts button.

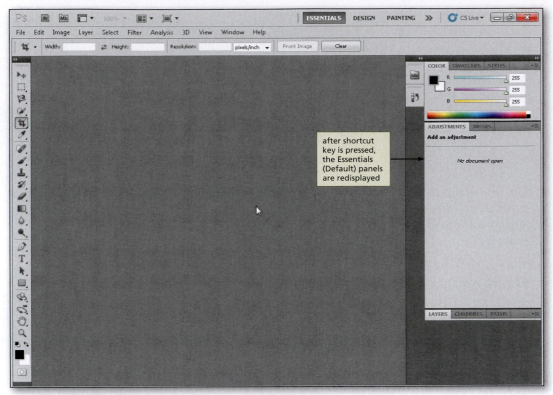

Figure 2–70

To Return to the Default Settings for Keyboard Shortcuts

It is a good idea, especially in a lab situation, to reset the keyboard shortcuts to their default settings. The following steps restore the default shortcut keys.

1

- Click Edit on the menu bar and then click Keyboard Shortcuts to display the Keyboard Shortcuts and Menus dialog box.

- On the Keyboards Shortcuts tab, click the Set box arrow to display the list (Figure 2–71).

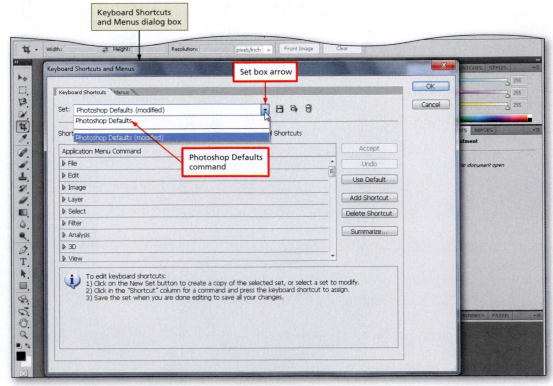

Figure 2–71

2
- Click Photoshop Defaults to choose the default settings for shortcuts. (Figure 2–72).

3
- When Photoshop displays a message asking if you want to save your changes, click the No button to cancel your changes.

- Click the OK button (Keyboard Shortcuts and Menus dialog box) to close the dialog box.

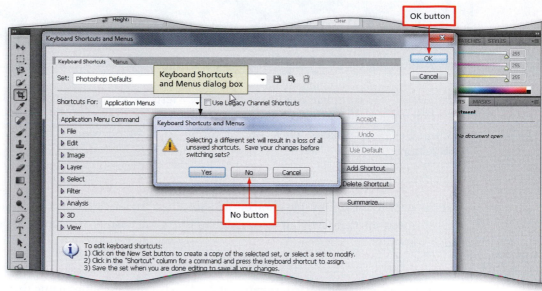

Figure 2–72

To Quit Photoshop Using a Shortcut Key

The following step quits Photoshop and returns control to Windows.

1 Press CTRL+Q to quit Photoshop.

Chapter Summary

In this chapter, you learned how to use selection tools, including the marquee tools, the lasso tools, the Quick Selection Tool, and the Magic Wand Tool. You worked with the Subtract from selection command, the Refine Edge dialog box, and the Grow command to edit the selection border. Upon completing the selection, you then learned many of the transformation commands, including rotating, scaling, and flipping. You used the Move Tool to move and copy selections. Each of the tools and commands had its own options bar with settings to control how the tool or command worked. You learned about the History panel and its states. Finally, you learned how to create and test a new keyboard shortcut.

The items listed below include all the new Photoshop skills you have learned in this chapter:

1. Use the Rectangular Marquee Tool (PS 83)
2. Use the Move Tool (PS 84)
3. Display Transformation Controls (PS 88)
4. Rotate a Selection (PS 88)
5. Use the Quick Selection Tool (PS 90)
6. Display the History Panel (PS 93)
7. Undo Changes Using the History Panel (PS 94)
8. Collapse the History Panel (PS 95)
9. Refine Edges (PS 96)
10. Duplicate the Selection (PS 98)
11. Scale a Selection (PS 99)
12. Display a Grid (PS 101)
13. Turn Off the Grid Display (PS 102)
14. Create a Guide (PS 103)
15. Select Using the Polygonal Lasso Tool (PS 105)
16. Grow the Selection (PS 107)
17. Select Using the Lasso Tool (PS 108)
18. Subtract from a Selection Using the Magic Wand Tool (PS 110)
19. Flip a Selection (PS 111)
20. Select Using the Magnetic Lasso Tool (PS 114)
21. Add to a Selection Using the Quick Selection Tool (PS 115)
22. Save in the PDF Format (PS 120)
23. Create a New Keyboard Shortcut (PS 122)
24. Test a New Keyboard Shortcut (PS 125)
25. Return to the Default Settings for Keyboard Shortcuts (PS 126)

Learn It Online

Test your knowledge of chapter content and key terms.

Instructions: To complete the Learn It Online exercises, start your browser, click the Address bar, and then enter the Web address **scsite.com/pscs5/learn**. When the Photoshop CS5 Learn It Online page is displayed, click the link for the exercise you want to complete and then read the instructions.

Chapter Reinforcement TF, MC, and SA
A series of true/false, multiple choice, and short answer questions that test your knowledge of the chapter content.

Flash Cards
An interactive learning environment where you identify chapter key terms associated with displayed definitions.

Practice Test
A series of multiple choice questions that test your knowledge of chapter content and key terms.

Who Wants To Be a Computer Genius?
An interactive game that challenges your knowledge of chapter content in the style of a television quiz show.

Wheel of Terms
An interactive game that challenges your knowledge of chapter key terms in the style of the television show *Wheel of Fortune*.

Crossword Puzzle Challenge
A crossword puzzle that challenges your knowledge of key terms presented in the chapter.

Apply Your Knowledge

Reinforce the skills and apply the concepts you learned in this chapter.

Moving and Duplicating Selections
Instructions: Start Photoshop and perform the customization steps found on pages PS 6 through PS 9. Open the Apply 2-1 Bread file in the Chapter 02 folder from the Data Files for Students and save it, in the PSD file format, as Apply 2-1 Bread Edited. You can access the Data Files for Students on the CD that accompanies this book; see the inside back cover of this book for instructions on downloading the Data Files for Students, or contact your instructor for information about accessing the required files.

You will create a grocery advertisement featuring bakery items. First, you will select individual items from within the file, and then you will transform and move them so that the finished design looks like Figure 2–73. You will place the rest of the images from back to front.

Perform the following tasks:
1. Because the checkered tablecloth is in the very back of the arrangement, you will start with it. Use the Rectangular Marquee Tool to select the checkered tablecloth.

2. Use the Move Tool to move the tablecloth to the top-center of the page. Do not deselect the tablecloth.

3. With the Move Tool still selected, press CTRL+T to display the bounding box. To distort the tablecloth and make it appear in perspective, CTRL+drag each of the lower corner sizing handles down and outward. Do not overlap any of the bread items. The result should be a trapezoid shape, as shown in Figure 2–73. If you make a mistake, press the ESC key and start again. When you are satisfied with the shape, press the ENTER key to confirm the transformation.

Figure 2–73

4. The croissant is the back-most item in the arrangement. Use the Polygonal Lasso Tool to select the croissant. (*Hint:* The croissant is the lower-right item in the Apply 2-1 Bread image.) Right-click the Quick Selection Tool button on the Tools panel, and then click Magic Wand Tool. On the options bar, click the 'Subtract from selection' button, then click the white area around the croissant to remove it.

5. Use the Move Tool to move the croissant to the upper-right portion of the tablecloth. ALT+drag a second croissant to a location below and to the left of the first, as shown in Figure 2–73. (*Hint:* Do not drag the center reference point.) Press CTRL+D to deselect it.

6. Repeat Steps 4 and 5 to select and move the French bread.

7. ALT+drag the French bread to the right to create a duplicate.

8. Select and move the remaining bread items until you are satisfied with the arrangement. For each bread item, use a selection tool that will approximate the shape of the bread. On the options bar, use the 'Add to selection' and 'Subtract from selection' buttons as necessary. Use the Magic Wand Tool to remove white space around the selection before moving it.

9. Right-click the Rectangular Marquee Tool button on the Tools panel, then click Elliptical Marquee Tool. Use the Elliptical Marquee Tool to select the Sale button. (*Hint:* Press and hold the SHIFT key as you select to maintain a perfect circle.)

10. Move the Sale button to the lower-right portion of the advertisement.

11. Use the Crop Tool to select the portion of the image to use for the final advertisement. (*Hint:* The remaining white space is unnecessary.)

12. Save the Apply 2-1 Bread Edited file, and then close Photoshop.

13. Submit the assignment in the format specified by your instructor.

Extend Your Knowledge

Extend the skills you learned in this chapter and experiment with new skills. You may need to use Help to complete the assignment.

Separating Objects from the Background

Instructions: Start Photoshop and perform the customization steps found on pages PS 6 through PS 9. Open the Extend 2-1 Flowers file in the Chapter 02 folder from the Data Files for Students and save it, in the PSD format, as Extend 2-1 Flowers Edited. You can access the Data Files for Students on the CD that accompanies this book; see the inside back cover of this book for instructions on downloading the Data Files for Students, or contact your instructor for information about accessing the required files.

The original flower image displays the flowers in their natural settings, with various colors in the background. After moving the frame and making a copy, you will select the flowers while preventing background colors from straying into the selection. Finally, you will position each flower in front of a frame as shown in Figure 2–74.

Figure 2–74

Perform the following tasks:

1. Use the Elliptical Marquee Tool to select the oval frame. (*Hint:* For more careful placement, while dragging to create the selection, you can press the SPACEBAR key to adjust the location of the drag and then release it to continue drawing the marquee.) Be careful to select only the frame, and eliminate any white around the edge of the selection using the Magic Wand Tool and the 'Subtract from selection' button.

2. Drag the selection to a location below the left side of the word, Flowers. Do not be concerned if you leave a slight shadow behind. Press CTRL+T to display the Transform options bar. Increase the selection to 110 percent in both width and height. Press the ENTER key to commit the transformation.

3. With the frame still selected, SHIFT+ALT+drag to create a duplicate and place it to the right of the original. (*Hint:* Recall that using the SHIFT key keeps the duplicate aligned with the original.)

4. Use appropriate selection tools to select the upper flower and its stem. (*Hint:* Use the Magic Wand Tool with a tolerance setting of 50 to select the contiguous pink and then add to the selection using other tools.) Click the 'Add to selection' button or the 'Intersect with selection' button to edit areas, if necessary. Do not include the background.

5. To ensure that the selection does not have any stray pixels around its border, use the Refine Edge dialog box to refine the edge by increasing the radius to .7 px.

6. As you create the selection, if necessary, press CTRL+ALT+Z to step back through the editing history and return the image to an earlier state.

7. Move the selected flower onto the left frame. Resize the flower if necessary.

8. Repeat steps 4 through 7 for the lower flower and the right frame. If you make an error, display the History panel and then click a previous state.

9. Crop the image to include only the word, Flowers, and the two framed flowers. Save the changes.

10. Use the Magic Wand Tool to select the blue color in the word, Flowers. (*Hint:* To select all of the letters, you will have to remove the check mark in the Contiguous box.) If parts of the image other than the word, Flowers, appear within the marquee, use the 'Subtract from selection' button to remove them.

11. Use Photoshop Help to investigate how to soften the edges of selections. Use the Refine Edge dialog box to soften the edges. Expand the selection and feather the edges.

12. Use Photoshop Help to investigate how to stroke a selection or layer with color. With the letters selected, use the Stroke command on the Edit menu to display the Stroke dialog box. Stroke the selection with a white color, 5 pixels wide, on the outside of the selection. If necessary, drag the Opacity slider to 100%.

13. Close the photo and close Photoshop. Send the revised photo to your instructor as an e-mail attachment.

Make It Right

Analyze a project and correct all errors and/or improve the design.

Correcting an Error in a Photo

Instructions: Start Photoshop and perform the customization steps found on pages PS 6 through PS 9. Open the Make It Right 2-1 Candles file in the Chapter 02 folder from the Data Files for Students and save it, in the PSD file format, as Make It Right 2-1 Candles Edited. You can access the Data Files for Students on the CD that accompanies this book; see the inside back cover of this book for instructions on downloading the Data Files for Students, or contact your instructor for information about accessing the required files.

Continued ⊃

Make It Right *continued*

A gift catalog would like to advertise its selection of candles, but the photo has one leaning candle that you must fix. Zoom in on the leaning candle. Select only the candle by dragging around it with the magnetic lasso (Figure 2–75). Use other selection tools as necessary, along with the 'Add to Selection' and 'Subtract from selection' buttons to include only the candle. Refine the edge. Drag a vertical guide to the middle of the candle to use as a straight reference. Display the transformation controls and then use the mouse to rotate the candle clockwise until it is straight, then center the candle on the candle holder using the Move Tool.

Save the project again. Submit the revised document in the format specified by your instructor.

Figure 2–75

In the Lab

Design and/or create a publication using the guidelines, concepts, and skills presented in this chapter. Labs are listed in order of increasing difficulty.

Lab 1: Using the Keyboard with the Magic Wand Tool

Problem: As e-cards gain popularity, the need for good graphics also has increased. A small e-commerce site has hired you as its photo specialist to assist with images and photos used in the greeting cards provided online. Your first assignment is to provide a clean image for a card whose greeting will read, "I'm off my rocker! I forgot your birthday!" A photographer has submitted a photo of a rocker, but the layout artist needs the background removed and the rocker scaled to approximately half of its original size. The layout artist has requested a PDF of your final product. You decide to practice using the function keys to perform most of the editing tasks. The edited photo is displayed in Figure 2–76.

Instructions: Perform the following tasks:

1. Start Photoshop. Set the default workspace and reset all tools.

2. Press CTRL+O to open the Lab 2-1 Rocker file from the Chapter 02 folder of the Data Files for Students, or from a location specified by your instructor.

3. Press SHIFT+CTRL+S to display the Save As dialog box. Save the file on your storage device with the name, Lab 2-1 Rocker Edited.

4. If the photo does not appear at 16.67% magnification, press CTRL+PLUS SIGN (+) or CTRL+HYPHEN (–) to zoom in or out as necessary.

5. To remove the wallpaper:

   a. Press the W key to choose the Magic Wand Tool. If the Quick Selection Tool is the active tool, press SHIFT+W to select the Magic Wand Tool.

   b. On the options bar, click the Contiguous box so it does not display a check mark. If necessary, set the Tolerance value to 32.

   c. Click the blue wallpaper and then press CTRL+X to remove it.

6. To remove the floor:

   a. On the options bar, click the Contiguous box so it displays a check mark.

   b. Click the floor. SHIFT+click other parts of the floor to add to the selection. (*Hint*: Be sure to click the entire floor, including the spaces between the chair legs.)

   c. Use the Navigator panel to zoom as necessary, or if your computer's mouse has a wheel, ALT+wheel back and forth to zoom. Press CTRL+X to remove the floor selection.

7. To remove the baseboard:

   a. Repeat Step 6 for the baseboard.

   b. If you make an error, or some areas are deleted by mistake, click Window on the menu bar, and then click History to display the History panel. Press CTRL+ALT+Z to step backward through the states in the History panel, or click the first state in the History panel and begin again with Step 5.

8. If necessary, using the Magic Wand Tool, SHIFT+click any remaining part of the photo that is not the rocker and remove it.

9. To select only the rocker:

   a. On the Magic Wand Tool options bar, click the New selection button, if necessary, and then click to remove the check mark in the Contiguous box. Click the white area of the photo.

   b. Press SHIFT+CTRL+I to select the inverse. The rocker now should appear inside the selection marquee.

10. To scale the rocker:

    a. Press CTRL+T to free transform the rocker selection. On the options bar, drag the W scrubby slider to 50%. Drag the H scrubby slider to 50%.

    b. Press the ENTER key to commit the transformations.

    c. Press CTRL+D to deselect, if necessary.

11. Press CTRL+S to save the file with the same name. If Photoshop displays a Photoshop Format Options dialog box, click the OK button.

12. To create the PDF file:

    a. Click File on the menu bar and then click Save As to display the Save As dialog box.

    b. Click the Format button to display the various formats.

Figure 2–76

Continued >

In the Lab *continued*

   c. Click Photoshop PDF (*.PDF;*.PDP) in the list to select the PDF format, and then click the Save button to continue the saving process.

   d. Click the OK button to display the Save Adobe PDF dialog box, and then click the Save PDF button to continue the saving process.

   e. When Photoshop displays the Save Adobe PDF dialog box, click the Yes button to finish saving.

13. Quit Photoshop by pressing CTRL+Q.

14. Send the PDF file as an e-mail attachment to your instructor, or follow your instructor's directions for submitting the lab assignment.

In the Lab

Lab 2: Creating a Graphic from Back to Front

Problem: A local author has asked for your help in creating a book cover graphic about clock collecting. He has several photos of clocks that he wants placed in specific locations and sizes. The final graphic is shown in Figure 2–77.

Instructions: Perform the following tasks:

1. Start Photoshop. Set the default workspace and reset all tools.

2. Open the file, Lab 2-2 Clocks, from the Chapter 02 folder of the Data Files for Students, or from a location specified by your instructor.

3. Use the Save As command to save the file on your storage device with the name Lab 2-2 Clocks Edited.

4. To select and transform the round clock face:

   a. Use the Elliptical Marquee Tool to select the round clock face. If necessary, use the Magic Wand Tool and the 'Subtract from selection' button to remove any white from around the edge of the clock.

   b. Use the Move Tool to move it to a location in the center of the white area.

   c. Display the bounding box and enlarge the selection to fill the area. Do not let it overlap any of the other clocks. Drag a side handle to make the clock more round.

5. To select and transform the mantle clock:

   a. Use the Quick Selection Tool to select the mantle clock. Zoom as necessary. Use the Magic Wand Tool and the 'Subtract from selection' button to remove the white areas from around the selection.

   b. Use the Move Tool to move it to a location just below the round clock face and slightly to the left.

   c. Display the bounding box and enlarge the selection to match Figure 2–77.

Figure 2–77

6. To select and transform the grandfather clock:

   a. Use the Rectangular Marquee Tool to select the grandfather clock. Use the Magic Wand Tool and the 'Subtract from selection' button to remove the white areas from around the selection.

   b. Use the Move Tool to move it to a location in front of, and on the right side of the round clock face.

   c. Display the bounding box and enlarge the selection to match Figure 2–77.

7. To select and transform the wall clock:

   a. Use the Lasso Tool to select the wall clock. Zoom as necessary. Use the Magic Wand Tool and the 'Subtract from selection' button to remove any white from around the edge of the clock.

   b. Use the Move Tool to move it to a location in the upper-left corner of the scene, as shown in Figure 2–77.

   c. Display the bounding box and enlarge the selection, if necessary.

8. Submit the document, shown in Figure 2–77, in the format specified by your instructor.

In the Lab

Lab 3: Creating a Money Graphic using Transformations

Problem: Your local bank is starting an initiative to encourage children to open a savings account using their loose change. The bank would like a before and after picture showing how money can grow with interest.

Instructions: Perform the following tasks:

Start Photoshop. Set the default workspace and reset all tools. Open the file, Lab 2-3 Coins, from the Chapter 02 folder of the Data Files for Students, or from a location specified by your instructor. Save the file on your storage device with the name Lab 2-3 Coins Edited.

Use the Elliptical Marquee Tool to select the quarter. (*Hint:* While dragging, if your selection marquee does not match the quarter exactly, press and hold the SPACEBAR key to move the selection.) Once the quarter is selected, ALT+drag to create several duplicate copies. Use Figure 2–78 as a guide. As you create the duplicates, press CTRL+T to display the transformation controls, and use the context menu commands to distort, rotate 90° CW, and apply perspective. Use the Magnetic Lasso Tool to select the dime. ALT+drag to create several duplicate copies. As you create the duplicates, press CTRL+T to display the transformation controls. Use the mouse to rotate, move, and drag a corner to create a slight distortion.

Figure 2–78

Continued >

In the Lab *continued*

Use the Quick Selection Tool to select the nickel. ALT+drag to create several duplicate copies. As you create the duplicates, press CTRL+T to display the transformation controls. Flip, rotate and skew some of the copies. Use the Magic Wand Tool to select the penny. Create several copies and apply transformations of your choosing. Save the file again, and submit it in the format specified by your instructor.

Cases and Places

Apply your creative thinking and problem-solving skills to design and implement a solution.

1: Creating a Poster for the Computer Lab

Academic

The computer lab at your school wants a poster reminding students to save their work often. The department chair has asked you to create a graphic of a computer mouse that seems to be eating data. He has taken a picture of a mouse from the lab and started the poster for you. A file named Case 2-1 Poster is located in the Chapter 02 folder of the Data Files for Students. Start Photoshop and use the selection tools to select the mouse. Flip the mouse horizontally. Then, using the 'Subtract from selection' button, remove the white part around the selection. Also, remove the dark gray bottom portion of the mouse from the selection. With the top portion of the mouse selected, warp the selection up and away from the bottom part of the mouse to simulate an open mouth. Move the selection close to the 0 and 1 data pattern. Save a copy of the poster as a PDF and send it as an e-mail attachment to your instructor.

2: Creating a New Shortcut

Personal

You have decided to create a new keyboard shortcut to reset all tools, rather than having to move the mouse to the options bar, right-click, and then choose to reset all tools. Because other family members work on your computer system, you would like to save the new shortcut in a separate set for your personal use. You also would like to see a complete listing of the Photoshop shortcuts for your system. Access the Keyboard Shortcuts and Menus dialog box. Click the Shortcuts For box arrow and then click Panel Menus in the list. Scroll down and double-click Tool Presets, and then click Reset All Tools in the list. Enter the shortcut, CTRL+SLASH (/). Click the 'Create a new set based on the current set of shortcuts' button and save the shortcuts with your name. Click the Summarize button and save the summary as, My Shortcut Summary. When the summary is displayed in the browser, print a copy for your records.

3: Applying Transformations to Indicate Motion

Professional

Hobby Express, a store that specializes in model trains and remote control toys, wants a new logo. They would like to illustrate the concept of a train engine racing to the store. The picture will appear on their letterhead, business cards, and advertising pieces. They would like a digital file so they can use the logo for other graphic purposes. Open the file Case 2-3 Engine and save it on your storage device. Use the Magic Wand Tool and the 'Add to selection' button to select the sky and the grass. Press the DELETE key. When Photoshop displays a Fill dialog box, verify that the Opacity is set to 100%, and then click the OK button. On the Select menu, click Inverse. Display the bounding box. Right-click the selection and then click Warp. When Photoshop displays the warp grid, locate the upper-left warp point that appears as a gray circle on the grid (not the square sizing-handle). Drag the warp point to the left until the smokestack bends slightly. Experiment with the Skew, Perspective, and Distort commands to make the engine look as if it were moving. The front of the engine should appear closer than the rear. The smokestack should curve backward to simulate motion. Save the photo again and print a copy for your instructor.

3 | Working with Layers

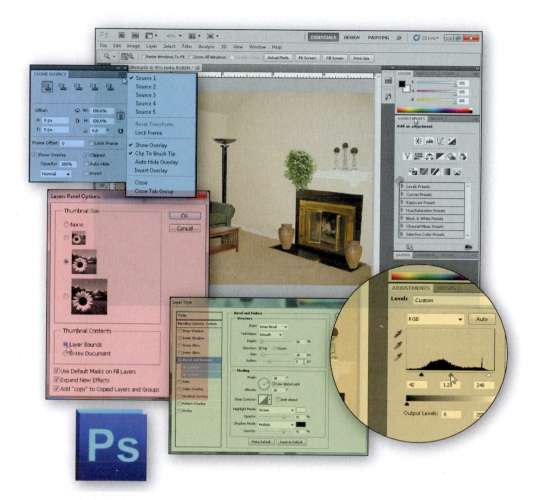

Objectives

You will have mastered the material in this chapter when you can:

- Use the Layers panel and change options
- Use the Layer via Cut command
- Set layer properties
- Hide, view, and rearrange layers
- Arrange and consolidate document windows
- Create a new layer from another image or selection
- Resize a layer

- Use the Eraser, Magic Eraser, and Background Eraser Tools
- Create layer masks
- Make level adjustments and opacity changes
- Apply adjustments using the Adjustments panel
- Create a layer style
- Use the Clone Stamp Tool
- Flatten a composite image

3 | Working with Layers

Introduction

Whether it is adding a new person to a photograph, combining artistic effects from different genres, or creating 3D animation, the concept of layers in Photoshop allows you to work on one element of an image without disturbing the others. A layer is an image superimposed or separated from other parts of the photograph. You might think of layers as sheets of clear film stacked one on top of one another. You can see through transparent areas of a layer to the layers below. The nontransparent, or opaque, areas of a layer are solid and obscure lower layers. You can change the composition of an image by changing the order and attributes of layers. In addition, special features, such as adjustment layers, layer masks, fill layers, and layer styles, allow you to create sophisticated effects.

Another tool that graphic designers use when they want to recreate a portion of another photo is the Clone Stamp Tool. As you will learn in this chapter, the Clone Stamp Tool takes a sample of an image and then applies, as you draw, an exact copy of that image to your document.

Graphic designers use layers and clones along with other tools in Photoshop to create **composite** images that combine or merge multiple images and drawings to create a new image, also referred to as a **montage**. Composite images illustrate the power of Photoshop to prepare documents for businesses, advertising, marketing, and media artwork. Composite images, such as navigation bars, can be created in Photoshop and used on the Web along with layered buttons, graphics, and background images.

Project — Room Furnishing

Chapter 3 uses Photoshop to create a composite image from several photographs by using layers. Specifically, it begins with a photo of an empty room and creates a composite image by inserting layers of furniture, a plant, a painting, and other decorative pieces to create a complete room design (Figure 3–1). The enhancements will show how the room will look when furnished. Wood flooring will replace the carpeting; a sofa, lamp, table, and other decorations will be added. Finally, adjustment layers will give the room eye appeal.

ile   Edit   Image   Layer   Select   Filter   Analysis   3D   View   Window   Help

Figure 3–1 (a)

Figure 3–1 (b)

Overview

As you read this chapter, you will learn how to create the composite room shown in Figure 3–1 by performing these general tasks:

- Create a layer using the Layer via Cut command.
- Insert layers from new images.
- Use the eraser tools.
- Add a layer mask.
- Create layer adjustments and layer masks.
- Apply layer styles.
- Clone from one image to another.
- Flatten the image.
- Save the photo with and without layers.

General Project Guidelines

When editing a photo, the actions you perform and decisions you make will affect the appearance and characteristics of the finished product. As you edit a photo, such as the one shown in Figure 3–1 on the previous page, you should follow these general guidelines:

1. **Gather your photos and plan your layers.** The graphics you choose should convey the overall message of your composite image. Choose high-quality photos with similar lighting characteristics. Create an ordered list of the layers you plan to include. Select images that are consistent with the visual effect you want to achieve as well as with customer requirements.

2. **Create layer adjustments.** Fine-tune your layers by creating layer adjustments. Look at each layer and evaluate how it fits into the background scene. Experiment with different adjustment tools until the layer looks just right. Decide whether to use destructive or nondestructive edits. Keep in mind the standard tonal dimensions of brightness, saturation, and hue.

3. **Edit layer styles.** Add variety to your layers by including layer styles such as shadow, glow, emboss, bevel, overlay, and stroke. Make sure the layer style does not overwhelm the overall image or detract from previous layer adjustments.

When necessary, more specific details concerning the above guidelines are presented at appropriate points in the chapter. The chapter also will identify the actions performed and decisions made regarding these guidelines during the creation of the edited photo shown in Figure 3–1.

Creating a Composite

Creating a composite with visual layers is a powerful effect. Photographers sometimes try to achieve the effect by using a sharp focus on objects in the foreground against an out-of-focus background. Others stage their photos with three layers of visual action. For example, at a baseball game, a person in the stands (foreground) may be observing a close call at first base (middle ground), while outfielders watch from afar (background). When those kinds of photographic techniques cannot be achieved, graphic artists use **composition techniques**, the layering of images and actions. Not only can you make realistic changes to parts of a photo, but you can add additional images and control their placement, blending, and special effects. In addition, you can make changes to a layer, independent of the layer itself, which is extremely helpful in composite production.

Simple layers may incorporate new objects or additional people. Layer effects create adjustments, add blending modes, or edit the coloring, fill, and opacity of the layer. Masks conceal or reveal part of a layer. All of the layering techniques are **nondestructive**, which means that no pixels are changed in the process; the effect is applied over the image or layer to create the change.

When an image duplication is required and layering a new copy does not achieve the required effect, some graphic artists **clone**, or reproduce, an image by painting a copy into the scene. As with masks, cloning allows you to control exactly how much of the image you want to use — even down to the smallest pixel. You also can use cloning to remove minor imperfections in a photo or to clone over intricate elements that do not fit into the picture.

The steps in this chapter create a composite image with layers; layer effects; and adjustments, masks, and cloning.

To Start Photoshop

If you are using a computer to step through the project in this chapter, and you want your screen to match the figures in this book, you should change your screen's resolution to 1024 × 768. For information about how to change the screen resolution, read Appendix C.

The following steps, which assume Windows 7 is running, start Photoshop based on a typical installation. You may need to ask your instructor how to start Photoshop for your computer.

1 Click the Start button on the Windows 7 taskbar to display the Start menu.

2 Type `Photoshop CS5` as the search text in the 'Search programs and files' text box, and watch the search results appear on the Start menu.

3 Click Adobe Photoshop CS5 in the search results on the Start menu to start Photoshop.

4 After a few moments, when the Photoshop window is displayed, if the window is not maximized, click the Maximize button on the title bar to maximize the window.

To Reset the Workspace

As discussed in Chapter 1, it is helpful to reset the workspace so that the tools and panels appear in their default positions. The following steps select the Essentials workspace.

1 Click the 'Show more workspaces and options' button on the Application bar to display the names of saved workspaces and then, if necessary, click Essentials to select the default workspace panels.

2 Click the 'Show more workspaces and options' button again to display the list and then click Reset Essentials to restore the workspace to its default settings and reposition any panels that may have been moved.

To Reset the Tools and the Options Bar

Recall that the Tools panel and the options bar retain their settings from previous Photoshop sessions. The following steps select the Rectangular Marquee Tool and reset all tool settings in the options bar.

1 If the tools in the Tools panel appear in two columns, click the double arrow at the top of the Tools panel.

2 If necessary, click the Rectangular Marquee Tool button on the Tools panel to select it.

3 Right-click the Rectangular Marquee Tool icon on the options bar to display the context menu and then click Reset All Tools. When Photoshop displays a confirmation dialog box, click the OK button to restore the tools to their default settings.

To Reset the Default Colors

Recall that Photoshop retains the foreground and background colors from session to session. Your colors might not display black over white on the Tools panel. The following step resets the default colors.

1 Press the D key to reset the default foreground and background colors.

To Open a Photo

To open a photo in Photoshop, it must be stored as a digital file on your computer or on an external storage device. The photos used in this book are stored in the Data Files for Students. You can access the Data Files for Students on the CD that accompanies this book. See the inside back cover of this book for instructions on downloading the Data Files for Students, or contact your instructor for information about accessing the required files.

The following steps open the file, Room, from a CD located in drive E.

1 Insert the CD that accompanies this book into your CD drive. After a few seconds, if Windows displays a dialog box, click its Close button.

2 With the Photoshop window open, click File on the menu bar, and then click Open to display the Open dialog box.

3 In the Open dialog box, click the Look in box arrow to display the list of available locations, and then click drive E or the drive associated with your CD.

4 Double-click the Chapter 03 folder to open it, and then double-click the file, Room, to open it.

5 When Photoshop displays the image in the document window, double-click the magnification box on the document window status bar, type 45, and then press the ENTER key to change the magnification (Figure 3–2).

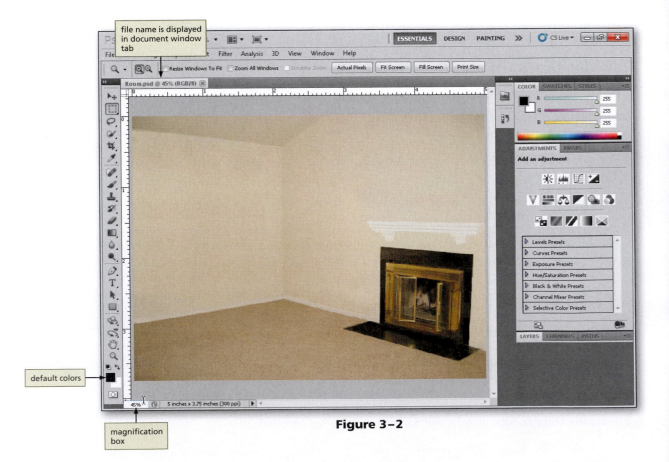

Figure 3–2

To View Rulers

The following steps display the rulers in the document window to facilitate making precise measurements.

1 If the rulers are not shown on the top and left sides of the document window, press CTRL+R to display the rulers in the workspace.

2 If necessary, right-click the horizontal ruler and then click Inches on the context menu to display the rulers in inches.

To Save a Photo

Even though you have yet to edit the photo, it is a good practice to save the file on your personal storage device early in the process. The following steps save the photo with the name Room Edited.

1 With your USB flash drive connected to one of the computer's USB ports, click File on the menu bar to display the File menu and then click Save As to display the Save As dialog box.

2 In the File name text box, type `Room Edited` to rename the file. Do not press the ENTER key after typing the file name.

3 Click the Save in box arrow and then click UDISK 2.0 (F:), or the location associated with your USB flash drive, in the list, if necessary.

4 Click the Save button in the Save As dialog box to save the file.

Creating a Composite Image Using Layers

Photoshop has many tools to help create composite images, photomontages, and collages. A composite, or composite image, is one that combines multiple photographs or images to display in a single combined file. Graphic artists use the newer term, **photomontage**, to refer to both the process and the result of creating a composite from photos.

One of the most powerful tools in Photoshop is layering. A **layer** is a section within a Photoshop document that you can manipulate independently from the rest of the document. Layers can be stacked one on top of the other, resembling sheets of clear film, to form a composite image.

Gather your photos and plan your layers.
One of the keys to successful image compositions is finding the best source material with similar lighting situations and tonal qualities. Choose high-quality photos and images that convey your overall message. Make sure you have permission to use the images if they are not original photographs taken by you or provided to you by a colleague or client. Obtain several versions of the same photo, if possible, including photos from different angles and with different lighting situations. Make two copies of each photo and store one as a backup. Crop unwanted portions of the photos before adding them as new layers.

Plan Ahead

Layer Comps
Graphic artists often create multiple versions, or compositions, of their work. A **layer comp** is a single view of the page layout with specific visible layers and attributes. You can use layer comps to demo versions of your composition to customers or colleagues, or simply to jump back and forth between different views and layers of your document. Similar to the History panel's snapshot, a layer comp takes a picture of the composite, using the Layers panel to show a particular stage of development.

Layers have been used by business and industry for years. Cartoonists create layers of physical transparencies to help with animation. The medical field uses overlays to illustrate anatomical features. Virtual simulations use layers to display processes. With Photoshop, layers are easy to create and export for these kinds of applications.

Recall that you used selections in Chapter 2 to move, copy, transform, and delete portions of a photo. Layers can perform all of the same functions performed by selecting, while providing added features. The most powerful feature of layers is the ability to revisit a portion of the image to make further changes, even after deselecting. Layers can be created, copied, deleted, displayed, hidden, merged, locked, grouped, repositioned, and flattened. Layers can be composed of images, patterns, text, shapes, colors, or filters. You can use layers to apply special effects, correct or colorize pictures, repair damaged photos, or import text elements. In previous chapters, you worked with images in a flat, single layer called the **Background layer**. In this chapter, you will create, name, and manipulate multiple layers on top of the Background layer.

Many layer manipulations are performed using the **Layers panel**, which lists all the layers, groups, and layer effects in an image (Figure 3–3). Each time you insert a layer onto an image, the new layer is added to the top of the panel. The default display of a layer on the Layers panel includes a visibility icon, a thumbnail of the layer, and the layer's name. To the right of the layer's name, a locking icon or other manipulations might appear.

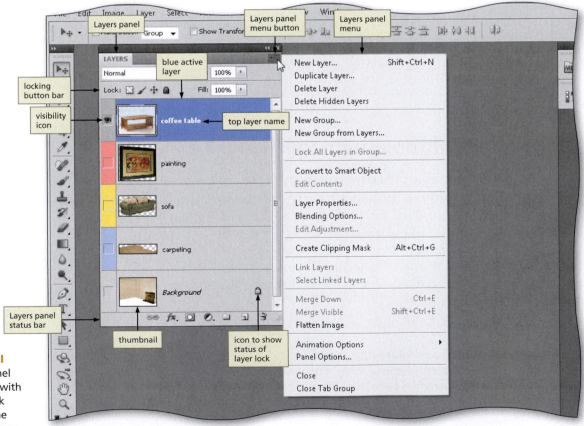

Figure 3–3

Layer Comps Panel
The Layer Comps panel includes a status bar with buttons to move back and forth through the comps, to update comps from the current view, to create them, and to delete them. The Layer Comps menu has some of those same commands, as well as others to duplicate a layer comp and set its properties.

Photoshop allows you to lock three different components of layers. The 'Lock transparent pixels' button confines editing to opaque layer portions. The 'Lock image pixels' button prevents modification of the layer's pixels using paint tools. The Lock position button prevents the layer from being moved. The Lock all button enables all of the three ways of locking the layer. A lock icon appears to the right of the name on the Layers panel on locked layers.

The Layers panel is used in several different manners: to show and hide layers, to create new layers, and to work with groups of layers. You can access additional commands and attributes by clicking the Layers panel menu button or by right-clicking a layer. The Layers panel defines how layers interact. As you use the buttons and boxes on the Layers panel, each will be explained.

While Photoshop allows background editing, as you have done in previous chapters, the Background layer cannot be moved, nor can its transparency be changed. In other words, the Background layer fills the document window, and there is no layer behind the background. Partially locked by default, the Background layer displays a hollow lock (Figure 3–3). If you want to convert the Background layer into a fully editable layer, double-click the layer on the Layers panel, and then click the OK button in the New Layer dialog box.

When working with layers, it is important to make sure you know which layer you are editing by looking at the active layer on the Layers panel or by looking at the layer name, appended to the file name on the document window tab. Many other layer commands appear on the Layer menu, including making adjustments to the layer, creating layer masks, grouping layers, and other editing and placement commands.

BTW

Layer Comps vs. History Snapshots
Layer comps include the visibility, position, and appearance of layers, not the edited steps. In addition, layer comps are saved with the document, whereas History panel snapshots are not. You can export layer comps to separate graphic or PDF files for easy distribution.

To Change Layers Panel Options

The Panel Options command, accessible from the Layers panel menu, allows you to change the view and size of the thumbnail related to each layer. A thumbnail displays a small visual preview of the layer on the Layers panel. The Panel Options dialog box allows you to choose small, medium, large, or no thumbnails. The following steps select a medium-sized thumbnail of each layer.

1

• Click the Layers panel menu button to display the Layers panel menu (Figure 3–4).

Q&A

Do I have to display thumbnails?

No, but displaying thumbnails of each layer allows you to see easily what the layer looks like and helps you to be more efficient when editing a layer. To improve performance and save monitor space, however, some Photoshop users choose not to display thumbnails.

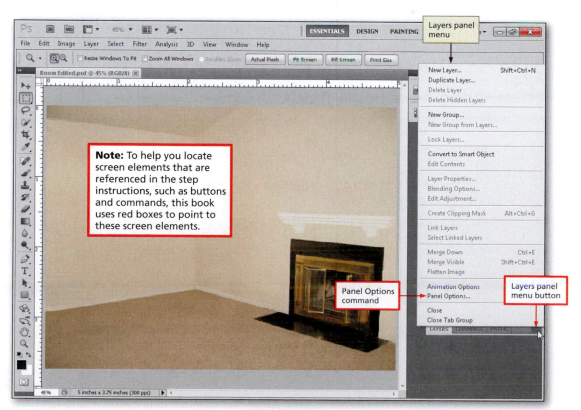

Figure 3–4

2

- Click Panel Options on the menu to display the Layers Panel Options dialog box.

- Click the medium-sized thumbnail to select it.

- Click the Layer Bounds option button, if necessary, to select it and change the look and feel of the Layers panel (Figure 3–5).

Q&A How does the Layer Bounds option change the interface?

The Layer Bounds option causes the Layers panel to display only the layer in the thumbnail, not the entire image.

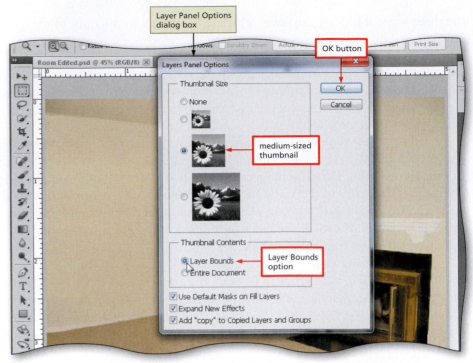

Figure 3–5

3

- Click the Layers panel tab to expand the panel.

- Click the OK button to close the Layers Panel Options dialog box (Figure 3–6).

Q&A Should I see a difference on the Layers panel?

Unless a previous user had already changed it, the size of the thumbnail should have changed on the Layers panel. Layer bounds will not appear until you create a layer other than the Background layer.

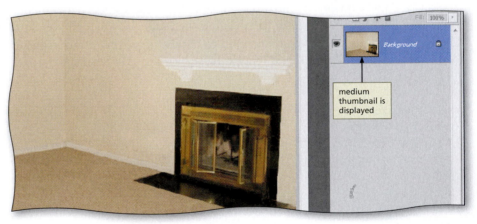

Figure 3–6

Creating a Layer Via Cut

There are several ways to create a new layer. You can:

- isolate a portion of the image and then cut or make a layer copy

- create a new layer by copying from a different image

- duplicate a layer that already exists

- create a new, blank layer on which you can draw or create text

When you add a layer to an image, a new layer appears above, or on top of, the currently selected layer, creating a **stacking order**. By default, Photoshop names and numbers layers sequentially; however, you can rearrange the stacking order to change the appearance of the image. The final appearance of an edited Photoshop document is a view of the layer stack from the top down.

To Create a Layer Via Cut

The following steps create a new layer that includes only the carpeting on the floor. You will use the Quick Selection Tool to select the area and then use the Layer via Cut command to isolate the floor from the rest of the photo, creating a new layer.

- On the Tools panel, select the Quick Selection Tool.

- If necessary, click the New selection button on the options bar to start a new selection.

- In the photo, drag slowly from the upper-left corner of the carpeting to the lower-right corner of the photo to select only the carpeting (Figure 3–7).

Q&A Why did Photoshop change to the 'Add to selection' button on the options bar?

Once you create a New selection, the most common task is to add more to the selection, so Photoshop selects that button automatically. If you want to start over, you can select the New selection button again.

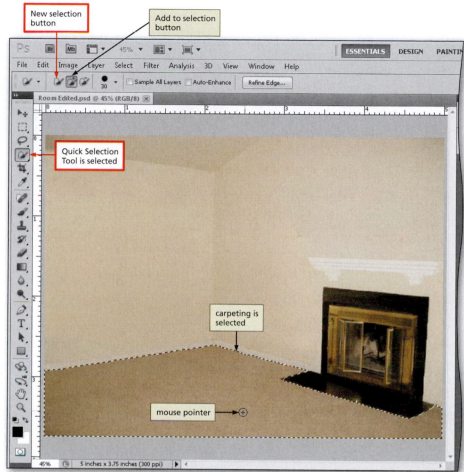

Figure 3–7

- Right-click the selection to display the context menu (Figure 3–8).

Q&A Could I use the New layer command?

No. The New layer command creates a blank layer.

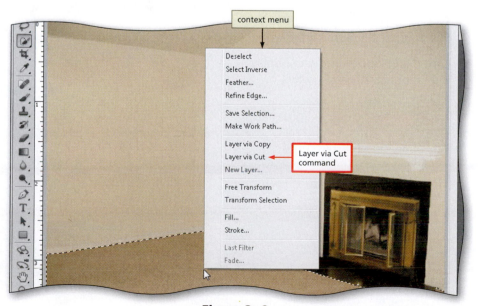

Figure 3–8

3

- Click Layer via Cut on the context menu to create the new layer (Figure 3–9).

Q&A

What is the difference between Layer via Cut and Layer via Copy?

The Layer via Cut command removes the selection from the background. The Layer via Copy command creates a copy on the Layers panel and leaves the original selection intact. Future edits to the Background, such as changing the color or lighting, will not affect a cut layer.

Figure 3–9

Other Ways

1. Create selection, on Layer menu, point to New, click Layer via Cut
2. Create selection, press SHIFT+CTRL+J

To Name and Color a Layer

It is a good practice to give each layer a unique name so you can identify it more easily. The name of the active layer appears on the Layers panel and on the title bar of the document window. Photoshop allows you to give each layer its own color identification as well. The following steps name and color a layer using the Layer Properties dialog box.

1

- Click the Layers panel menu button (shown in Figure 3–9) to display the menu.

- Click Layer Properties to display the Layer Properties dialog box.

- Type **carpeting** in the Name box to name the layer, carpeting.

- Click the Color box arrow to display the list of identification colors (Figure 3–10).

 Experiment

- One at a time, click each of the colors and watch the changes on the Layers panel.

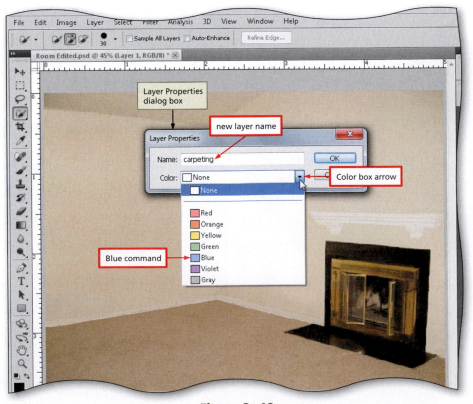

Figure 3–10

• Click Blue in the list to choose a blue identification color (Figure 3–11).

Figure 3–11

• Click the OK button to apply the new settings on the Layers panel (Figure 3–12).

Other Ways

1. Right-click layer, click Layer Properties, type new name, choose new color, click OK

2. To name layer, on Layers panel, double-click layer name, type new name, press ENTER

3. To color layer, on Layers panel, right-click visibility area, click color

Figure 3–12

To Hide and Show a Layer

Sometimes you want to hide a layer to view other layers to make editing decisions. The following steps hide and show the Background layer.

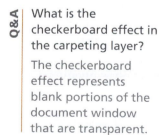

• Click the 'Indicates layer visibility' button to the left of the Background layer to hide the layer in the document window and to remove the visibility icon (Figure 3–13).

Q&A

What is the checkerboard effect in the carpeting layer?

The checkerboard effect represents blank portions of the document window that are transparent.

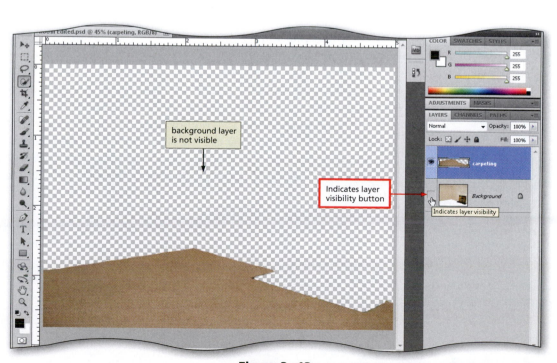

Figure 3–13

2

● Click the 'Indicates layer visibility' button again to show the Background layer in the document window and display the visibility icon (Figure 3–14).

Q&A

What is the white area on the Background layer thumbnail?

When you cut or delete from a locked layer such as the Background layer, the default background color shows through; in this case, it is the default white color. Because other layers will eclipse the white, you do not have to remove it.

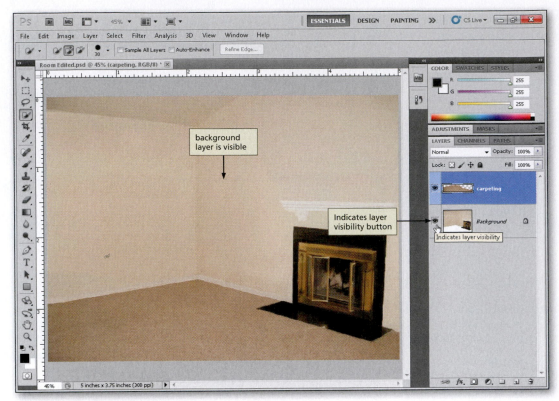

Figure 3–14

Other Ways

1. Right-click visibility icon, click Hide this layer or Show this layer

2. On Layer menu, click Hide Layers or Show Layers

Creating a Layer from Another Image

When you create composite images, you might want to create layers from other images. It is important to choose images that closely match or complement color, lighting, size, and perspective if you want your image to look natural. While you can adjust disparate images to improve how well they match, it is easier to start with as close a match as possible, ideally with similar lighting situations and tonal qualities.

Many sources exist for composite images and they come in many different file types and sizes. For example, you can use your own digital photos, scanned images, images from royalty-free Web sites, or you can draw your own. If you use a photo or image from the Web, make sure you have legal rights to use the image. Legal rights include permission from the photographer or artist to use the image, or purchasing these rights, through a contract, from an online store.

The basic process of creating a new layer from another image involves opening a second image, selecting the area you wish to use, and then moving it to the original photo in a drag-and-drop, or cut-and-paste, fashion. Once the layer exists in the destination photo, you might need to do some editing to remove portions of the layer, to resize it, or to make tonal adjustments.

BTW

Creating Layer Groups
Layer groups help you manage and organize layers in a logical manner. To create a layer group, click the Create New Group button on the Layers panel. A new layer will appear with a folder icon. You then can drag layers into the folder or use the Layers panel menu to insert a new layer. You can apply attributes and masks to the entire group.

To Open a Second Image

To add a sofa as a layer to the Room Edited image, you will need to open a new file, Sofa, from the Data Files for Students, or from a location specified by your instructor. The following steps open the Sofa file, which is stored in the PSD format.

1 Press CTRL+O to display the Open dialog box.

2 In the Open dialog box, if necessary, click the Look in box arrow, and then navigate to the Chapter 03 folder of the Data Files for Students, or a location specified by your instructor.

3 Double-click the file named Sofa to open it (Figure 3–15).

Figure 3–15

Displaying Multiple Files

Photoshop has more than 25 different ways to arrange document windows when more than one file is open. You also can create a custom workspace by moving and manipulating document windows manually.

For example, you might want to display two document windows, horizontally or vertically, in order to drag and drop from one image to another. You might want to compare different versions or views of photos beside each other in the document window. Or, when creating a panorama, you might want to preview how certain photos will look side by side.

When you are finished viewing multiple document windows in the workspace, you can **consolidate**, or view only one window at a time.

To Arrange the Document Windows

The following steps display the Room Edited and Sofa windows beside each other using the Arrange Documents button on the Application bar.

1

- On the Application bar, click the Arrange Documents button to display its list (Figure 3–16).

Q&A

Why are some of the arrangements grayed out?

Because you have only two document windows open, the only arrangements enabled are the ones that display two windows.

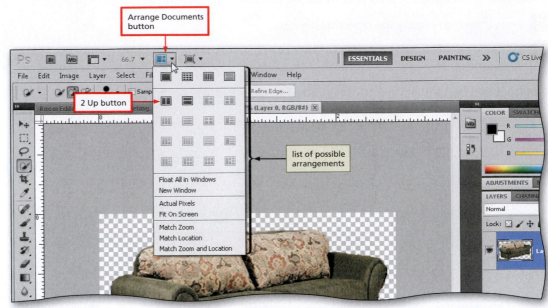

Figure 3–16

2

- Click the first 2 Up button in the list to display the windows beside each other (Figure 3–17).

Figure 3–17

Other Ways

1. On Window menu, click Arrange, click Tile

To Create a Layer by Dragging an Entire Image

When you drag a selection from one document window to the other, Photoshop creates a new layer in the destination document window, on top of the other layers. If you want to include the entire image from the source window, use the Move Tool to drag from any location in the source window to the destination window. Dragging between document windows is an automatic duplication rather than a true move. The original, source image remains unchanged.

The following step moves the entire image from the source window, Sofa, to the destination window, Room Edited.

- Press the v key to activate the Move Tool.

- Drag the sofa image into the Room Edited window and drop it in the room (Figure 3–18).

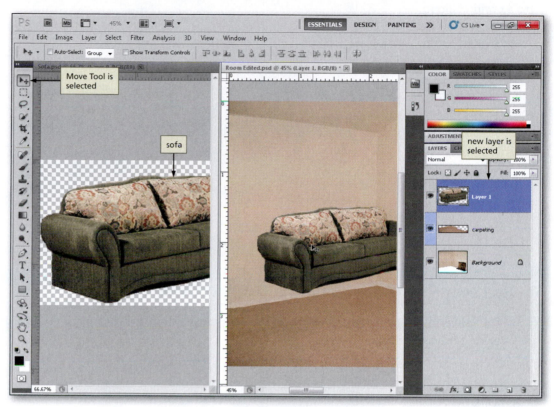

Figure 3–18

To Close the Sofa Document Window

Because you are finished with the Sofa image, the following step closes the Sofa window.

1 Click the Close button on the Sofa document window tab. If Photoshop asks you to save the file, click the No button.

Other Ways

1. In source window, create selection, on Edit menu click Copy, in destination window on Edit menu click Paste

BTW

The Layers Panel Context Menus
The Layers panel has many ways to work with layers. For example, right-clicking the layer name displays a different context menu from the one you see when right-clicking the thumbnail. Double-clicking the layer name allows you to rename the layer; double-clicking the thumbnail opens the Layer Style dialog box.

To Position a Layer

The following step drags the sofa to a new location.

1

• With the new layer still selected on the Layers panel, and the Move Tool still selected on the Tools panel, drag the sofa to a position along the left wall, on the floor (Figure 3–19).

Q&A

Is it acceptable for some of the sofa to disappear off the edge of the document window?

Yes. Your goal is to make it look as natural as possible, as if it is sitting on the floor.

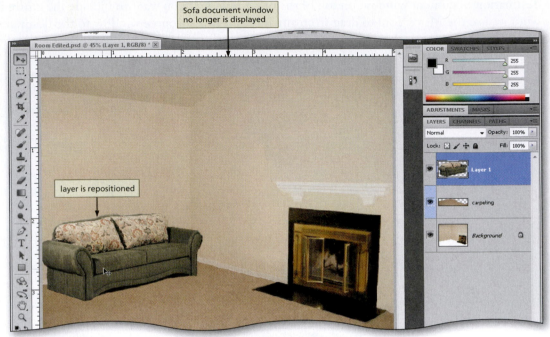

Figure 3–19

To Set Layer Properties Using the Context Menu

The following steps set the layer properties for the sofa, this time using the context menu displayed by right-clicking the layer itself.

1

• On the Layers panel, right-click the name of the layer, Layer 1, to display the context menu (Figure 3–20).

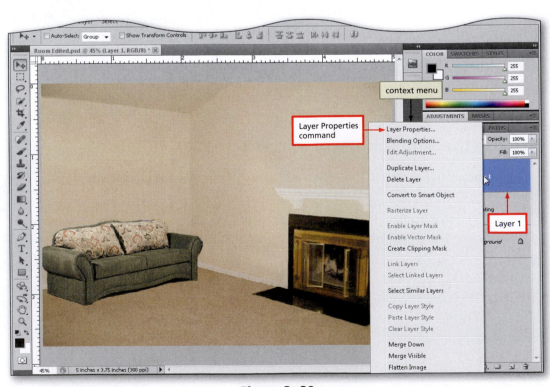

Figure 3–20

• Click Layer Properties on the menu to display the Layer Properties dialog box.

• Type **sofa** in the Name box to name the layer.

• Click the Color box arrow, and then click Yellow in the list to choose a yellow identification color (Figure 3–21).

• Click the OK button to display the new settings on the Layers panel.

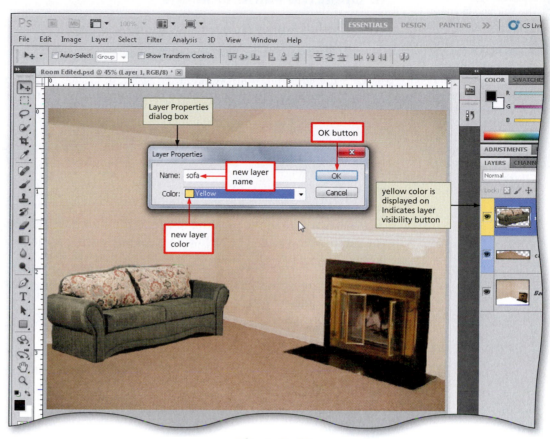

Figure 3–21

To Save the File

Because you have created layers and made changes to the image, it is a good idea to save the file again. The following step saves the file again.

1 Press CTRL+S to save the Room Edited file with the same name. If Photoshop displays a dialog box about compatibility, click the OK button.

Other Ways

1. Click Layers panel menu button, click Layer Properties, type new name, choose new color, click OK button

2. Click Layer on the menu bar, click Layer Properties, type new name, choose new color, click OK button

Break Point: If you wish to take a break, this is a good place to do so. You can quit Photoshop now. To resume at a later time, start Photoshop, open the file called Room Edited, and continue following the steps from this location forward.

Creating a Layer by Dragging a Selection

Sometimes you do not want to move an entire image from one window to another. When you want only a part of an image, you create a selection, as you learned in Chapter 2, and then move the selection to the destination window. Once the selection exists in the destination window, some editing, such as scaling, erasing, or adjusting, commonly is necessary.

BTW

JPG File Type
The Painting image is stored as a JPG file. Recall that JPG stands for Joint Photographic Experts Group and is the file type typically generated by digital cameras. The JPG format supports many different color modes. JPG retains all color information in an RGB image, unlike the GIF format.

To Open the Painting Image

The following steps open a file named Painting.

① Press CTRL+O to display the Open dialog box.

② Click the Look in box arrow, and then navigate to the Chapter 03 folder of the Data Files for Students, or a location specified by your instructor, if necessary.

③ Double-click the file named Painting to open it.

To Select the Painting

When adding the painting image to the Room Edited image, you will not need the surrounding wall. The following steps select the painting only, using the Rectangular Marquee Tool.

① If necessary, right-click the current marquee tool and then click Rectangular Marquee Tool on the context menu to select it.

② If necessary, click the New selection button on the options bar to start a new selection.

③ Drag around the painting. Avoid including the wall in the selection. If you make a mistake while selecting, press the ESC key and then begin again (Figure 3–22).

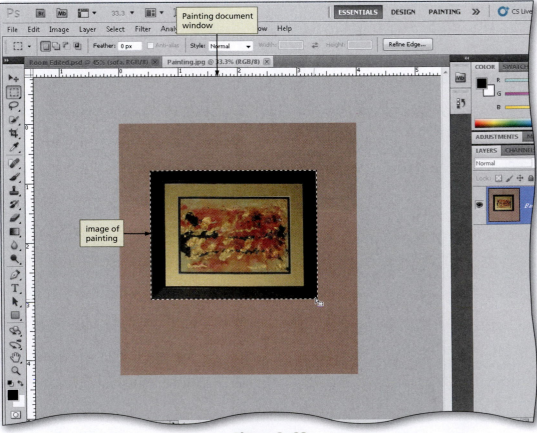

Figure 3–22

To Create a Layer by Dragging a Selection

The following steps move the selection. To facilitate dragging the selection between windows, you will view the windows above and below one another.

1

- On the Application bar, click the Arrange Documents button (shown in Figure 3–16 on page PS 152) to display its list, and then click the second 2 Up button to display the windows above and below one another (Figure 3–23).

Experiment

- Click the Arrange Documents button and then click the Tile All Horizontally button. Open a third file and then try some of the other configurations. When you are done, close the third file. Click the Arrange Documents button and then click the second 2 Up button.

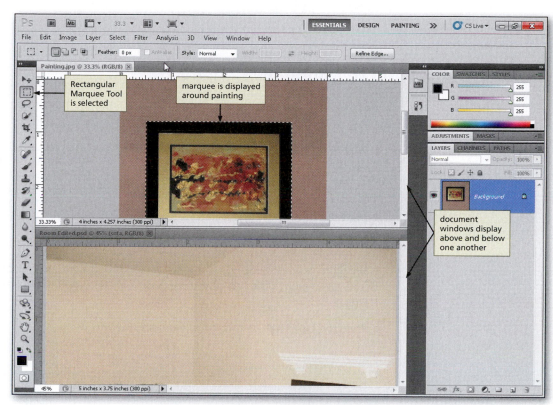

Figure 3–23

2

- Press the V key to activate the Move Tool.

- Drag the selection and drop it in the Room Edited window (Figure 3–24).

Q&A

Why is the painting so large?

The photos used in composites may come from a variety of sources and camera types, with a variety of different resolutions, and with different physical sizes. Photos generated by digital cameras, with lots of megapixels, create very large files.

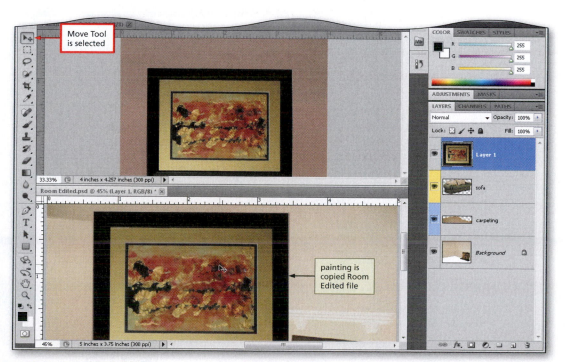

Figure 3–24

To Close the Painting Window

The following step closes the Painting window.

1 Click the Close button on the Painting document window tab. If Photoshop displays a dialog box asking if you want to save the changes, click the No button.

To Transform the Painting

The following steps resize the layer. Also, to make the painting appear more natural in the setting, you will skew the layer using skills discussed in Chapter 2.

1 With the new layer still selected on the Layers panel, press CTRL+T to display the bounding box.

2 SHIFT+drag a corner sizing handle until the selection is approximately 50% smaller.

3 Drag the layer to a location above the sofa.

4 Right-click the selection and then click Skew on the context menu.

5 Drag the lower-left sizing handle down to skew the painting. Drag other sizing handles, if necessary, until the top of the painting appears parallel with the ceiling, as shown in Figure 3–25.

6 Press the ENTER key to commit the transformation.

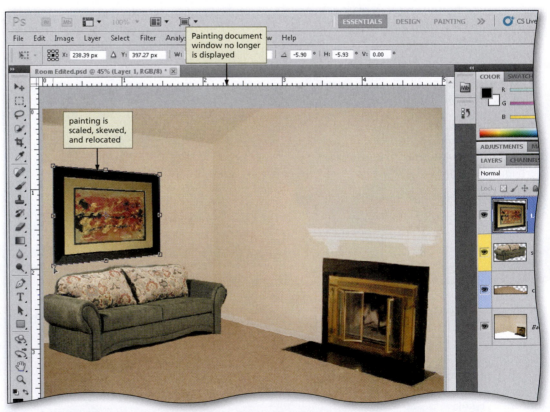

Figure 3–25

To Set the Painting Layer Properties

The following steps set the painting layer properties.

1 Right-click Layer 1 on the Layers panel. Click Layer Properties on the context menu.

2 Type `painting` in the Name box. Click the Color box arrow, and then click Red.

3 Click the OK button to apply the settings.

The Eraser Tools

In the painting layer, you eliminated the background before moving it to the composite by using a selection technique. Other times, however, a new layer still may have extra color or objects that are not appropriate for the composite image. The image might be shaped oddly, making selecting tedious, or there might be other images in the background that come along with the selection, no matter what you do. In those cases, dragging the image into a layer and then erasing part of that layer gives you more freedom and control in how the layer appears.

On the Tools panel, when you right-click the Eraser Tool button, Photoshop displays the three eraser tools. To alternate among the three eraser tools, press SHIFT+E. To access the eraser tools after using a different tool, press the E key.

The eraser tools are described in Table 3–1.

Table 3–1 Eraser Tools

Tool	Purpose	Shortcut	Button
Eraser Tool	erases pixels beneath the cursor or brush tip	E SHIFT+E toggles through all three eraser tools	
Background Eraser Tool	erases sample color from the center of the brush	E SHIFT+E toggles through all three eraser tools	
Magic Eraser Tool	erases all similarly colored pixels	E SHIFT+E toggles through all three eraser tools	

When using the eraser tools, it is best to erase small portions at a time. That way each erasure is a separate state on the History panel. If you make mistakes, you can click earlier states on the panel. Small erasures also can be undone. To undo an erasure, press CTRL+Z, or click Edit on the menu bar, and then click Undo Eraser.

To Open the Coffee Table Image

The following step opens a file named Coffee Table in preparation for using the eraser tools.

1 Open the Coffee Table file from the Chapter 03 folder of the Data Files for Students, or a location specified by your instructor, if necessary.

BTW

PNG File Type
The Coffee Table image is stored as a PNG file. Recall that PNG stands for Portable Network Graphics and is a cross-platform file type similar to GIF. It differs in that you can control the opacity of transparent colors. PNG files interlace, or fill in, faster on Web pages.

To Create the Coffee Table Layer

1 On the Application bar, click the Arrange Documents button to display its list, and then click the first 2 Up button to display the windows beside each other.

2 With the Coffee Table window still active, click the Move Tool button on the Tools panel, if necessary.

3 Drag the entire coffee table image and drop it in the Room Edited window. Zoom to 33% magnification (Figure 3–26).

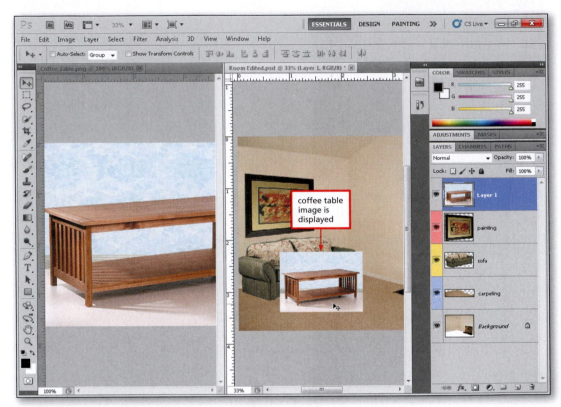

coffee table image is displayed

Figure 3–26

To Close the Coffee Table Window

The following step closes the original the Coffee Table window.

1 Close the Coffee Table document window. If Photoshop displays a dialog box asking if you want to save the changes, click the No button.

To Set the Layer Properties

The following steps set the layer properties.

1 Display the Layer Properties dialog box.

2 Name the layer **coffee table**, and choose a gray identification color.

3 Close the Layer Properties dialog box.

Using the Magic Eraser Tool

The Magic Eraser Tool erases all similarly colored pixels with one click. The Magic Eraser Tool options bar (Figure 3–27) gives you the choice of contiguous or non-contiguous pixels and allows you to enter a tolerance value to define the range of erasable color. A lower tolerance erases pixels within a range of color values very similar to the pixel you click. A higher tolerance erases pixels within a broader range. Recall that the Anti-alias check box creates a smooth edge that can apply to both selecting and erasing. **Opacity** refers to the level at which you can see through a color to reveal the layer beneath it. When using the eraser tools, an opacity setting of 100% completely erases pixels. A lower opacity partially erases pixels.

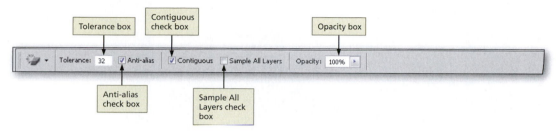

Figure 3–27

To Erase Using the Magic Eraser Tool

The following steps use the Magic Eraser Tool to remove the background from the coffee table image.

1

• Zoom to 100% magnification and scroll as necessary to view the coffee table layer.

• With the coffee table layer still selected, right-click the Eraser Tool button on the Tools panel to display the context menu (Figure 3–28).

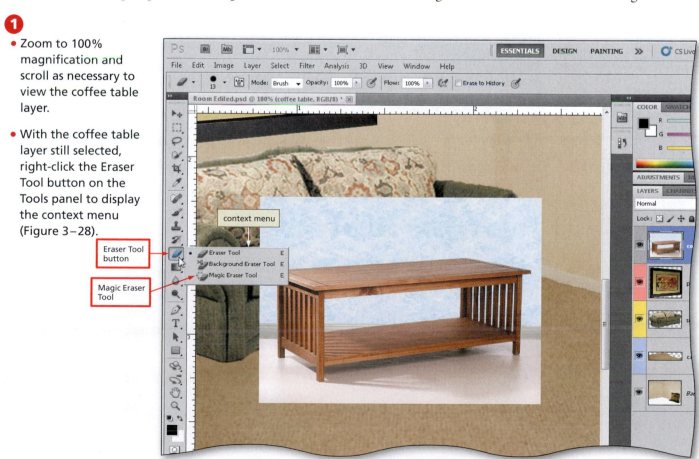

Figure 3–28

2

• Click the Magic Eraser Tool to select it.

• On the Magic Eraser options bar, type 4 0 in the Tolerance box.

• If necessary, click the Anti-alias check box to display the check mark.

• Click the Contiguous check box so it does not display a check mark (Figure 3–29).

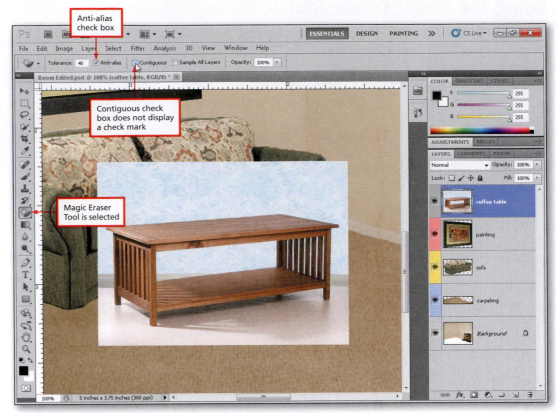

Figure 3–29

3

• Click the wallpaper to delete all of the blue color.

• If some blue remains in your layer, click it (Figure 3–30).

Q&A How should I position the Magic Eraser Tool mouse pointer?

Position the center of the starburst tip over the pixel color to erase using the Magic Eraser Tool mouse pointer.

Other Ways

1. Press SHIFT+E until Magic Eraser Tool is selected, click document

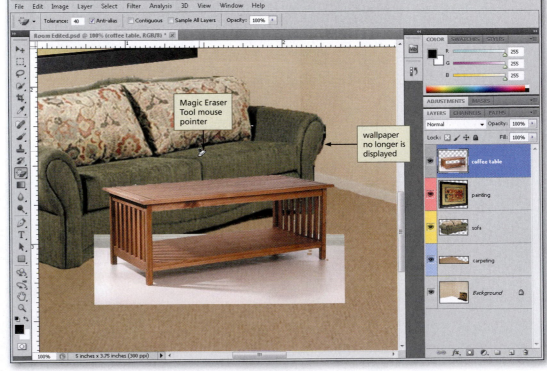

Figure 3–30

Using the Eraser Tool

The Eraser Tool changes pixels in the image as you drag through them. On most layers, the Eraser Tool simply erases the pixels or changes them to transparent, revealing the layer beneath. On a locked layer, such as the Background layer, the Eraser Tool changes the pixels to the background color.

The Eraser Tool options bar (Figure 3–31) displays a Mode box in which you can choose one of three shapes for erasure: brush, block, and pen. The brush shape gives you the most flexibility in size, and many different brush tips are available. The default brush tip is a circle. Block mode is a hard-edged, fixed-sized square with no options for changing the opacity or flow; however, it does give you quick access to a square to erase straight lines and corners. The pencil mode is similar to the brush mode, except that the pencil does not spread as much into adjacent pixels.

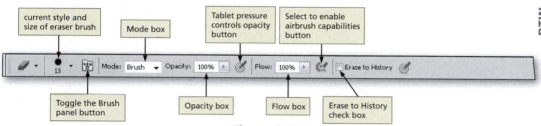

Figure 3–31

As with the Magic Eraser Tool options bar, an Opacity box allows you to specify the depth of the erasure. The Flow box specifies how quickly the erasure is performed. In addition, you can erase to a saved state or snapshot in the History panel.

As you erase with the brush shape, the RIGHT BRACKET ( ]) and LEFT BRACKET ([ ) keys increase and decrease the size of the eraser, respectively.

To Display Only the Current Layer

Some users find it easier to erase in a layer when only that layer appears in the document window. The following step hides all but the current layer.

• On the Layers panel, ALT+click the coffee table layer visibility icon, so only the coffee table is displayed (Figure 3–32).

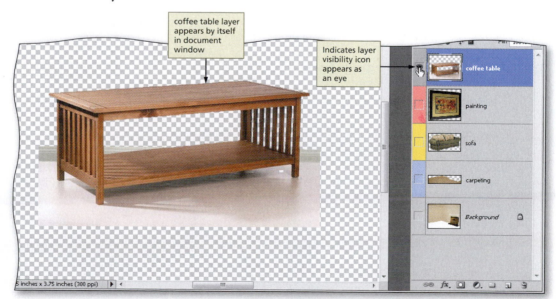

Figure 3–32

To Select the Eraser Tool and Resize the Mouse Pointer

The following steps select the Eraser Tool in preparation for erasing more of the layer.

1 Right-click the Magic Eraser Tool button on the Tools panel, and then click Eraser Tool on the context menu.

2 Move the mouse pointer into the document window.

3 If the mouse pointer is extremely small, press the RIGHT BRACKET (]) key several times to resize the eraser until the mouse pointer changes from a dot to a small circle (Figure 3–33).

Figure 3–33

To Erase Using the Eraser Tool

The following steps erase the white floor beneath the coffee table using the Eraser Tool.

1
• Drag the mouse across a portion of the floor to erase it. Do not drag across the coffee table (Figure 3–34).

Q&A How should I position the Eraser Tool mouse pointer?

By default the Eraser Tool mouse pointer appears as a circle. When you click or drag, Photoshop erases everything within the circle. You can change the size of the mouse pointer using the bracket keys.

Figure 3–34

2

- Continue dragging to erase more of the floor and the molding, using the LEFT BRACKET ([) and RIGHT BRACKET (]) keys to change the size of your eraser. Do not erase completely along the very edge of the coffee table (Figure 3–35).

 **Experiment**

- Drag a short erasure over the coffee table that creates an error. Then press CTRL+Z to undo the erasure.

Figure 3–35

To Erase Using the Block Mouse Pointer

The following steps delete flooring and shadows that are very close to the coffee table using a block mouse pointer.

1

- Click the Mode box arrow on the options bar to display its list (Figure 3–36).

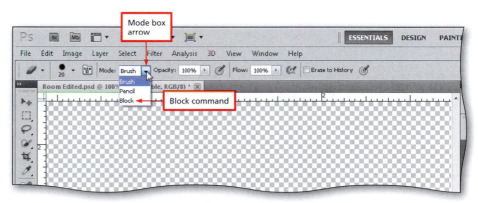

Figure 3–36

2

- Click Block to choose a block mouse pointer.

- Drag close to the coffee table to erase the rest of the flooring and shadows (Figure 3–37).

Q&A Can I change the size of the block?

No, the block eraser mouse pointer cannot be resized. You can change the magnification, however, to help you erase smaller portions using the block.

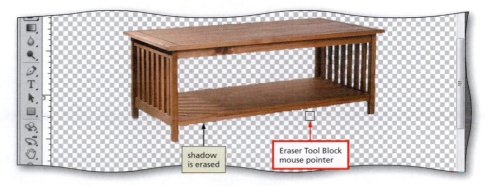

Figure 3–37

Other Ways
1. Press SHIFT+E until Eraser Tool is selected, click document

To View All Layers

The following steps show all of the layers.

1 ALT+click the coffee table visibility icon to show all of the layers.

2 If viewing all of the layers reveals other areas of the coffee table that need to be erased, drag to erase them. Zoom and scroll as necessary.

To Transform the Coffee Table Layer

The following steps transform the coffee table layer in order to make it fit the perspective of the room.

1 With the coffee table layer still selected, zoom out as necessary, and then press CTRL+T to turn on the bounding box.

2 Right-click within the bounding box to display the context menu, and then choose Perspective.

3 Drag the left-center sizing handle down to change the perspective so it resembles Figure 3–38.

4 If necessary, move the coffee table to a location in front of the sofa.

5 Press the ENTER key to confirm the transformation.

6 If necessary, zoom to 45% magnification.

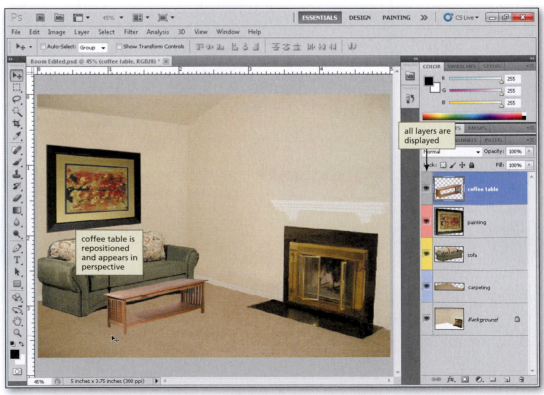

Figure 3–38

Using the Background Eraser Tool

The Background Eraser Tool erases the background while maintaining the edges of an object in the foreground, based on a set color that you choose for the background. The Background Eraser Tool samples the color in the center of the mouse pointer, called the **hot spot**. As you drag, the tool erases that color, leaving the rest of the layer as foreground. You release the mouse and drag again to sample a different color. On the Background Eraser Tool options bar (Figure 3–39) you can use the tolerance setting to control the range of colors that will be erased, sample the color selections, and adjust the sharpness of the boundaries by setting limits. The three sampling buttons on the Background Eraser Tool options bar sample in different ways. When you use the Sampling: Continuous button, it samples colors and erases continuously as you drag; the Sampling: Once button erases only the areas containing the color you first click; and the Sampling: Background Swatch button erases only areas containing the current color on the Tools panel, Color panel, or Swatches panel.

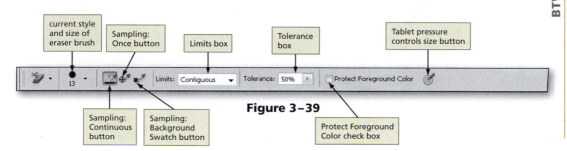

Figure 3–39

To Open the Ivy Image

The following step opens a file named Ivy in preparation for using the Background Eraser Tool.

1 Open the Ivy file from the Chapter 03 folder of the Data Files for Students, or from a location specified by your instructor.

To Create the Ivy Layer

To create the ivy layer, you first will move the entire image into the Room Edited document window.

1 On the Application bar, click the Arrange Documents button to display its list, and then click the first 2 Up button to display the windows beside each other.

2 Activate the Move Tool.

3 Drag the ivy image and drop it in the Room Edited window.

To Close the Ivy Window

The following step closes the Ivy window because you are finished with it.

1 Close the Ivy document window. If Photoshop displays a dialog box asking if you want to save the changes, click the No button.

To Set the Layer Properties

The following steps set the layer properties.

1 Double-click the new layer name in the Layers panel. Type **ivy** and then press the ENTER key to name the layer.

2 Right-click the 'Indicates layer visibility' button and choose the green identification color from the context menu (Figure 3–40).

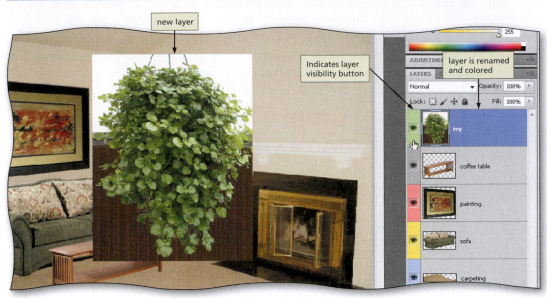

Figure 3–40

To Erase Using the Background Eraser Tool

The following steps use the Background Eraser Tool to remove the paneling from behind the ivy plant. If you make a mistake while erasing, click the previous state on the History panel or press CTRL+Z and begin erasing again.

1

• With the ivy layer still selected, right-click the Eraser Tool button on the Tools panel and then click Background Eraser Tool on the context menu to select the tool.

• On the options bar, click the Sampling: Once button.

• Click the Limits box arrow to display its list (Figure 3–41).

Q&A

How should I position the Background Eraser Tool mouse pointer?

Position the center of the starburst tip over the pixel color to erase using the Magic Eraser Tool mouse pointer.

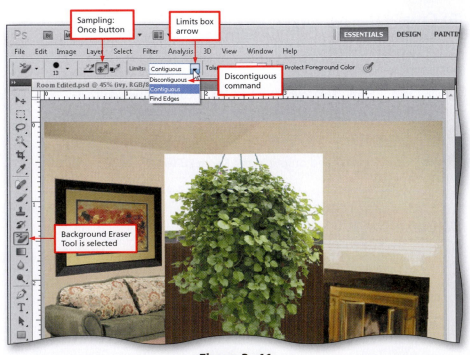

Figure 3–41

2
- Click Discontiguous to choose the setting.
- Enter 2 5 in the Tolerance box to lower the Tolerance setting, which will erase a more narrow range of color.
- If necessary, click to display a check mark in the Protect Foreground color check box.
- Move the mouse pointer to the document window and then press the RIGHT BRACKET (]) key several times to increase the size of the eraser, if necessary (Figure 3–42).

What does discontiguous mean?

Discontiguous means non-contiguous, in this case pixels of the same color that are not physically located together. In the ivy layer, parts of the brown panel appear behind the ivy and are not connected color-wise to the other brown paneling.

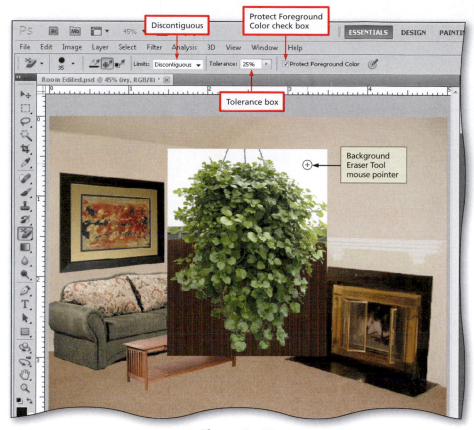

Figure 3–42

3
- Position the mouse pointer directly over a portion of the paneling.
- Click and hold the mouse button. Drag across the layer, including the ivy, to erase some of the paneling (Figure 3–43).

What is the purpose of the Protect Foreground Color check box?

When checked, the Protect Foreground Color check box gives you even more control of the background erasing. When colors are very similar, you can ALT+click the color you want to keep, then drag the color you wish to erase.

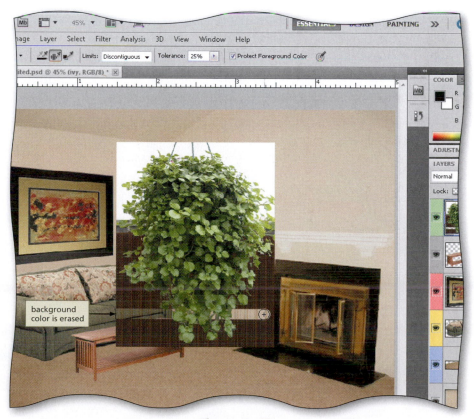

Figure 3–43

4

- Position the mouse pointer directly over a portion of the paneling.

- Click and hold the mouse button. Drag to erase the rest of the paneling.

- If some color remains, zoom as necessary to position your mouse directly over the color. Click and drag to erase the rest of the color (Figure 3–44).

Q&A

Some of the paneling still remains. How do I delete it?

Use the Eraser Tool or the Magic Erase Tool to erase the small portions. Zoom and change the size of your mouse pointer as necessary.

all paneling is erased

Figure 3–44

Other Ways

1. Press SHIFT+E until Background Eraser Tool is selected, set options bar, click document

To Finish the Ivy Layer

The following steps erase the rest of the background.

1 With the ivy layer still selected on the Layers panel, use a combination of eraser tools and techniques to erase the white portion of the layer, the hanging wires, and the chair rail molding.

2 Resize the layer as necessary and move it to a location on the left side of the fireplace mantel (Figure 3–45).

background is removed and layer is scaled and repositioned

Figure 3–45

To Add a Pole Lamp to the Room

The following steps add a pole lamp layer to the room.

1 Open the file named Pole Lamp from the Chapter 03 folder of the Data Files for Students, or from a location specified by your instructor.

2 Use the techniques you have learned to create a new layer and place the pole lamp in the Room Edited document window.

3 Name the new layer `pole lamp`, and color the layer orange.

4 Close the Pole Lamp document window.

To Rearrange Layers

The following step rearranges the layers on the Layers panel, so the pole lamp appears behind the end of the sofa.

1

- Select the pole lamp layer on the Layers panel, if necessary.

- Press CTRL+LEFT BRACKET ([) several times to move the layer down and place it below the sofa layer.

- In the document window, move the pole lamp to the right end of the sofa, in the corner of the room (Figure 3–46).

 Experiment

- Drag individual layers on the Layers panel to new locations in the stack, and watch how that changes the document window. When you are finished, rearrange the layers to appear as shown in Figure 3–46.

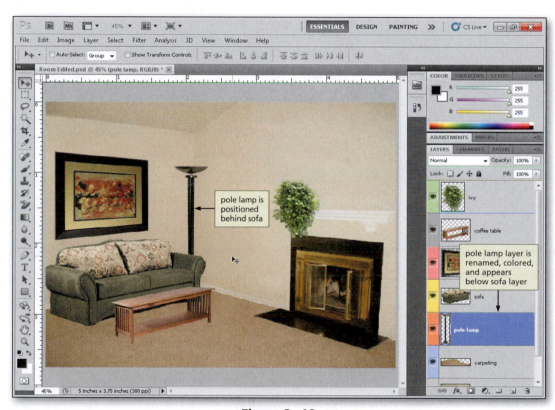

Figure 3–46

BTW

Arranging Layers
To rearrange layers, change their visibility, or better organize them, drag the layer up or down on the Layers panel. The top layer on the Layers panel appears in front of any other layers in the document window. The Layer menu also contains an Arrange submenu to help you organize your layers.

To Add Mantle Decorations to the Room

The following steps add a mantle decoration layer to the room.

1 Open the file named Mantle Decorations from the Chapter 03 folder of the Data Files for Students, or from a location specified by your instructor.

2 Use the techniques you have learned to create a new layer, edit it as necessary, and place the mantle decorations on the mantle in the Room Edited document window.

3 Name the new layer, `mantle decorations`, and color the layer violet.

4 Close the Mantle Decorations document window (Figure 3–47).

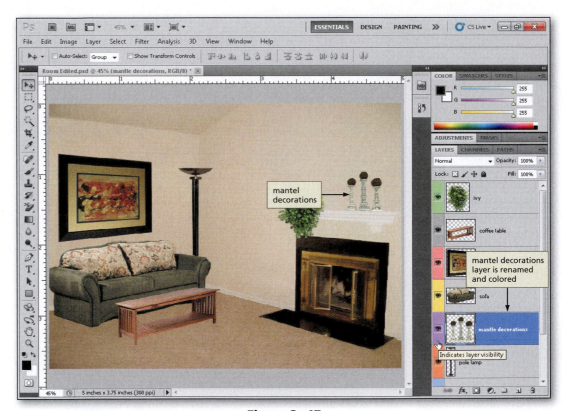

Figure 3–47

To Save the File

Many layers have been added to the composite image. The following step saves the file.

1 Save the Room Edited file with the same name.

Break Point: If you wish to take a break, this is a good place to do so. You can quit Photoshop now. To resume at a later time, start Photoshop, open the file named Room Edited and continue following the steps from this location forward.

Layer Masks

Another way to edit layers is by creating a mask. A **mask** shows or hides portions of a layer; it also can protect areas of the layer from inadvertent editing. For example, in a graphic of an exotic animal, you might want to mask all of the area except the animal, rather than permanently delete the background. Or, if you wanted to layer a musical score over the top of a piano graphic, you might mask the edges of the paper so the notes look like they blend into the piano. A mask does not alter the layer as the Eraser Tool did; it merely overlays a template to conceal a portion of the layer. That way, if you change your mind and need to display more of the layer, you can. Nothing has been erased permanently. With the Eraser Tool, you would have to delete the layer, open a backup copy, recreate the layer, and then begin to edit again. With masks, you simply edit the mask.

Photoshop provides two types of masks. **Layer masks** or **pixel masks** are resolution-dependent bitmap images, created with the painting or selection tools. **Vector masks** are resolution independent, created with a pen or shape tool. In this chapter, you will create a layer mask.

When you add a mask, a layer mask thumbnail appears on the Layers panel in **grayscale**, which means each pixel in the mask uses a single color on a scale from black to white. When selecting the layer mask thumbnail, the default colors change to white over black and the eraser tools are inactive. To mask, you paint on the layer with black. If you change your mind and want to unmask, you paint with white. Painting with gray displays various levels of transparency in the layer.

To Open the Potted Plant File

The following steps open the Potted Plant file in preparation for creating a layer mask.

1 Open the file named Potted Plant from the Chapter 03 folder of the Data Files for Students, or from a location specified by your instructor.

2 Display the windows side by side.

3 Drag the potted plant into the room. Scroll in the Room Edited document window as necessary and drag the potted plant to place it on the left side of the fireplace.

4 Name the new layer `left potted plant`, and color the layer green.

5 Because you will use the Potted Plant document window again, do not close it.

To Consolidate Windows

Sometimes, after viewing multiple document windows, you may want to view only one window, without closing the others. The steps on the next page consolidate to the Room Edited document window, while leaving the Potted Plant document window open.

① Right-click the tab at the top of the Room Edited document window to display the context menu (Figure 3–48)

② Click Consolidate All to Here to view only that document window.

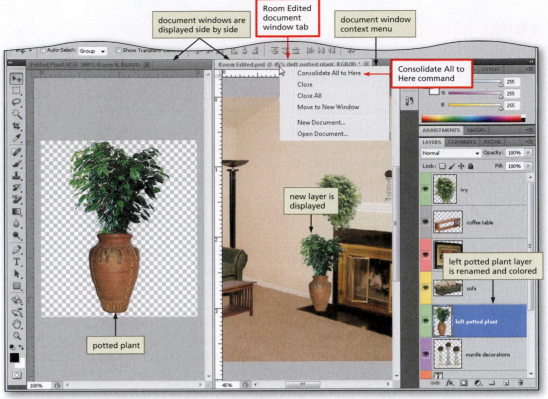

Figure 3–48

To Create a Layer Mask

The following steps mask the plant in the potted plant layer to reveal only the pot. That way, potential decorators can see what the room would look like with and without the plant.

① With the left potted plant layer selected, click the 'Add layer mask' button on the Layers panel status bar to create a layer mask (Figure 3–49).

Q&A What is the new notation on the Layers panel?

Photoshop adds a layer mask thumbnail to the selected layer on the panel. The link icon **links**, or connects, the mask to the layer. A link icon appears between the layer thumbnail and the mask thumbnail. Also notice that the default colors on the Tools panel are reversed.

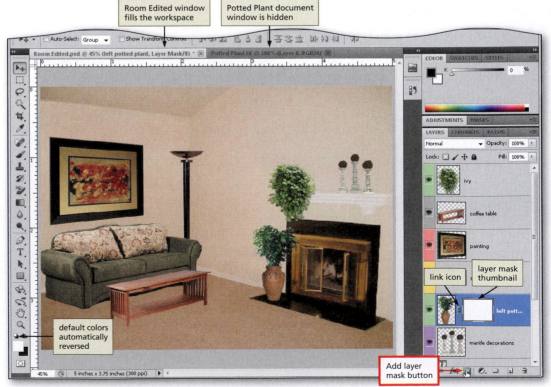

Figure 3–49

2

- If necessary, press the x key to choose black over white.

- Press the B key to activate the brush and then move the mouse pointer into the document window.

- Press the RIGHT BRACKET (]) key to increase the size of the brush's circle, as necessary.

- Drag the mouse across the plant itself. Do not drag across the pot (Figure 3–50).

Q&A

Why does the layer mask use a brush tip mouse pointer?

Layer masks use painting techniques to mask out portions of the image.

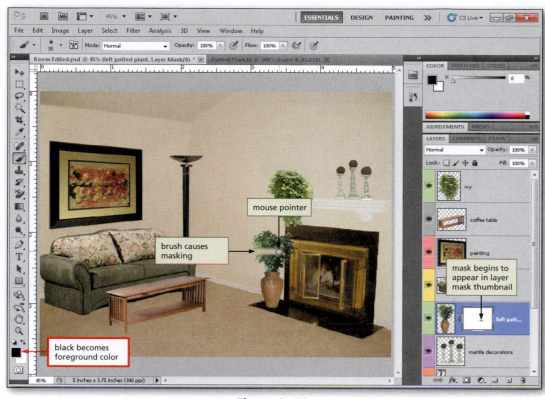

Figure 3–50

3

- Continue dragging through the layer to remove everything except the pot. Zoom the magnification and adjust the size of the brush mouse pointer as necessary (Figure 3–51).

Q&A

Why is my erasing brush fuzzy?

Your brush may be set on a soft setting that creates fuzzy or hazy erasures. To create an erasure with a more solid edge, click the Brush Preset picker on the options bar, and then drag the Hardness slider to the right.

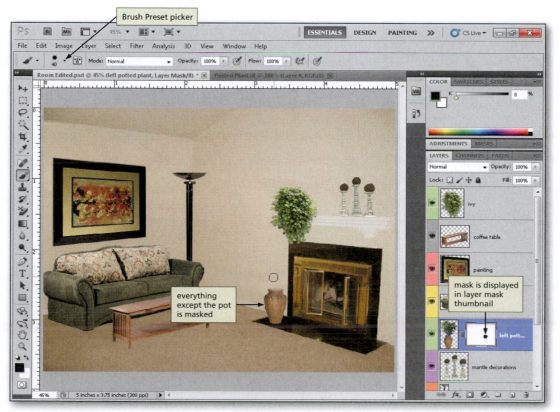

Figure 3–51

To Correct a Masking Error

The following steps create a masking error and then unmask the area by painting with white.

1
● Drag across the pot to mask a portion of the pot (Figure 3–52).

Figure 3–52

2
● Press the x key to switch the foreground and background colors so you are painting with white.

● Drag across the same portion of the pot to unmask it (Figure 3–53).

Figure 3–53

Other Ways

1. On Layer menu, point to Layer Mask, click Reveal All

The Masks Panel

The Masks panel (Figure 3–54) provides additional controls to adjust a layer mask. You can change the density of the mask to allow more or less of the masked content to show through. For example, if you wanted to create a special effects layer to show a time-line or to animate a process, you could create several layer masks with varying percentages of density. Additionally, you can create a **selection layer mask**; instead of painting in the layer mask, the selection border dictates the transparent portion of the layer. The Masks panel allows you to invert the mask in the same way you invert a selection, and allows you to feather the edges and refine the mask border.

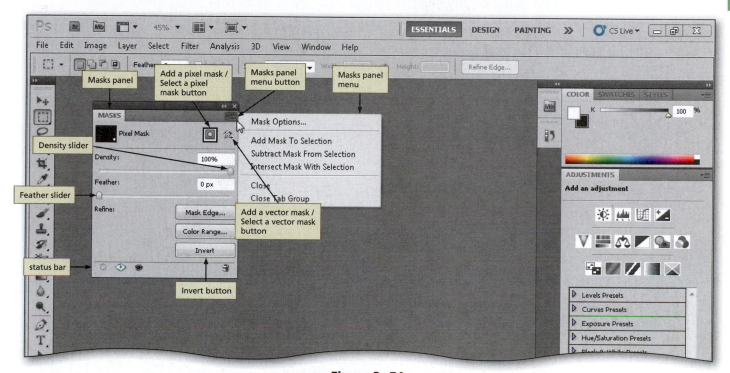

Figure 3–54

To Copy and Paste Using Shortcut Keys

The following steps copy and paste a second potted plant into the Room Edited image, creating another layer.

1 Press CTRL+TAB to view the Potted Plant document window.

2 Press CTRL+A to select the entire image.

3 Press CTRL+C to copy the image.

4 Press CTRL+TAB to view the Room Edited document window.

5 Press CTRL+V to paste the potted plant image.

6 Press the V key to activate the Move Tool and then move the second potted plant to a location on the right side of the fireplace.

7 Name the new layer **right potted plant**, and color it green.

8 Close the Potted Plant document window. If Photoshop displays a dialog box asking if you want to save the changes, click the No button.

BTW

Manipulating Masks
Once you have created a mask, you might want to perform other manipulations on the mask. For example, if you want to unlink a mask to move it independently of its layer, click the link icon on the Layers panel. To unlink a mask temporarily, SHIFT+click the link icon. If you want to mask the entire layer completely, you can ALT+click the Add layer mask button. In that case, you would paint with white in the mask to reveal portions of the mask. To make the mask permanent and reduce overall file size, apply the mask using a command on the mask's context menu.

To Display the Masks Panel

The following steps display the Masks panel.

1
- Click Window on the menu bar to display the Window menu (Figure 3–55).

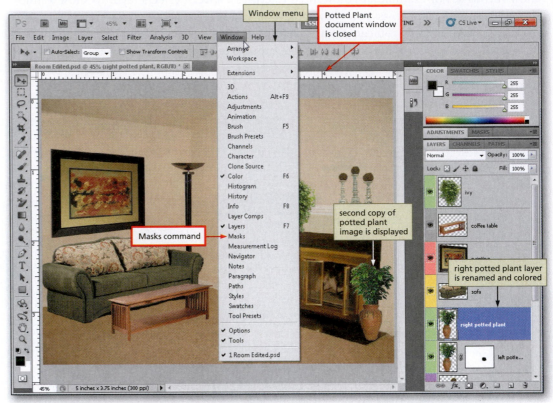

Figure 3–55

2
- Click Masks to display the Masks panel (Figure 3–56).

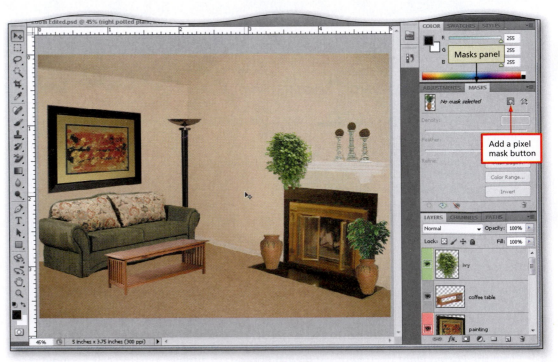

Figure 3–56

To Use the Masks Panel

The following step creates a selection and then use the Masks panel to edit mask properties.

- On the Tools panel, select the Rectangular Marquee Tool and create a selection around the right pot, but not the plant.

- On the Masks panel, click the 'Add a pixel mask' button to create the selection layer mask (Figure 3–57).

Experiment

- Click the Invert button to display the inverted mask. Click the Invert button again to return to the pot. Drag the Density slider to various percentages and watch the mask fade. Drag the Feather slider to various pixels and watch the edge of the mask soften and blend with less contrast.

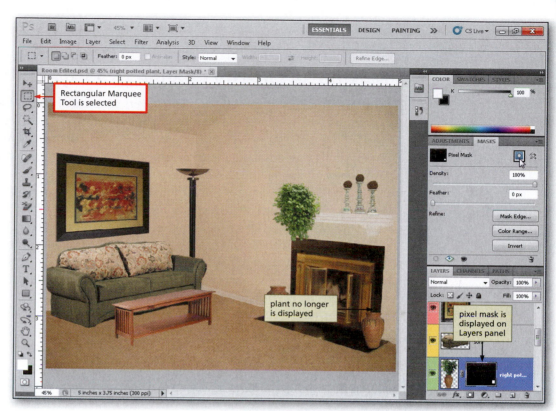

Figure 3–57

Fine-Tuning Layers

Sometimes layers need special adjustments in order to fit into their new surroundings in the document window. This fine-tuning usually involves **tonal adjustments** that affect the range of color, lighting, opacity, level, or fill; **style adjustments** such as special effects or blends; or **filter adjustments** that let you apply predetermined pictures, tiles, or patterns. With the correct adjustment, a layer seems to meld into the image, maintaining a consistency of appearance for the overall composite image.

When you do not want to alter the pixels in an image permanently, you can create an extra layer in which to make changes while preserving the original pixels. An **adjustment layer** is a new layer added to the image to affect a large-scale tonal change. You can create adjustment layers for the entire composite image or just a specific layer.

> **Create layer adjustments.**
> Layer adjustments allow you to fine-tune your layers. Evaluate layers to see if a change in levels, brightness, saturation, or hue would help them to fit into the background scene. Use nondestructive edits when possible, so if the client does not like the adjustment, you can remove it.

BTW

Smart Objects
You can convert a layer into a smart object, which is a nondestructive layer that does not change the original pixels. They are useful for warping, scaling, or rotating both raster and vector graphic layers. To convert a layer into a smart object, right-click the layer, and then click Convert to Smart Object on the context menu.

Plan Ahead

Adjustment layers have several advantages. They are nondestructive, which means you can experiment with various settings and reedit the adjustment layer at any time. Adjustment layers reduce the amount of damage you do to an image by making direct edits. You can copy adjustments to other layers and images, saving time and maintaining consistency.

If you want to make permanent tonal, style, or filter changes to the pixels themselves, you can edit the layer directly. Features such as opacity, fill, and blending modes can be changed on the Layers panel. These changes can be undone using the History panel, but become permanent when you save the image.

Making an Opacity Change to a Layer

Some adjustment tools specific to layers are located on the Layers panel. The Opacity box allows you to change the opacity or transparency of a layer. You can control exactly how solid the objects on a specific layer appear. For example, if you wanted to display an American flag superimposed over a memorial or monument, you might change the flag layer's opacity to 50 percent. The monument easily would be visible through the flag.

The Fill box changes the fill of a layer's opacity as well, but it only changes the pixels in the layer rather than changing any applied layer styles or blending modes. If you have no layer styles or blending modes, you can use either the Opacity or Fill box. When you click either the Opacity box arrow or the Fill box arrow, a slider is displayed to adjust the percentage. You also can type a percentage in either box.

The Blending mode box arrow displays a list of blending modes for the selected layer or layers. **Blending modes** define how an object interacts with other objects, such as the Background layer. You will learn more about blending modes in a later chapter.

BTW

Moving Masks
To move the mask, first click the link icon on the Layers panel to unlink the mask from the layer. Select the Move Tool. Then, in the document window, drag the layer to reposition it. When the mask is positioned correctly, click between the layer and layer mask on the Layers panel to relink them.

To Make an Opacity Change to a Layer

The following step lightens the color in the ivy by lowering the opacity, to make it fit better into the room design.

- Zoom to display the ivy in the document window at 100% magnification.

- On the Layers panel, scroll as necessary to select the ivy layer.

- On the Layers panel, point to the word, Opacity, and then drag the scrubby slider to the left until the Opacity box displays 85% to lighten the color of the ivy (Figure 3–58).

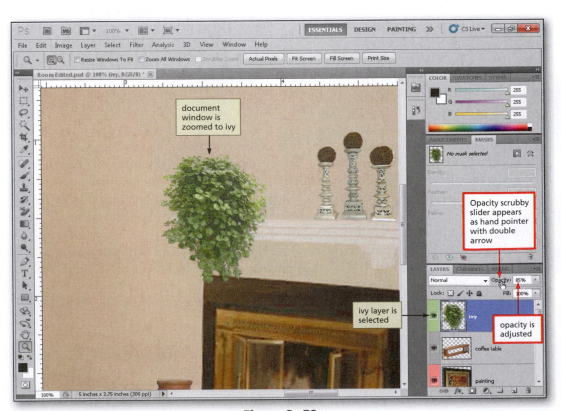

Figure 3–58

The Adjustments Panel

Other tools that nondestructively adjust image lighting and shading are located on the Adjustments panel (Figure 3–59).

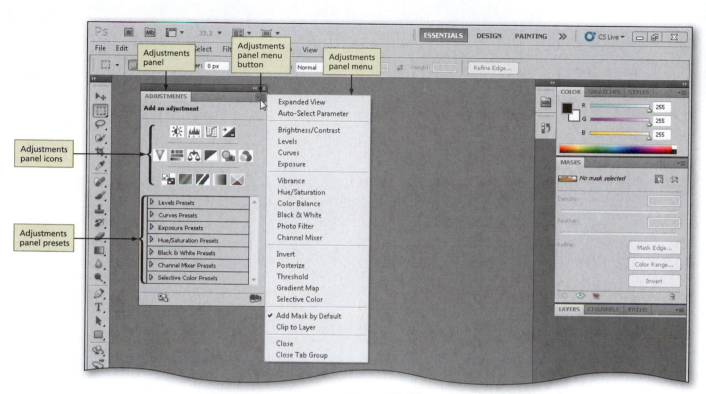

Figure 3–59

Clicking an adjustment icon or a preset displays the settings for the specific adjustment, including channel selectors, eyedroppers, sliders, and input boxes, among others. Buttons on the Adjustments panel status bar allow you to specify visibility, delete the adjustment, return to the main Adjustments panel, or create a **clip** that applies the adjustment to a layer rather than to the entire image.

Some adjustments also display their settings using a dialog box, if accessed from outside the Adjustments panel with a shortcut key or a menu command.

Table 3–2 displays a list of the adjustments available on the Adjustments panel. Many of the adjustments are available using a menu command as well.

Table 3–2 Adjustments Panel Icons			
Adjustment	**Description**	**Shortcut (if available)**	**Icon**
Brightness/Contrast	changes general brightness (shadows and highlights) and overall contrast (tonal range)		
Levels	adjusts color balance for shadows, midtones, highlights, and color channels	CTRL+L	
Curves	adjusts individual points in the tonal range of black to white	CTRL+M	
Exposure	changes exposure, which adjusts the highlights; changes offset, which darkens the shadows and midtones; changes gamma, which adjusts the midtones		
Vibrance	adjusts vibrance and color saturation settings so shifting to primary colors, or clipping, is minimized		
Hue/Saturation	changes hue, saturation, and lightness of entire image or specific colors	CTRL+U	
Color Balance	adjusts the overall midtone of colors in an image	CTRL+B	
Black & White	converts a color image to grayscale	ALT+SHIFT+CTRL+B	
Photo Filter	simulates effects of using a filter in front of a camera lens		
Channel Mixer	modifies and adjusts individual color channels		
Invert	converts every color to its inverse or opposite	CTRL+I	
Posterize	specifies the number of tonal levels in each channel		
Threshold	converts images to high-contrast black and white		
Gradient Map	maps colors to a specified gradient fill		
Selective Color	changes the mixture of colors in each of the primary color components		

While you will use some of the adjustment features in this chapter, you will learn more about these commands in future chapters.

Level Adjustments

A **level adjustment** is one way to make tonal changes to shadows, midtones, and highlights. A **shadow** is a darkened shade in an image. A **midtone**, also called **gamma**, is the midpoint gray between shadows and highlights. A **highlight** is a portion of an image that is strongly illuminated and may appear as the lightest or whitest part of the image. To change levels, Photoshop uses black, gray, and white sliders to adjust any or all of the three tonal input levels. A **histogram**, or frequency distribution bar chart, indicates the amount of color in the tonal ranges. When adjusting levels using the histogram, a general guideline is to drag the black and white (or shadow and highlight) sliders to the first indication, or outlier, of strong tonal change in the histogram. Then, experiment with the gray (or midtone) slider to change the intensity value of the middle range of gray

BTW

Level Sliders
In the Levels dialog box, the Input Level sliders on each end map the black point (on the left) and white point (on the right) to the settings of the Output sliders. The middle Input slider adjusts the gamma or midtone in the image, changing the intensity values of the middle range of gray tones without dramatically altering the highlights and shadows. As you move any of the Input Level sliders, the black point, midtone, and white point change in the Output sliders; all the remaining levels are redistributed.

tones without dramatically altering the highlights and shadows. Becoming proficient at adjusting levels takes practice. Furthermore, adjustments are subjective; the impact of some effects is a matter of opinion.

To Display the Adjustments Panel

The following step displays the Adjustments panel.

1

- Zoom to 45% and select the sofa layer on the Layers panel.

- Click the Adjustments panel tab to display its icons, buttons, and settings (Figure 3–60).

Q&A Why did the Layers panel collapse when I clicked the Adjustments panel?

Both the Layers panel and the Adjustments panel need a larger portion of the workspace than other panels. Photoshop automatically adjusts the size of the panel when you click the tab, to show as much of the panel as possible.

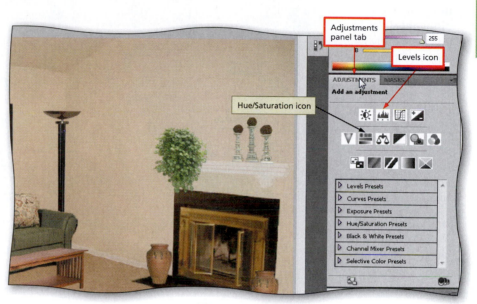

Figure 3–60

To Make a Levels Adjustment

In the sofa layer of the image, you will adjust the levels to make the layer better fit into the picture and bring out the cushion colors. The following steps make level adjustments to the sofa.

1

- Click the Levels icon on the Adjustments panel (shown in Figure 3–60) to display the level settings and options.

- Click the Clip to Layer button on the Adjustments panel status bar to adjust only the sofa layer (Figure 3–61).

Experiment

- Drag the three sliders to see how they affect the sofa layer.

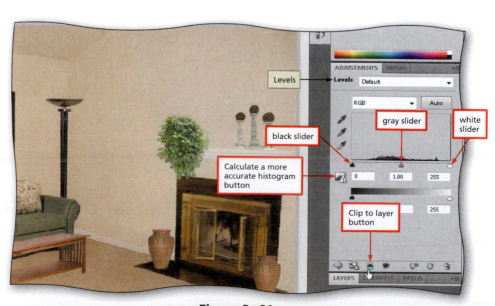

Figure 3–61

2
- Click the 'Calculate a more accurate histogram' button to make the level change more visible.

- In the input area, drag the white highlight slider to approximately 240, aligning it with the first visible change on the right side of the histogram.

- Drag the black shadow slider to approximately 42 to adjust the shadow input level.

- Drag the gray midtone slider to 1.20 to adjust the midtone colors (Figure 3–62).

Q&A

My visible changes were at different levels. Did I do something wrong?

No, your histogram may differ, depending on your previous erasures.

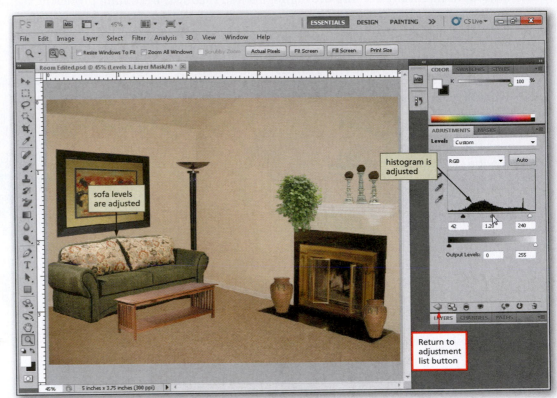

Figure 3–62

3
- Click the 'Return to adjustment list' button to display all of the adjustment icons and settings on the Adjustments panel.

Q&A

Did the Layers panel change?

Yes, you will see an extra layer created just above the sofa layer, with a clipping symbol to imply the relationship.

> **Other Ways**
>
> 1. Press CTRL+L, adjust levels, click OK

Hue and Saturation

Another way to adjust a layer or image is to change the hue or saturation. **Hue** is the shade of a color in an image. **Saturation** is the intensity of a hue and is highly dependent on the chosen color model; but in general, pastels have low saturation, and bright colors have high saturation. You will learn more about color models and the color wheel in later chapters and by reading Appendix B.

To Adjust the Hue and Saturation

The following steps adjust the hue and saturation of the coffee table layer.

1

- Click the Layers panel tab to display the Layers panel, and then select the coffee table layer.

- Click the Adjustments panel tab to display the Adjustments panel, and then click the Hue/ Saturation icon (shown in Figure 3–60 on page PS 183) on the Adjustments panel.

- Click the Clip to Layer button on the Adjustments panel status bar to adjust only the layer.

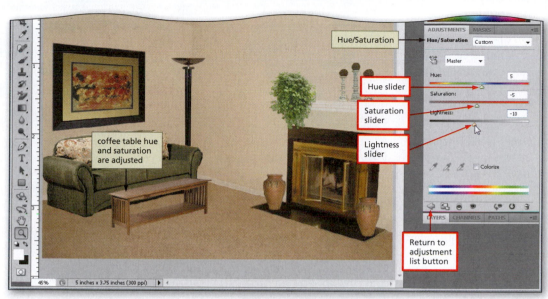

Figure 3–63

- Drag the Hue slider to +5. Drag the Saturation slider to −5. Drag the Lightness slider to −10 (Figure 3–63).

🔍 Experiment

- Drag the sliders to view the affect of hue and saturation settings to the layer. When you are done experimenting, drag the sliders to the settings listed in the step.

2

- Click the 'Return to adjustment list' button to display all of the adjustment icons and settings on the Adjustments panel.

Brightness and Contrast

Brightness refers to color luminance or intensity of a light source, perceived as lightness or darkness in an image. Photoshop measures brightness on a sliding scale from −150 to +150. Negative numbers move the brightness toward black. Positive numbers compress the highlights and expand the shadows. For example, the layer might be an image photographed on a cloudy day; conversely, the image might appear overexposed by having been too close to a photographer's flash. Either way, editing the brightness might enhance the image.

Contrast is the difference between the lightest and darkest tones in an image, involving mainly the midtones. When you increase contrast, the middle-to-dark areas become darker, and the middle-to-light areas become lighter. High-contrast images contain few color variations between the lightest and darkest parts of the image; low-contrast images contain more tonal gradations.

To Adjust the Brightness and Contrast

Sometimes it is easier to create a layer adjustment from the Layers panel. The following steps edit the brightness and contrast of the Background layer using the 'Create new fill or adjustment layer' button on the Layers panel.

Other Ways

1. Select layer, press CTRL+U, complete adjustments, right-click layer, click Create Clipping Mask

---

BTW

Layer Selection
Sometimes a menu or panel will cover the Layers panel, or a layer might be scrolled out of sight. You always can identify which layer you are working with by looking at the document window tab as shown in Figure 3–64 on the next page. The name of the current layer appears in parentheses.

1

• Display the Layers panel and scroll as necessary to select the Background layer.

• On the Layers panel, click the 'Create new fill or adjustment layer' button to display the list of adjustments (Figure 3–64).

Q&A What is the difference between clicking the Brightness/Contrast button on the Adjustments panel and clicking the 'Create new fill or adjustment layer' button?

There is no difference when adjusting the brightness or contrast. The list of adjustments accessed from the Layers panel includes a few more settings than the Adjustments panel.

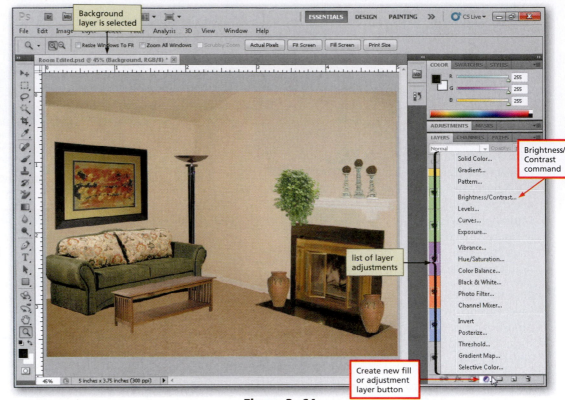

Figure 3–64

2

• Click Brightness/Contrast in the list to display the settings and access the Adjustments panel.

• Click the Clip to Layer button on the Adjustments panel status bar to adjust only the Background layer.

• Drag the Brightness slider to +10 and the Contrast slider to −10 to brighten the room (Figure 3–65).

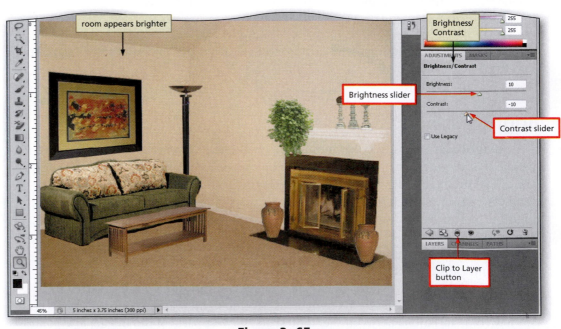

Figure 3–65

Other Ways

1. On Adjustments panel, click Brightness/Contrast icon, click third button on status bar, adjust settings

2. On Layer menu, point to New Adjustment Layer, click Brightness/Contrast, click OK, adjust settings

To View Adjustment Layers

- Display the Layers panel, and then scroll as necessary to select the coffee table layer and view the adjustment layers (Figure 3–66).

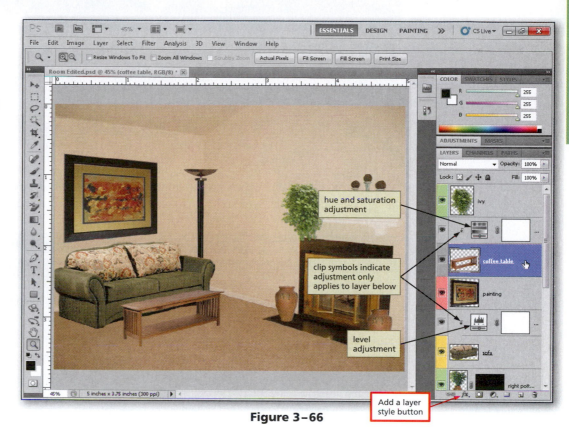

Figure 3–66

Layer Styles

Similar to a layer adjustment, a **layer style** is applied to a layer rather than changing the layer's actual pixels. Layer styles, or layer effects, affect the appearance of the layer by adding depth, shadow, shading, texture, or overlay. A layer can display multiple styles or effects.

> **Edit layer styles.**
> Layer styles add dimension, texture, and definition to your layers. Styles such as shadow, glow, emboss, bevel, overlay, and stroke commonly distinguish the layer rather than making it fit in. Choose the settings carefully and think about direction, angle, distance, and spread. Make sure the layer style does not overwhelm the overall image or detract from previous layer adjustments.

**Plan
Ahead**

Table 3–3 lists the layer styles.

BTW

Copying and Moving Layer Styles
To copy a layer style, right-click the source layer and then click Copy Layer Style on the context menu. Right-click the destination layer and then click Paste Layer Style. To move a layer style, drag the fx icon from one layer to another on the Layers panel.

Table 3–3 Layer Styles	
Style	**Description**
Drop Shadow	creates a shadow behind the layer
Inner Shadow	creates a shadow inside the edges of the layer
Inner Glow	adds a glow around the inside edge of the layer

Table 3–3 Layer Styles (Continued)	
Style	**Description**
Outer Glow	adds a glow around the outside edge of the layer
Bevel and Emboss	adds highlights and shading to a layer
Satin	applies interior shading to create a satin finish
Color Overlay	adds a color over the layer
Gradient Overlay	inserts a gradient in front of the layer
Pattern Overlay	fills the layer with a pattern
Stroke	outlines the layer with a color, gradient, or pattern

Each of the layer styles has its own set of options and properties. Table 3–4 describes some of the layer style options. The options apply to many of the styles.

Table 3–4 Layer Style Options	
Option	**Description**
Angle	sets a degree value for the lighting angle at which the effect is applied
Anti-alias	blends the edge pixels of a contour or gloss contour
Blend Mode	determines how a layer style blends with its underlying layers
Color	assigns the color of a shadow, glow, or highlight
Contour	allows you to create rings of transparency such as gradients, fades, beveling and embossing, and sculpting
Depth	sets the depth of a bevel or pattern
Distance	specifies the offset distance for a shadow or satin effect
Fill Type	sets the content of a stroke
Global Light	allows you to set an angle to simulate the direction of the light
Gloss Contour	creates a glossy, metallic appearance on a bevel or emboss effect
Gradient	indicates the gradient of a layer effect
Highlight or Shadow Mode	specifies the blending mode of a bevel or emboss highlight or shadow
Jitter	varies the color and opacity of a gradient
Layer Knocks Out Drop Shadow	controls the drop shadow's visibility in a semitransparent layer
Noise	assigns the number of random elements in the opacity of a glow or shadow
Opacity	sets the opacity or transparency
Pattern	specifies the pattern
Position	sets the position of a stroke
Range	controls which portion or range of the glow is targeted for the contour
Size	specifies the amount of blur or the size of the shadow
Soften	blurs the results of shading to reduce unwanted artifacts
Source	specifies the source for an inner glow
Style	specifies the style of a bevel or emboss

BTW

The Angle Radius Icon
In the Layer Style dialog box, the Angle setting adjusts the direction of the layer style on a 360-degree scale: 180 degrees both clockwise and counterclockwise. In addition to entering a degree setting, the Angle radius icon (Figure 3–68) allows you to drag to the desired direction.

When a layer has a style applied to it, an fx icon appears to the right of the layer's name on the Layers panel. You can expand the icon on the Layers panel to view all of the applied effects and edit them when changing the style.

As you can tell from Table 3–3 and Table 3–4, there are a large number of layer styles and settings in Photoshop. As you use them, many of these settings will be explained in future chapters.

To Add a Layer Style

The following steps add a layer style to the ivy. You will create an inner bevel to give the ivy more depth.

1
- On the Layers panel, select the ivy layer.

- Zoom to 100% magnification.

- Click the 'Add a layer style' button (shown in Figure 3–66 on page PS 187) on the Layers panel status bar to display the menu (Figure 3–67).

Figure 3–67

2
- Click Bevel and Emboss to display the Layer Style dialog box. If necessary, drag the title bar of the dialog box to the right, so the ivy is visible.

- In the Layer Style dialog box, enter 50 in the Depth box to decrease the strength of the shading.

- Enter 10 in the Size box and 5 in the Soften box to edit the bevel (Figure 3–68).

3
- Click the OK button to close the Layer Style dialog box.

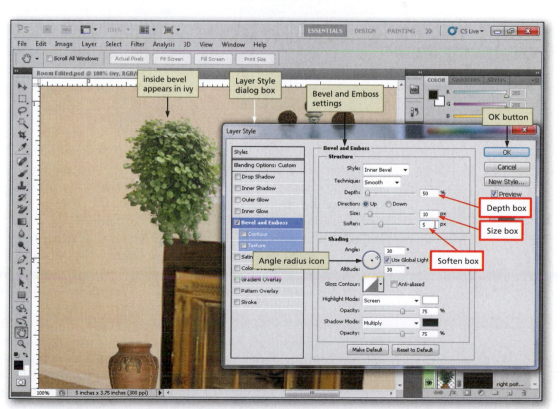

Figure 3–68

To Hide Layer Effects on the Layers Panel

The following step uses the 'Reveal layer effects in the panel' button to hide the effects on the Layers panel.

1

• On the Layers panel, in the ivy layer, click the 'Reveals layer effects in the panel' button to hide the added effects on the Layers panel (Figure 3–69).

Figure 3–69

The Clone Stamp Tool

The Clone Stamp Tool reproduces portions of an image, changing the pixels in a specific area. After clicking the Clone Stamp Tool button on the Tools panel, you press and hold ALT while clicking the portion of the picture that you wish to copy. Photoshop takes a **sample** of the image, remembering where you clicked. You then move the mouse pointer to the position where you wish to create the copy. As you drag with the brush, the image is applied. Each stroke of the tool paints on more of the sample. The Clone Stamp Tool is useful for duplicating specific parts of an object or correcting defects in an image. You can clone from image to image, or clone locations within the same document window.

The Clone Source panel (Figure 3–70) appears when you click Clone Source on the Window menu. The panel has options to rotate or scale the sample, or specify the size and orientation. The Clone Source panel makes it easy to create variegated patterns using multiple sources. You can create up to five different clone sources to select the one you need quickly, without re-sampling each time. For example, if you are using the Clone Stamp Tool to repair several minor imperfections in an old photo, you can select your various samples first, and then use the sources as needed. The Clone Source panel also helps you create unique clones positioned at different angles and perspectives from the original.

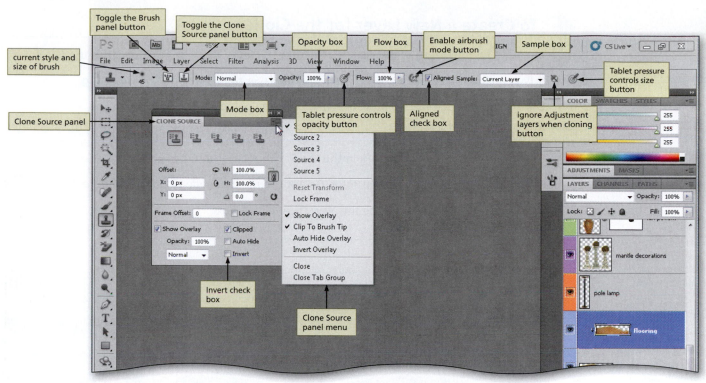

Figure 3–70

The Clone Stamp Tool options bar (Figure 3–70) displays some of the same settings that you used with layer masks, along with an Aligned check box and Sample box. When you align, the sample point is not reset if you start dragging in a new location; in other words, the sampling moves to a relative point in the original image. Otherwise, the sample point begins again as you start a new clone. The default value is to sample only the current layer or background. When you select All Layers in the Sample box, the clone displays all layers. One restriction when using the Clone Stamp Tool from one image to another is that both images have to be in the same color mode, such as RGB or CMYK. The color mode of an image appears on the document window tab. You will learn more about color modes in a later chapter.

On the Clone Stamp Tool context menu, a second kind of stamp, the Pattern Stamp Tool, allows you to paint with a pattern chosen from Photoshop's pattern library. A **pattern** is a repeated or tiled image, used to fill a layer or selection. On the Pattern Stamp Tool options bar, a Pattern Picker box arrow displays installed patterns. You can import additional patterns into the Pattern Picker box.

To Open the Flooring File and Arrange the Windows

To finish the composite image of the room, you will remove the carpet and add wood flooring to the room. The following steps open the Flooring file.

1 Open the Flooring file from the Chapter 03 folder of the Data Files for Students, or from a location specified by your instructor.

2 Arrange the windows so that windows appear one above the other and drag the border between the two document windows so more of the Room Edited window is displayed.

3 In the Room Edited window, select the carpeting layer and zoom to 45% magnification. Scroll to display the carpeting.

To Create a New Layer for the Clone

The following steps create a new flooring layer that clips to the carpeting layer.

1 ALT+click the visibility icon on the carpeting layer to display only the carpeting.

2 Press SHIFT+CTRL+N to display the New Layer dialog box.

3 Name the layer, flooring.

4 Click to display a check mark in the Use Previous Layer to Create Clipping Mask check box.

5 Choose a blue identification color. Do not change the mode or opacity (Figure 3–71).

6 Click the OK button to close the New Layer dialog box.

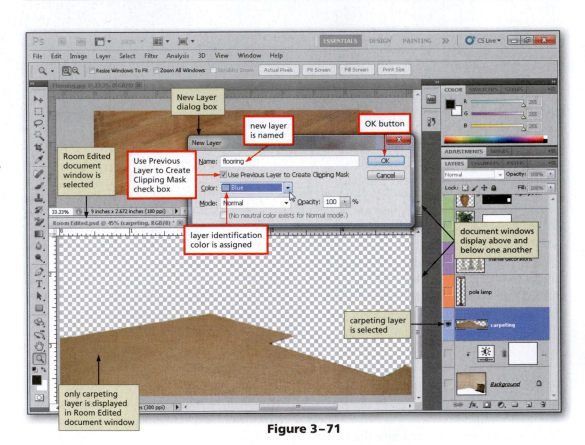

Figure 3–71

To Create a Clone

Using the Clone Stamp Tool, you will sample the Flooring image and then clone it to the carpeted area in the Room Edited image, as shown in the following steps.

As you clone the flooring, adjust the magnification of the image to view the corners and small areas clearly. If you make a mistake while cloning, press CTRL+Z to undo the most recent clone stroke or access the History panel and click a previous state. Then begin cloning again.

1

- Click the Flooring document window tab to make the window active.

- Click Window on the menu bar, and then click Clone Source to display the Clone Source panel.

- On the Clone Source panel, click the Invert box to remove its check mark, if necessary.

- On the Tools panel, right-click the Clone Stamp Tool button to display its context menu (Figure 3–72).

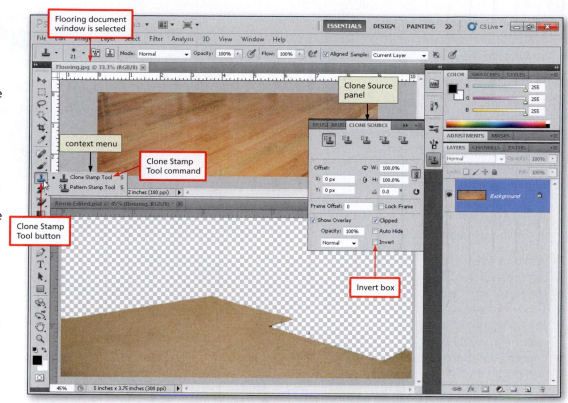

Figure 3–72

2

- Click Clone Stamp Tool on the context menu.

- On the options bar, click the Aligned check box so it displays a check mark, if necessary.

- Move the mouse pointer to the Flooring document window and ALT+click on the left edge of the flooring, approximately halfway down to sample the wood grain (Figure 3–73).

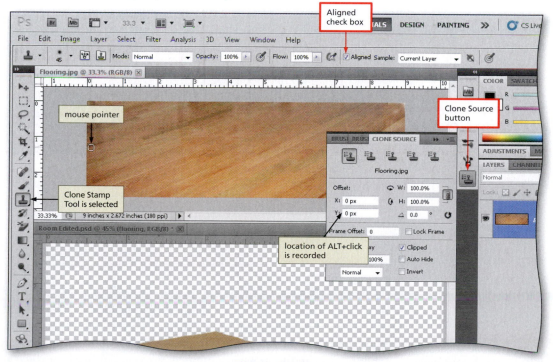

Figure 3–73

Q&A   How do I know if I indicated the clone source correctly?

As you ALT+click, the Clone Stamp Tool displays a crosshair mouse pointer and the Clone Source panel displays the source of the clone.

3

- Click the Clone Source button in the vertical docking to collapse the panel.

- Click the Room Edited document window tab to make it active.

- With the flooring layer still selected, and the carpeting layer visible, move the mouse pointer into the document window.

- Working from left to right, drag to replace the carpeting. Zoom, scroll, and adjust the pointer size as necessary to fill in corners. Use short strokes, so if you make a mistake, you can press CTRL+Z to undo the error (Figure 3–74).

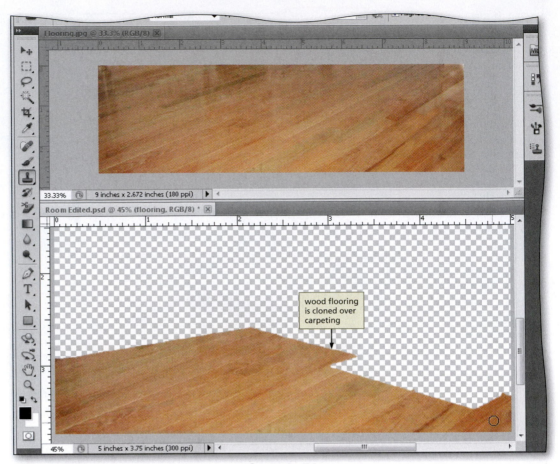

Figure 3–74

BTW

Aligned Check Box
When checked, the Aligned check box allows you to use short strokes as you clone. The clone will not start over if you lift the mouse button to drag in another location. Aligning is helpful for cloning areas with a pattern.

To Close the Flooring Window

The following step closes the Flooring window and redisplays all the layers.

1 Close the Flooring document window. If Photoshop asks if you want to save changes to the document, click the No button.

2 Display all of the layers in the Room Edited document.

BTW

Photoshop Help
The best way to become familiar with Photoshop Help is to use it. Appendix D includes detailed information about Photoshop Help and exercises that will help you gain confidence in using it.

Flattening a Composite Image

When you **flatten** a composite image, Photoshop reduces the file size by merging all visible layers into the background, discarding hidden layers, and applying masks. A flattened file is easier to print, export, and display on the Web. It is a good practice, however, to save the layered version in PSD format before flattening in case you want to make further changes to the file. It is very important to remember that once a file is flattened and saved, no changes can be made to individual layers. If you flatten an image and then change your mind, if the file still is open, you can click the previous state on the History panel to restore all of the layers.

If you want to save each layer as a separate file, click File on the menu bar, point to Scripts, and then click Export Layers to Files. This script is useful if you think you might want to use your layers in other composite images.

The Layer menu has many of the same commands as the Layers panel menu. The choice of which to use is a matter of personal preference, and the location of your mouse pointer at the time. After saving the composite image, you will use the Layer menu to flatten the visible layers. Finally, you will save the flattened file in TIF format with the name, Room Complete.

To Save the Composite Image

The following steps save the Room Edited file with its layers.

1 With your USB flash drive connected to one of the computer's USB ports, click File on the menu bar and then click Save As.

2 When the Save As dialog box is displayed, type **Room Composite** in the File name text box. Do not press the ENTER key after typing the file name.

3 If necessary, click the Format box arrow and then choose Photoshop (*.PSD, *.PDD) in the list.

4 If necessary, click the Save in box arrow and then click UDISK 2.0 (F:), or the location associated with your USB flash drive, in the list.

5 Click the Save button in the Save As dialog box. If Photoshop displays an options dialog box, click the OK button.

BTW

Quick Reference

For a table that lists how to complete the tasks covered in this book using the mouse, context menu, and keyboard, see the Quick Reference Summary at the back of this book or visit the Photoshop CS5 Quick Reference Web page (scsite.com/pscs5/qr).

To Flatten a Composite Image

The following steps use the Layer menu to flatten the composite image.

1

• Click Layer on the menu bar to display the Layer menu (Figure 3–75).

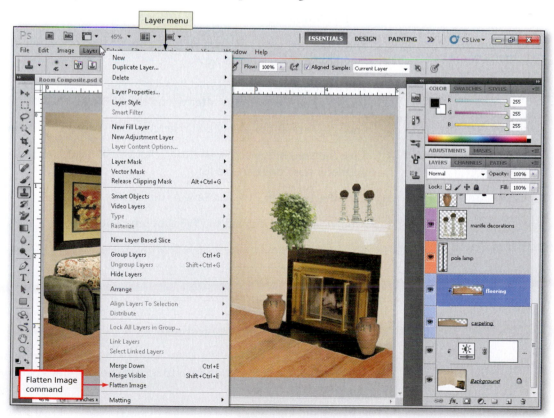

Figure 3–75

2

• Click Flatten Image on the Layer menu to flatten the layers. If Photoshop displays a confirmation dialog box, click the Yes button (Figure 3–76).

Q&A

What is the difference between flatten and merge?

The Merge command flattens specific layers together. The Flatten command uses all of the layers and merges into a Background layer.

Other Ways

1. Right-click any layer, click Flatten Image
2. Click Layers panel menu button, click Flatten Image

image appears without layers

Figure 3–76

To Save a File in the TIFF Format

Printing Composites
On desktop printers, it usually is better to print a flattened image than a composite image. If you want to print the flattened TIFF image, click File on the menu bar and then click Print One Copy on the File menu to print the image on the default printer.

The following steps save the flattened image as a TIFF file.

1 With your USB flash drive connected to one of the computer's USB ports, click File on the menu bar and then click Save As.

2 When the Save As dialog box is displayed, type **Room TIFF** in the File name text box. Do not press the ENTER key after typing the file name.

3 Click the Format box arrow and then click TIFF (*.TIF, *TIFF) in the list.

4 Click the Save in box arrow and then click UDISK 2.0 (F:), or the location associated with your USB flash drive, in the list.

5 Click the Save button in the Save As dialog box.

6 When Photoshop displays the TIFF Options dialog box, click the OK button to finish saving the file.

To Quit Photoshop

The final step quits Photoshop.

1 Click the Close button on the right side of the Photoshop title bar. If Photoshop displays a dialog box, click the No button to ignore the changes since the last time you saved the photo.

Chapter Summary

In virtually decorating a room, you gained a broad knowledge of Photoshop's layering capabilities. First, you were introduced to the concept of layers. You created a layer via cut, a layer from another image, and a layer from a selection, using the Layers panel to set options, select, rename, color, view, and hide layers. Then you used the eraser tools to erase unneeded portions of the layer. You learned how to hide portions of layers and fine-tuned layers with layer masks, adjustments, and styles. Finally, you used the Clone Stamp Tool to add wood flooring into the composite image. The file was flattened and saved in the TIF format.

The items listed below include all the new Photoshop skills you have learned in this chapter:

1. Change Layers Panel Options (PS 145)
2. Create a Layer Via Cut (PS 147)
3. Name and Color a Layer (PS 148)
4. Hide and Show a Layer (PS 149)
5. Arrange the Document Windows (PS 152)
6. Create a Layer by Dragging an Entire Image (PS 153)
7. Position a Layer (PS 154)
8. Set Layer Properties Using the Context Menu (PS 154)
9. Create a Layer by Dragging a Selection (PS 157)
10. Erase Using the Magic Eraser Tool (PS 161)
11. Display Only the Current Layer (PS 163)
12. Erase Using the Eraser Tool (PS 164)
13. Erase Using the Block Mouse Pointer (PS 165)
14. Erase Using the Background Eraser Tool (PS 168)
15. Rearrange Layers (PS 171)
16. Consolidate Windows (PS 173)
17. Create a Layer Mask (PS 174)
18. Correct a Masking Error (PS 176)
19. Display the Masks Panel (PS 178)
20. Use the Masks Panel (PS 179)
21. Make an Opacity Change to a Layer (PS 180)
22. Display the Adjustments Panel (PS 183)
23. Make a Levels Adjustment (PS 183)
24. Adjust the Hue and Saturation (PS 185)
25. Adjust the Brightness and Contrast (PS 185)
26. View Adjustment Layers (PS 187)
27. Add a Layer Style (PS 189)
28. Hide Layer Effects on the Layers Panel (PS 190)
29. Create a Clone (PS 192)
30. Flatten a Composite Image (PS 195)

Learn It Online

Test your knowledge of chapter content and key terms.

Instructions: To complete the Learn It Online exercises, start your browser, click the Address bar, and then enter the Web address `scsite.com/pscs5/learn.` When the Photoshop CS5 Learn It Online page is displayed, click the link for the exercise you want to complete and then read the instructions.

Chapter Reinforcement TF, MC, and SA
A series of true/false, multiple choice, and short answer questions that tests your knowledge of the chapter content.

Flash Cards
An interactive learning environment where you identify chapter key terms associated with displayed definitions.

Practice Test
A series of multiple choice questions that test your knowledge of chapter content and key terms.

Who Wants To Be a Computer Genius?
An interactive game that challenges your knowledge of chapter content in the style of a television quiz show.

Wheel of Terms
An interactive game that challenges your knowledge of chapter key terms in the style of the television show *Wheel of Fortune*.

Crossword Puzzle Challenge
A crossword puzzle that challenges your knowledge of key terms presented in the chapter.

Apply Your Knowledge

Reinforce the skills and apply the concepts you learned in this chapter.

Creating Layers in a Poster

Instructions: Start Photoshop and perform the customization steps found on pages PS 6 through PS 9. Open the Apply 3-1 Storage History file from the Chapter 03 folder of the Data Files for Students. You can access the Data Files for Students on the CD that accompanies this book. See the inside back cover of this book for instructions on downloading the Data Files for Students, or contact your instructor for information about accessing the required files.

The purpose of this exercise is to create a composite poster showing the history of external storage devices by creating layers. The edited photo is displayed in Figure 3–77.

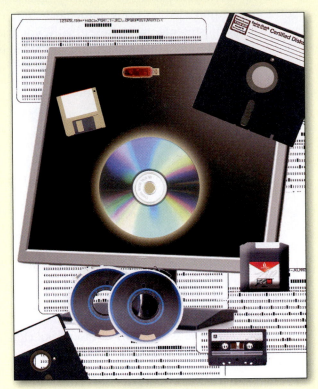

Figure 3–77

Perform the following tasks:
1. Press SHIFT+CTRL+S to open the Save As dialog box. Enter the name, **Apply 3-1 Storage History Composite**. Do not press the ENTER key. Click the Format box arrow and then select the Photoshop PSD format, if necessary. Click the Save in box arrow and then select your USB flash drive location. Click the Save button to save the file in the PSD format. Table 3–5 lists the other files, layer names, identification colors, and manipulations that you will use in this assignment.

Table 3–5 Storage Device Layers

File Name	Layer Name	Layer Color	Layer Manipulations
Apply 3-1 CD	CD	Violet	Layer Style	Outer Glow
Apply 3-1 Flash Drive	flash drive	Green	Layer Style	Inner Glow Mask lid
Apply 3-1 Zip Disk	zip disk	Orange	Layer Style	Bevel and Emboss
Apply 3-1 Tape	tape	Yellow	Adjustments	Hue 10, −10, 0
Apply 3-1 Cassette Tape	cassette tape	Yellow	Adjustments	Brightness/Contrast
Apply 3-1 Small Floppy	small floppy	Blue	erase background and rotate
Apply 3-1 Medium Floppy	medium floppy	Blue	erase background and rotate
Apply 3-1 Large Floppy	large floppy	Blue	erase background and rotate
Apply 3-1 Punched Card	punched card	Red	clone

2. To create the CD layer:

   a. Press CTRL+O to display the Open dialog box. Navigate to the Data Files for Students and then double-click the file named Apply 3-1 CD to open it.

   b. On the Photoshop Application bar, click the Arrange Documents button and click the first 2 Up button to arrange the document windows side by side.

   c. Press V to activate the Move Tool. Drag the image from the Apply 3-1 CD document window into the Apply 3-1 Storage History Composite document window. Close the Apply 3-1 CD file.

   d. Name and color the layer as directed in Table 3–5.

   e. Click the 'Add a layer style' button on the Layers panel status bar, and then click Outer Glow. Change the Opacity to **75%** and the Size to **150 px**. Use the default values for all other settings.

3. To create the flash drive layer:

   a. Press CTRL+O to display the Open dialog box. Navigate to the Data Files for Students and then open the file named Apply 3-1 Flash Drive.

   b. On the Photoshop Application bar, click the Arrange Documents button and click the second 2 Up button to arrange the document windows one above the other.

   c. Drag the flash drive image into the Apply 3-1 Storage History Composite document window. Close the Apply 3-1 Flash Drive file.

   d. Name and color the layer as directed in Table 3–5.

   e. Click the 'Add a layer style' button on the Layers panel status bar, and then click Inner Glow. Change the Opacity to **75%** and the Size to **25 px**. Use the default values for all other settings.

   f. Resize the flash drive and position it as shown in Figure 3–77.

   g. Click the 'Add layer mask' button. If black is not the foreground color, press the X key to exchange colors. Press the B key to access the brush and then paint over the flash drive cover to mask it.

4. To create the zip disk layer:

   a. Open the file, Apply 3-1 Zip Disk.

   b. Arrange the document windows side by side.

   c. Drag the image from the new window into the Apply 3-1 Storage History Composite document window. Close the Apply 3-1 Zip Disk file.

   d. Name and color the layer.

   e. Click the 'Add a layer style' button on the Layers panel status bar, and then click Bevel and Emboss. Click the Style box arrow and then click Inner Bevel, if necessary. Change the Size to **90 px**. Use the default values for all other settings.

   f. Position the casette tape image layer as shown in Figure 3–77.

5. To create the tape layer:

   a. Open the file, Apply 3-1 Tape. Select all of the image and copy.

   b. Paste the image into the Apply 3-1 Storage History Composite document window. Close the Apply 3-1 Tape file.

   c. Name and color the layer.

   d. Click Window on the menu bar and then click Adjustments to display the Adjustments panel. Click the Hue/Saturation icon to display the settings. On the panel's status bar, click the Clip to Layer button. Adjust the Hue to **10**, the Saturation to **−10** and the Lightness to **0**. Click the 'Return to adjustment list' button to redisplay the Adjustments panel.

   e. Scale and position the tape image layer as necessary.

Continued >

Apply Your Knowledge *continued*

6. To create the cassette tape layer:

   a. Open the file, Apply 3-1 Cassette Tape.

   b. Arrange the document windows and drag the image from the new window into the Apply 3-1 Storage History Composite document window. Close the Apply 3-1 Cassette Tape file.

   c. Name and color the layer.

   d. On the Adjustments panel, click the Brightness/Contrast icon and then click the Clip to Layer button. Adjust the Brightness to 35. Click the 'Return to adjustment list' button to display the Adjustments panel.

   e. Click the Adjustments button in the vertical docking to collapse the Adjustments panel.

   f. Position the layer to match Figure 3–77.

7. To create the floppy disk layers.

   a. One at a time, open each of the floppy disk files listed in Table 3–5.

   b. Copy and paste the image into the Apply 3-1 Storage History Composite document window.

   c. Name and color each layer.

   d. Use the eraser tools to erase extraneous background.

   e. Scale, position and rotate the images as shown in Figure 3–77.

8. To clone the punched card:

   a. Select the Background layer. Create a new layer by pressing CTRL+SHIFT+N. Name the layer, punched card. Do not check the Use Previous Layer to Create Clipping Mask check box. Choose a red identification color. Do not change the mode or opacity. Click the OK button to close the New Layer dialog box. Press CTRL+LEFT BRACKET ([) to move the punched card layer below the Background layer. ALT+click the visibility icon on the punched card layer to display only that layer.

   b. Open the file, Apply 3-1 Punched Card.

   c. Arrange the document windows above and below one another.

   d. Press the s key to activate the Clone Stamp Tool. On the options bar, click to display the Aligned check mark, if necessary.

   e. ALT+click in the punched card document window, close to the top-left corner.

   f. Drag in the Apply 3-1 Storage History Composite document window to create a clone.

   g. Repeat Steps e and f to create four more clones at various locations in the window. (*Hint:* in this montage, it is ok for part of a cloned image to run off the edge of the document window.)

9. Close the Apply 3-1 Punched Card window.

10. On the Layers panel of the Apply 3-1 Storage History Composite window, click the 'Indicates layer visibility' button beside each layer to display the layers.

11. Save the file again by pressing CTRL+S.

12. On the Layers panel, click the Layers panel menu button to display the menu. Click Flatten Image on the menu to flatten all of the layers.

13. Press SHIFT+CTRL+S to open the Save As dialog box. Type **Apply 3-1 Storage History Complete** in the Name box. Click the Format box arrow and then click TIFF in the list. Click the Save button. If Photoshop displays a dialog box, click the OK button.

14. Turn in a hard copy of the project to your instructor.

15. Quit Photoshop.

Extend Your Knowledge

Extend the skills you learned in this chapter and experiment with new skills. You may need to use Help to complete the assignment.

Instructions: Start Photoshop. Set the default workspace, default colors, and reset all tools. Open the file Extend 3-1 Marketing Graphic from the Chapter 03 folder of the Data Files for Students. You can access the Data Files for Students on the CD that accompanies this book. See the inside back cover of this book for instructions on downloading the Data Files for Students, or contact your instructor for information about accessing the required files.

The purpose of this exercise to create layer comps for client evaluation. The current graphic has layers for the background, inside, and outside of the box. You are to insert the trophy graphic and scale it to fit the box. Then create layer comps showing the inside and the outside. The edited photo is shown in Figure 3 – 78.

Perform the following tasks:

1. Save the file with the name, Extend 3-1 Marketing Graphic Composite. If necessary, click the Format box arrow and click Photoshop in the list. Browse to your USB flash drive storage device. Click the Save button. If Photoshop displays a Format Options dialog box, click the OK button.

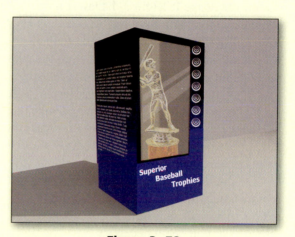

Figure 3–78

2. Show and hide the various layers using the visibility icon to gain familiarity with the graphic.

3. Make the Background layer and inside layer visible; hide all other layers. Select the inside layer.

4. Open the file Extend 3-1 Trophy from the Chapter 03 folder of the Data Files for Students. Use the Arrange Documents button to display the windows side by side.

5. Use the Move Tool to drag the trophy from its own window into the Extend 3-1 Marketing Graphic Composite document window. Scale the trophy to fit in the box. Make the outside layer visible and make sure the trophy can be seen through the opening in the outer box. Name the layer, trophy.

6. Make the front panel layer visible and select it. Adjust the Opacity setting so the layer looks more transparent, as if it were plastic.

7. Make the gleam layer visible. Adjust the Opacity and Fill settings as necessary. Save the file.

8. Use Help to learn about Layer Comps. Also read the BTW boxes on pages PS 144 and PS 145. Open the Layer Comps panel and create the layer comps described in Table 3 – 6.

Table 3–6 Marketing Graphic Layer Comps	
Layer Comp Name	**Visible Layers**
Empty Box	Background, inside
Inner Box with Trophy	Background, inside, trophy
Outer Box with Trophy	Background, inside, trophy, outside, shadow
Complete Graphic	All layers

Continued >

Extend Your Knowledge *continued*

9. Save the file again.

10. For extra credit, copy the trophy layer and scale it to approximately 30 percent of its original size. In the Layers panel, move the layer above the outside layer. Position the trophy in the lower-middle portion of the box. Warp the layer to make it wrap around the corner of the box. Create a layer comp named Complete with Wrapped Logo and include all layers.

11. Submit this assignment in the format specified by your instructor.

Make It Right

Analyze a project and correct all errors and/or improve the design.

Instructions: Start Photoshop and perform the customization steps found on pages PS 6 through PS 9. Open the Make It Right 3-1 Desert file from the Chapter 03 folder of the Data Files for Students. You can access the Data Files for Students on the CD that accompanies this book. See the inside back cover of this book for instructions on downloading the Data Files for Students, or contact your instructor for information about accessing the required files.

The photo has layers that are invisible, layers that need transformation, and layers that need to be moved, trimmed, and adjusted for levels (Figure 3–79).

Save the file on your storage device in the PSD format with the name, Make It Right 3-1 Desert Composite. For each invisible layer, reveal the layer, correct any order problem by dragging the layer to an appropriate position on the Layers panel, erase or mask parts of the layer as necessary, and move the layer to a logical position.

Use the Adjustments panel and tools such as Levels, Brightness/Contrast, and Hue/Saturation to create adjustment layers. (*Hint:* Do not forget to click the Clip to Layer button on the Adjustments panel status bar, so the adjustment will apply to that layer only.) Make any other adjustments or layer style changes as you deem necessary. Save the file again and submit it in the format specified by your instructor.

Figure 3–79

In the Lab

Design and/or create a project using the guidelines, concepts, and skills presented in this chapter. Labs are listed in order of increasing difficulty.

Lab 1: Making Level Adjustments Using Masks

Problem: A local tourist company has hired you to create its latest brochure about historic homes. You encounter a photo that is too dark to use in the brochure. You decide to try adjusting the levels to lighten the steps, grass, and shrubs in the photo and prepare it for print in the brochure. The edited photo is shown in Figure 3–80.

Instructions: Perform the following tasks:

Figure 3–80

1. Start Photoshop. Set the default work-space, default colors, and reset all tools.

2. Open the file Lab 3-1 Historic Home from the Chapter 03 folder of the Data Files for Students. You can access the Data Files for Students on the CD that accompanies this book. See the inside back cover of this book for instructions on downloading the Data Files for Students, or contact your instructor for information about accessing the required files.

3. Click the Save As command on the File menu. Type **Lab 3-1 Historic Home Composite** as the file name. Click the Format box arrow and click Photoshop in the list. Browse to your USB flash drive storage device. Click the Save button. If Photoshop displays a Format Options dialog box, click the OK button.

4. On the Tools panel, select the Quick Selection Tool. Drag very slowly to select only the house, sky, clouds, and trees. Do not include the shrubs, grounds, or steps in the selection. If necessary, use the marquee or lasso tools, adding or subtracting to the selection as necessary.

5. Click Select on the menu bar and then click Inverse to select the inverse of the house, trees, and sky, which would be the steps, shrubs, and grounds.

6. Click Layer on the menu bar, point to New, and then click Layer via Cut.

7. On the Layers panel, rename the layer, grounds. Use a green identification color.

8. With the layer selected, open the Adjustments panel and click the Levels icon. On the panel's status bar, click the Clip to Layer button. In the Input Levels area, drag the white slider to the left until the grounds are lighter and the features easily discerned.

9. Press CTRL+S to save the photo again. If Photoshop displays the Photoshop Format Options dialog box, click the OK button.

10. Flatten the image.

11. Press SHIFT+CTRL+S to access the Save As dialog box. Choose the TIFF format and name the file Lab 3-1 Historic Home Complete. If Photoshop displays a warning dialog box about layers, click the OK button.

12. Print a copy and turn it in to your instructor.

In the Lab

Lab 2: Creating a Toy Company Advertisement

Problem: You are to create a composite photo for a toy company, adding and adjusting layers, as shown in Figure 3–81.

Figure 3–81

Instructions: Perform the following tasks:

1. Start Photoshop and reset the workspace, default colors, and all tools.

2. Open the Lab 3-2 Robot Background file from the Chapter 03 folder of the Data Files for Students and save it as Lab 3-2 Robot Composite. You can access the Data Files for Students on the CD that accompanies this book. See the inside back cover of this book for instructions on downloading the Data Files for Students, or contact your instructor for information about accessing the required files.

3. To clone over the shadow on the right side of the image:

   a. Select the Clone Stamp Tool. On the options bar, click the Aligned check box so it does not display a check mark.

   b. ALT+click the ground approximately one inch below the shadow to create the sample for the clone. Drag over the shadowed area, including any rocks, to create a cloned area and hide the shadow. (*Hint:* Use the left and right bracket keys to adjust the size of the mouse pointer as needed.)

4. To create a sky layer:

   a. Use the Magic Wand Tool and the 'Add to selection' button to select all of the sky.

   b. On the Layer menu, point to New, and then click Layer via Cut.

   c. On the Layers panel, double-click the layer name and type **sky** to rename the layer. Right-click the visibility icon and choose Blue in the list.

5. To add the robot body:

   a. Open the Lab 3-2 Robot Body file from the Chapter 03 folder of the Data Files for Students.

   b. On the Application bar, use the Arrange Documents button to display the windows side by side.

   c. Use the Move Tool to drag the robot body from the Lab 3-2 Robot Body document window to the Lab 3-2 Robot Composite document window. (Hint: Holding down the shift key as you drag automatically centers the image and creates a new layer.) After creating the layer, close the Lab 3-2 Robot Body document window.

   d. Name the layer, robot, and use a violet identification color.

6. Repeat Step 5 to add the shadow graphic using the file, Lab 3-2 Robot Shadow file. Position it behind the robot near the feet, as shown in Figure 3–81. Name the layer, shadow, and use a gray identification color. Close the Lab 3-2 Robot Shadow document window.

7. To move the layer behind the robot, on the Layers panel, drag the shadow layer just below the robot layer.

8. Repeat Step 3 to add the earth graphic using the file, Lab 3-2 Robot Earth file. Position it in the upper-right corner of the scene. Name the layer, earth, and use a green identification color.

9. Repeat Step 3 to add the title graphic using the file, Lab 3-2 Robot Title file. Position the words centered above the robot's head. Name the layer, title, and use a yellow identification color.

10. To create an adjustment layer and make the background appear more like a moonscape:

    a. On the Layers panel, select the Background layer.

    b. Open the Adjustments panel.

    c. Click the Hue/Saturation button to display the settings.

    d. On the Adjustments panel status bar, click the Clip to Layer button to create a new adjustment layer for the background.

    e. Change the Hue to +20 and the Saturation to –80.

    f. On the status bar, click the 'Return to adjustment list' button.

11. To create an adjustment layer and make the sky layer appear black:

    a. Select the sky layer.

    b. On the Adjustments panel, click the Brightness/Contrast button to display the controls, and then click the Clip to Layer button. Click the Use Legacy check box to select it.

    c. Drag both the Brightness and Contrast sliders to the left to create a black sky.

    d. On the Adjustments panel status bar, click the 'Return to adjustment list' button.

12. To add a layer effect to the title layer:

    a. Select the title layer.

    b. Click the 'Add a layer style' button on the Layers panel status bar, and then click Stroke to open the Layer style dialog box. (*Hint:* You may want to read about the Stroke command in Photoshop Help.) Drag the Layer Style dialog box title bar so you can view the robot and the dialog box.

    c. In the Layer Style dialog box, click the Color box to display the Select stroke color dialog box. Drag the Select stroke color dialog box title bar so you can view the robot and the dialog box, if necessary.

    d. Click one of the yellow eyes on the robot to select the yellow color. (*Hint:* The mouse pointer looks like an eyedropper when selecting a color.)

    e. Click the OK button to close the Select stroke color dialog box and then click the OK button to close the Layer Style dialog box.

13. Save the composite file again with all the layers.

14. Flatten the image.

15. Press SHIFT+CTRL+S to open the Save As dialog box. Type `Lab 3-2 Robot Complete` in the Name box. Click the Format box arrow and then click TIFF in the list. Click the Save button. If Photoshop displays a dialog box, click the OK button.

16. Quit Photoshop.

In the Lab

Lab 3: Creating a Contest Entry with Layers

Problem: You would like to enter your hamster in a creative pet photo contest. You decide to use Photoshop's layering capabilities to dress up your hamster as shown in Figure 3–82.

Figure 3–82

Instructions: Perform the following tasks:
1. Start Photoshop. Set the default workspace, default colors, and reset all tools.
2. Open the file Lab 3-3 Hamster from the Chapter 03 folder of the Data Files for Students. You can access the Data Files for Students on the CD that accompanies this book. See the inside back cover of this book for instructions on downloading the Data Files for Students, or contact your instructor for information about accessing the required files. Rename the file, Lab 3-3 Hamster Composite and save it as a PSD file on your storage device.
3. Using the file Lab 3-3 Pipe, create a new layer by dragging from one window to another. Edit the layer to remove the background and then scale and position the layer as shown in Figure 3–82. Repeat the process using the file Lab 3-3 Magnifying Glass file. Finally, use the file Lab 3-3 Hat to create a hat layer. Select the right third (back) of the hat and create a new layer via cut. Move the new layer, below the hamster layer, so that part of the hat appears behind the hamster's ear. Set layer properties to name and color each layer as desired.
4. Make any other adjustments to the layers that you feel would enhance the photo. When you are satisfied with your layers, save the image again. Flatten the image, save it as a TIFF file, named Lab 3-3 Hamster Complete, and then submit a copy to your instructor.

Cases and Places

Apply your creative thinking and problem-solving skills to design and implement a solution.

1: Cloning within the Same Document

Academic

Earlier in this chapter, a suggestion was made to create a flag with 50 percent opacity superimposed over a memorial. Open the files named Case 3-1 Memorial and Case 3-1 Flag, located in the Chapter 03 folder of the Data Files for Students. (Alternatively, locate or take a photo of a memorial in your city or a building on your campus. If necessary, obtain permission to use a digital photo or scan the image.) Arrange the windows. Select only the flag and then drag it as a new layer into the memorial photo. Resize the layer to fit across the memorial. Change the opacity to 40 percent. Make other corrections as necessary. Save the composite photo and print a copy.

2: Creating a Graphic with Opacity Changes

Personal

You recently took a photo of a deer at the local forest preserve. To make the picture more interesting, you decide to create a layer and clone the deer. Open the photo named Case 3-2 Deer, located in the Chapter 03 folder of the Data Files for Students. Click the Layer command on the menu bar, point to New, and then click Layer. Name the layer, deer. Click the Background layer, choose the Clone Stamp Tool, and take a sample of the middle of the deer. Click the new layer and clone the deer. On the Edit menu, click Free Transform and resize the cloned deer so it appears to be farther away. Flip the clone horizontally. Rename the file and save it in the TIF format on your storage device.

3: Creating a Greeting Card Graphic with Masking

Professional

You have been hired as an intern with a greeting card company. You were given several photos to use in preparing holiday cards. The photo named, Case 3-3 Santa Scene, is located in the Chapter 03 folder of the Data Files for Students. You want to use the figure of Santa Claus only, on the front of a card. Rename and save the photo in the PSD format on your USB flash drive storage device. Create a rectangular marquee selection around the figure. Use the Layer via Cut command and name the new layer, Santa. Hide the background. Create a layer mask, painting with black to display only the figure. Print with the background hidden.

Appendix A
Project Planning Guidelines

Using Project Planning Guidelines

The process of communicating specific information to others is a learned, rational skill. Computers and software, especially Adobe Photoshop CS5, can help you develop ideas and present detailed information to a particular audience.

Using Adobe Photoshop CS5, you can edit photos and create original graphics. Computer hardware and productivity software, such as Adobe Photoshop CS5, reduces much of the laborious work of drafting and revising projects. Some design professionals use sketch pads or storyboards, others compose directly on the computer, and others have developed unique strategies that work for their own particular thinking and artistic styles.

No matter what method you use to plan a project, follow specific guidelines to arrive at a final product that presents an image or images clearly and effectively (Figure A–1). Use some aspects of these guidelines every time you undertake a project, and others as needed in specific instances. For example, in determining content for a project, you may decide an original graphic would communicate the idea more effectively than an existing photo. If so, you would create this graphical element from scratch.

Determine the Project's Purpose

Begin by clearly defining why you are undertaking this assignment. For example, you may want to correct camera errors and adjust image flaws. Or you may want to create a graphic for a specific publishing or marketing purpose. Once you clearly understand the purpose of your task, begin to draft ideas of how best to communicate this information.

Analyze Your Audience

Learn about the people who will use, analyze, or view your work. Where are they employed? What are their educational backgrounds? What are their expectations? What questions do they have? Design experts suggest drawing a mental picture of these people or finding photographs of people who fit this profile so that you can develop a project with the audience in mind.

> **PROJECT PLANNING GUIDELINES**
>
> **1. DETERMINE THE PROJECT'S PURPOSE**
> *Why are you undertaking the project?*
>
> **2. ANALYZE YOUR AUDIENCE**
> *Who are the people who will use your work?*
>
> **3. GATHER POSSIBLE CONTENT**
> *What graphics exist, and in what forms?*
>
> **4. DETERMINE WHAT CONTENT TO PRESENT TO YOUR AUDIENCE**
> *What image will communicate the project's purpose to your audience in the most effective manner?*

Figure A–1

By knowing your audience members, you can tailor a project to meet their interests and needs. You will not present them with information they already possess, and you will not omit the information they need to know.

Example: Your assignment is to raise the profile of your college's nursing program in the community. Your project should address questions such as the following: How much does the audience know about your college and the nursing curriculum? What are the admission requirements? How many of the applicants admitted complete the program? What percent of participants pass the state nursing boards?

Gather Possible Content

Rarely are you in a position to develop all the material for a project. Typically, you would begin by gathering existing images and photos, or designing new graphics based on information that may reside in spreadsheets or databases. Design work for clients often must align with and adhere to existing marketing campaigns or publicity materials. Web sites, pamphlets, magazine and newspaper articles, and books could provide insights of how others have approached your topic. Personal interviews often provide perspectives not available by any other means. Consider video and audio clips as potential sources for material that might complement or support the factual data you uncover. Make sure you have all legal rights to any photographs you plan to use.

Determine What Content to Present to Your Audience

Experienced designers recommend writing three or four major ideas you want an audience member to remember after viewing your project. It also is helpful to envision your project's endpoint, the key fact or universal theme that you wish to emphasize. All project elements should lead to this ending point.

As you make content decisions, you also need to think about other factors. Presentation of the project content is an important consideration. For example, will your brochure be printed on thick, colored paper or transparencies? Will your photo be viewed in a classroom with excellent lighting and a bright projector, or will it be viewed on a notebook computer monitor? Determine relevant time factors, such as the length of time to develop the project, how long editors will spend reviewing your project, or the amount of time allocated for presenting your designs to the customer. Your project will need to accommodate all of these constraints.

Decide whether a graphic, photograph, or artistic element can express or emphasize a particular concept. The right hemisphere of the brain processes images by attaching an emotion to them, so in the long run, audience members are more apt to recall themes from graphics rather than those from the text.

Finally, review your project to make sure the theme still easily is identifiable and has been emphasized successfully. Is the focal point clear and presented without distraction? Does the project satisfy the requirements?

Summary

When creating a project, it is beneficial to follow some basic guidelines from the outset. By taking some time at the beginning of the process to determine the project's purpose, analyze the audience, gather possible content, and determine what content to present to the audience, you can produce a project that is informative, relevant, and effective.

Appendix B

Graphic Design Overview

Understanding Design Principles

Understanding a few basic design principles can catapult you to the next level of digital artistry. Beyond knowing how to use software, a graphic designer must know how to create effective and readable layouts no matter what the product type. In this Appendix, you will learn the design principles, color theory, typography, and other technical knowledge required to create usable and successful graphic designs.

A major goal in graphic design work, whether for print or Web page layout, is to guide the viewer's eyes toward some key point. Another major goal of design work is to convey a certain emotion — a project can have the effect of making the viewer feel relaxed, energetic, hungry, hopeful, or even anxious. By implementing a few basic principles of design, you can control your viewers' physical focus so they look where you want them to look as you steer them toward a desired emotion. Design principles typically include the following:

- Balance
- Contrast
- Dominance
- Proximity
- Repetition
- Closure
- Continuance
- Negative space
- Unity

Balance

Visual elements can be **balanced** within a design, just as items may be balanced on either side of a scale. Unbalanced designs can cause viewers to feel anxious or uncomfortable, or even like they are falling sideways out of their seats. Balance may be achieved symmetrically or asymmetrically. Symmetrical balance mirrors a visual element to achieve equilibrium (Figure B–1). Asymmetrical balance can be achieved by balancing a small, dark element with a large, light element (Figure B–2) or balancing one large element with several smaller elements (Figure B–3).

with symmetrical balance, the left and right halves are mirror reflections, and the two trees, which are identical in size and shape, balance the composition

Figure B–1

left-heavy design with sparse right sidebar that is too white to add much weight

balanced design with a darker right sidebar adding weight to the right side

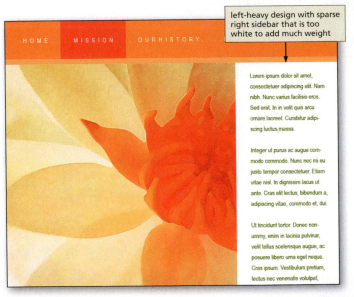
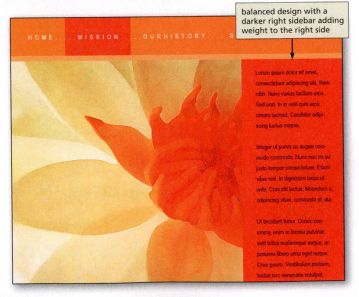

Figure B–2

large photo at right is asymmetrically balanced by the multiple small thumbnails on left

Figure B–3

Contrast

Contrast describes the visual differences between elements; it adds variety to a design and helps to draw the viewer's focus. Differences in color, scale, quantity, or other characteristics of visual elements help to achieve contrast. The element that is different from the others draws the viewer's attention. In Figure B–4, the words in white contrast against the other words on the page, and the viewer's eye is drawn to the contrasting sentence.

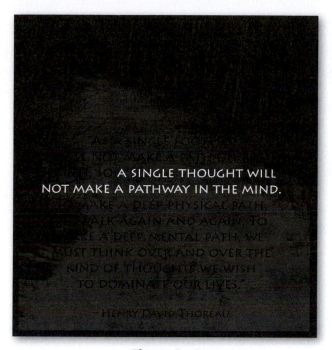

Figure B–4

Dominance

Dominance is a critical principle in controlling viewer focus. The dominant element in a design is the one to which a viewer's eyes and attention usually move first. An element's position within a design or its contrast to other elements can establish dominance. If you want your viewer to focus on a certain area of your design or on a specific design element, make it dominant, like the yellow V.I.P. banner in the discount card shown in Figure B–5.

grabbing your attention with its contrasting color, the V.I.P. banner is the dominant element in the design even though it is not the largest

Figure B–5

Proximity

Proximity describes the relative space between elements. Related elements should be close to each other. Headings should be close to their related paragraph text, and product names should be close to their photos and prices. As shown in Figure B–6, when related items are not within close proximity of each other (Figure B–6a), the viewer may not know the items are related. When elements are too close, the design looks cluttered and text can become difficult to read. Strive for balance in your proximity, as in Figure B–6b.

(a) Items Without Proximity Are Not Clearly Related

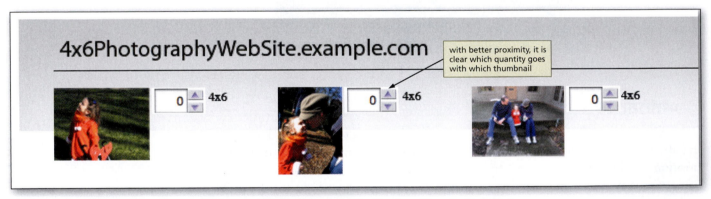

(b) Items With Close Proximity Are Clearly Related

Figure B–6

BTW

Natural Repetition
Repetition occurs naturally in the petals around a flower, patterns on snakeskin, and polygons on turtle shells.

Repetition

Repeating a visual element helps to tie a design together. **Repetition** of color, shape, texture, and other characteristics can help to unify your design (Figure B–7), create patterns, or impart a sense of movement. Most Web sites repeat a design theme across all the pages so users know they are on the same site as they navigate from page to page. Repeated colors and layouts help to unify the overall Web site design.

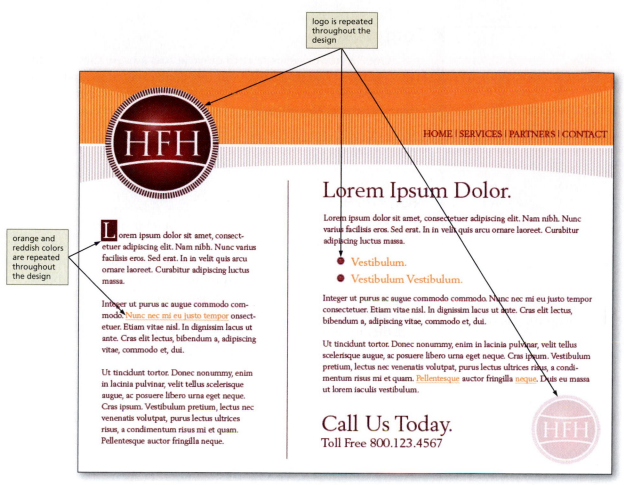

logo is repeated throughout the design

orange and reddish colors are repeated throughout the design

Figure B–7

Closure

Not everything in a design must be composed of solid lines. Composing objects from small parts and spaces allows a design to breathe and creates visual interest. Under the concept of **closure**, the human brain will fill in the blanks to close or complete the object (Figure B–8).

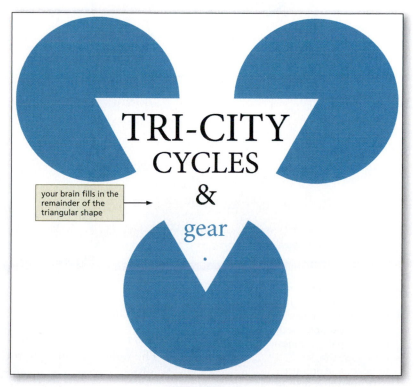

your brain fills in the remainder of the triangular shape

Figure B–8

large dominant dancer captures your attention and her arms direct your eyes straight to the message

Figure B–9

Continuance

Once a viewer's eyes start to move across a page, they tend to keep moving — and you can exploit this **continuance** to guide their eyes exactly where you want them to go. A dominant object can capture the viewer's initial focus, and diagonal lines within that dominant object can guide the viewer's eyes toward the focal point of your design (Figure B–9).

Negative Space

Negative space refers to the space in your design that does not contain information, or the space between elements. For example, the space between the vertical heading and descriptive text or the space between a logo and the vertical heading, as shown in Figure B–10, is negative space. Without negative space, your design will feel cluttered, and viewers will have difficulty identifying on the focal point. Note that negative space, also called **white space**, does not literally translate to "white space," as negative space does not have to be white (Figure B–10).

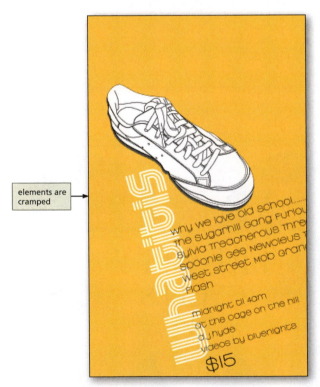

elements are cramped

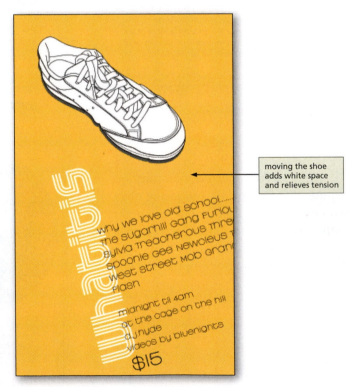

moving the shoe adds white space and relieves tension

Figure B–10

Unity
Unity is not limited to elements in a specific piece of work; it can apply to multiple pieces. For example, a business card, Web site, letterhead, and product packaging that feature a similar color and style can help unify a business's identity.

Unity

Unity refers to the concept that all elements within a design work well together to form a whole. The individual images, textures, text, and negative space join together to create a single unified message or meaning. Unity can be created by applying a combination of basic design principles. Balanced elements alone do not produce a visually appealing design. The same is true for elements with appropriate proximity and negative space, good contrast, or clear dominance. No single design principle is responsible for a pleasing design. Instead, the combination of these principles creates a single unified design. Without unity, a design degrades into chaos and loses meaning. Of course, that is not a bad thing if chaos is the intentional message.

Layout Grids

A graphic designer needs to know where to place elements within a document or Web page. The use of grids makes it easy to align objects to each other and can help with balance and proximity. There are many standard grids that can be applied to Web page layouts or print layouts for standard paper sizes. One very popular grid system uses thirds, which is derived from the golden ratio.

Rule of Thirds and Golden Ratio The rule of thirds specifies that splitting a segment into thirds produces an aesthetically pleasing ratio. The rule of thirds is derived from a more complex mathematical concept called the golden ratio, which specifies segment ratios of long segment divided by short segment equal to about 1.618 — which is close enough to the rule of thirds that designers typically apply the rule of thirds rather than break out their slide rulers (Figure B–11).

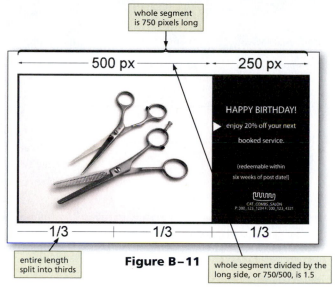

whole segment is 750 pixels long

entire length split into thirds

Figure B–11

whole segment divided by the long side, or 750/500, is 1.5

Dominant Object Placement
Placing an object at a certain location within a grid, such as the intersection of thirds or slightly above and to the right of center, helps to establish dominance.

Color Theory

Color can have a profound effect on the overall message a design conveys. Certain colors evoke specific emotions, and the way colors are combined can make the difference between readable copy and copy that is unable to be read.

Color Properties

Before you begin to work with color, it is important to understand the properties of color, which include hue, saturation, shade, tint, and value.

Hue refers to the tone, or actual color, such as red, yellow, or blue. Many color theorists interpret hue to mean pure color. A pure color, or hue, can be modified to create color variations. A basic color wheel, shown in Figure B–12, displays hue.

Saturation refers to the intensity of a color. As hues become less saturated, they create muted tones and pastels as they approach gray. As hues become more saturated, they appear very bright (Figure B–13).

Figure B–12

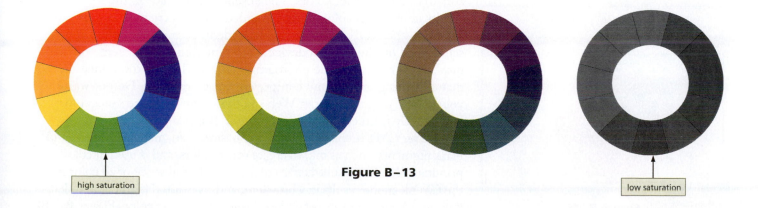

high saturation

low saturation

Figure B–13

desaturated hues can have calming effect

Figure B–14

oversaturated hues can be hard on the eyes

Figure B–15

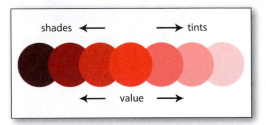

shades ← → tints

value

Figure B–16

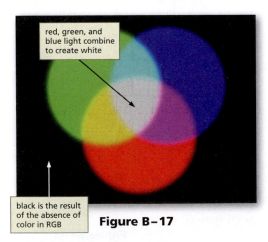

red, green, and blue light combine to create white

black is the result of the absence of color in RGB

Figure B–17

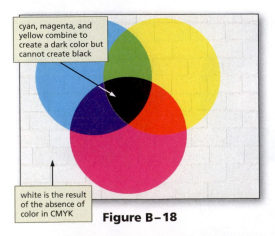

cyan, magenta, and yellow combine to create a dark color but cannot create black

white is the result of the absence of color in CMYK

Figure B–18

Desaturated colors can produce mellow tones and evoke calm feelings (Figure B–14). Oversaturated colors can produce almost neon colors and cause excitement (Figure B–15). Sometimes it is appropriate to use very bright colors, such as in a picture book for children or a high-energy advertisement for a sports drink. Other times, bright, saturated colors produce the wrong feeling for your work.

A **shade** is a mixture of a hue and black, producing a darker color. A **tint** is a mixture of a hue and white, producing a lighter color. A color's **value** describes its overall lightness or darkness. A tint has a higher value, while a shade has a lower value (Figure B–16). Mixing a hue with its shades, tints, and variations of saturation can lead to very harmonious color combinations.

Color Modes

A color mode describes the way in which colors combine to create other colors. The most commonly used color modes are RGB, CMYK, and LAB. Each mode has its strengths and weaknesses, and each is appropriate for a specific type of work.

The **RGB** color mode mixes red, green, and blue light to create other colors. Computer monitors and TV screens use the RGB color mode. All images used on a Web site must use the RGB color mode because few Web browsers can display CMYK images. RGB is an additive color mode, meaning colored light combines (light waves are added) to create other colors. The absence of all color in the RGB mode results in black. As colored light is added, white is created, as shown in Figure B–17. RGB is also device dependent, because the colors you see depend on the viewing device. Different computer screens will display colors in the same photograph differently due to variances in the manufacturing process and component wear over time. Do not waste your time trying to get your Web site to display the same exact colors consistently from computer to computer. It is not possible.

The **CMYK** color mode mixes physical cyan, magenta, yellow, and black pigments (such as ink) to create other colors, and is used in color printing. CMYK is a subtractive color mode. The absence of all color in the CMYK mode results in white light, and, as colored pigment is added, light wavelengths are absorbed or subtracted, creating color (Figure B–18).

Cyan, magenta, and yellow alone cannot create black; thus, the need for pure black in the CMYK mode.

Unlike RGB and CMYK, which combine individual well-defined colors, the **LAB** color mode combines levels of lightness with two color channels, a and b. One color channel ranges from green to magenta, while the other includes blue through yellow. By combining color ranges with lightness values, LAB is able to closely approximate the true human perception of color and thus is able to produce more colors than either RGB or CMYK. This makes it an ideal color mode for photographers wanting to have access to every possible color in a photograph. LAB typically is used during photographic retouching and color correction. The image then is converted to RGB or CMYK for use with electronic media or print.

BTW

LAB
LAB is sometimes written as L*a*b for lightness, color channel a, and color channel b.

Psychological Considerations of Color

Colors can evoke both positive and negative emotions in people, and the influence of a color can differ among individuals and cultures. While the effect of color on people is not an exact science, there are some generalities.

White often is associated with cleanliness, purity, and hope. Doctors and brides in most Western cultures wear white. However, white is associated with death and mourning attire in some Eastern cultures. White is the most popular background color and offers great contrast for highly readable dark text.

Black often is used to represent evil, death, or mourning, but also mystery, intelligence, elegance, and power. Black text on a white background is the easiest to read.

Red is used in Western cultures to signify love, passion, and comfort — but also is used to represent sin, hell, and danger. Use dark reds to imply indulgence or fine living and brownish reds for designs dealing with Thanksgiving, harvest, or the fall season in general.

Green symbolizes many positives such as growth, tranquility, luck, money, ecology, environmentalism, and health, but it also symbolizes jealousy. Green can have a calming effect.

Blue often is cited as the favorite color by men. Like green, it evokes feelings of calmness and serenity. Blue implies authority, stability, loyalty, and confidence. However, it is one of the least appetizing colors, as there are few naturally blue foods. It also is associated with sadness and bad luck, as evidenced in blues music or phrases like "I've got the blues."

Yellow generally makes people happy. It is a highly visible and active color. However, too much yellow can lead to frustration and eye fatigue. Babies cry more in yellow rooms. Avoid using yellow as a page background and use it instead in smaller areas to draw attention.

Print Considerations for Color

The printing process cannot reproduce every color. Gamut refers to the range of printable colors and colors that cannot be printed are said to be *out of gamut*. If an out of gamut color exists in your document, the printer you are using will simply get as close to it as it can — but it will not be exact. Depending on the printer you have installed, the actual color produced can vary. Photoshop identifies out of gamut colors in the Color Picker with a small icon. If your document contains out of gamut colors, you have two options: change or replace the out of gamut color with one that is in gamut; or accept that the final print may not be exactly what you expected.

Web Considerations for Color

When working with color for the Web, the most important thing to remember is that colors will appear differently on different computers. Web sites look similar, but not exactly the same, from computer to computer. Years ago, Web designers used only the **Web-safe colors**, which was a set of 216 colors that supposedly appear the same on all monitors. This was due to the limitations of video subsystems at the time, as computer monitors could display only 256 specific colors. Microsoft Windows supported 256 specific colors, and Apple Macintosh supported a different 256 colors. Of the two sets, 216 were the same across both platforms; these 216 became the Web-safe palette. However, designers soon realized that only 22 of those 216 were truly the same between Windows and Macintosh; this subset was called the **really Web-safe colors**.

Photoshop displays a warning in the Color Picker for non-Web-safe colors. Modern computers (as well as cell phone browsers) can display millions of distinct colors, so limiting yourself to 216 Web-safe colors is no longer a necessity. In fact, it is extremely limiting, because the 216 Web-safe colors are generally very bright or very dark with few choices for pastels or saturation and value variances. Most designers do not use Web-safe colors for their designs.

Relativity

A color's relative lightness/darkness value can appear different depending on what other color neighbors it. The gray block in Figure B–19 looks lighter when against the brown background and darker when against the light yellow background. Keep this in mind as you choose background/foreground relationships. A certain hue (or tint or shade) might look great when it is by itself, but you may not be so fond of it when used in close proximity to another certain color.

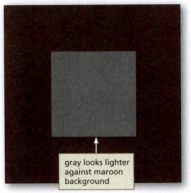

gray looks lighter against maroon background

gray looks darker against pale yellow background

Figure B–19

Color Schemes and Matching

Choosing colors that work well together and enforce the design's message can be challenging but worth the effort. Successful color matching requires an understanding of **color schemes**, which simply describes an organized method of matching colors based on their positions on a color wheel. The color scheme can make or break a design.

Figure B–12 on page APP 9 displayed a color wheel. While there are various color wheel models, the most popular uses the primary colors red, blue, and yellow (Figure B–20a). Primary colors combine to create the secondary colors green, orange, and purple (Figure B–20b). A primary and a secondary color combine to create a tertiary (third level) color (Figure B–20c). More complex color wheels can include gradients to show varying saturation, tints, and shades (Figure B–21).

(a) Primary Colors   **(b) Secondary Colors**   **(c) Tertiary Colors**

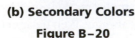

Figure B–20

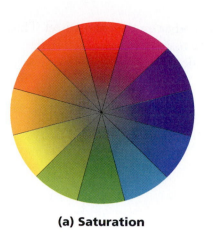

(a) Saturation

(b) Tints

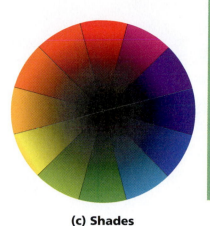

(c) Shades

Figure B–21

Color Schemes   A **monochromatic color scheme** is one that uses a single hue with a variety of shades and tints (Figure B–22). This is an easy color scheme to create. While a monochromatic color scheme can appear soothing, the lack of hue variance can leave it looking a bit boring.

BTW

Color Scheme Web Sites
Stand-alone color scheme software programs are available for purchase, but Adobe offers a free online service at kuler.adobe.com that lets you browse color schemes created by other users, modify them, and create and save your own.

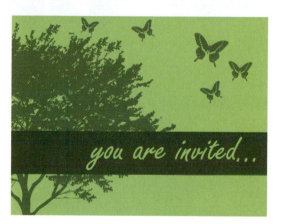

Figure B–22

A **complementary color scheme** uses colors directly across from each other on the color wheel. Their high contrast can look vibrant but also can be hard on the eyes. Avoid using complementary pairs in a foreground/background relationship, as shown in Figure B–23. Adjusting the saturation or substituting tints and shades makes this color scheme more workable.

bright complementary colors do not work well in a foreground/background relationship

adjusting the arrangement of the colors or using a variety of values or saturation can help

Figure B–23

An **analogous color scheme** uses colors next to each other on the color wheel. This color scheme is generally very appealing and evokes positive feelings (Figure B–24). Be careful not to choose colors that are too far apart. A very wide range of analogous colors can appear mismatched.

Figure B–24

The **split-complementary scheme** uses a base color and, instead of its direct complement, the two colors on either side of its complement (Figure B–25). This scheme offers a lot of hue variance, and therefore excitement. However, if all the hues are overly saturated, split-complementary colors can be very harsh. Try keeping one hue saturated and use tints, shades, or desaturated colors for the rest of the scheme.

Figure B–25

Other color schemes such as triadic, tetradic, neutral, and an infinite number of custom schemes also exist. Using a color matching resource such as software or a Web site is a good way to help you get started choosing colors and allows you to experiment to see what you and your client like.

Typography

Typography is the art of working with text. Perhaps the two most important factors for graphic designers to address when working with text are visual appeal and readability. A dull text heading will not entice viewers to read the rest of the advertisement, but a text heading that looks beautiful can be useless if it is not readable (Figure B–26).

Readability

Readability is the measurement of how comfortable or easy it is for readers to read the text. Many factors contribute to overall readability. Commonly accepted readability factors include the following:

- Large text passages written in lowercase are easier to read than long text passages in uppercase.
- Regular text is easier to read than italicized text.
- Black text on a white background is easier to read than white text on a black background.
- Legibility affects readability.
- Line length, letterforms, and appearance all influence readability.

Before learning the details of readability, you must understand some type basics. A **font** is a set of characters of a specific family, size, and style. For example, the description Times New Roman, 11 points, italic is a font. What most people consider a font is actually a **typeface** (Times New Roman, in this example). A font represents only a single specific size and style within a family, while a typeface is a set or family of one or more fonts.

Legibility refers to the ease with which a reader can determine what a letter actually is. If readers cannot figure out the letter, they cannot read the text, resulting in low readability and failed message delivery. The difference between legibility and readability is subtle. Figure B–27 shows an exit sign — something that needs to be legible.

Line length refers to the physical length of a line of text. When lines are too long, the reader's eyes can get lost trying to go all the way back to the left side of the page to find the next line. There is no conclusive magic number for how long a line of text should be. Optimal line lengths differ for adults and children, and for people with dyslexia and without. The best choices for line length differ based on the media of the message; printed newspapers, books, text on a Web site, and the subject lines in an e-mail message all require different line lengths. Some studies recommend line lengths based on physical lengths in inches, while other studies recommend a maximum number of characters per line. However, many designers follow the guideline that line lengths should not exceed 70 characters (about two-and-a-half alphabets' worth of characters).

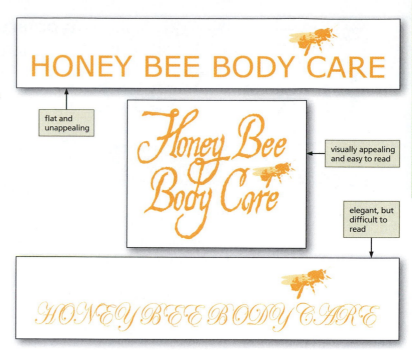

flat and unappealing

visually appealing and easy to read

elegant, but difficult to read

Figure B–26

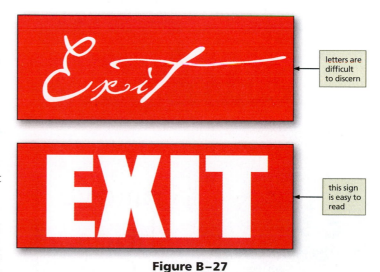

letters are difficult to discern

this sign is easy to read

Figure B–27

BTW

DON'T YELL
Not only is typing in all uppercase difficult to read, but it connotes yelling at your reader.

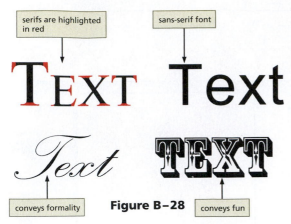

serifs are highlighted in red

sans-serif font

conveys formality

Figure B–28

conveys fun

Typeface Categories

Typefaces are organized into several categories, including serif, sans-serif, script, and display. Serif fonts include additional appendages, while sans-serif fonts do not (Figure B–28). It is generally accepted that large passages of serif text in print are easy to read, while sans-serif text is easier to read on a Web page. Because headlines are typically small, either serif or sans-serif is appropriate. Varying the headline typeface style from the body copy typeface style is an effective method of adding some visual excitement to an otherwise dull page of text. Script fonts look like handwriting, and display fonts are decorative.

In addition to differences in readability, the choice of a serif, sans-serif, or other font can help to create an emotion much like the selection of a color scheme. Wedding invitations often use a script font to signify elegance, while headlines using display fonts can grab a reader's attention. The same phrase written in different typefaces can have different implications (Figure B–29). Similarly, differences in the size, weight (boldness), or spacing of a font also can influence emotion or meaning (Figure B–30).

typeface implies a fancy party or elegant gathering

typeface implies the event will be fun, zany, or whimsical

Figure B–29

you are asked to remove your shoes, but you are still made to feel welcome

you are being ordered to remove your shoes, and emphasis on remove and before may cause resentment

Figure B–30

Designing for Web vs. Print

Graphic designers must be aware of subtle differences in how print and Web projects are created and perceived when designing for these media. While many design principles are common to both, it takes a different mindset to successfully create a design for either medium. Print designs are static, as the layout never varies from print to print (though differences in color may appear due to inconsistencies with the printer or printing press). The appearance of Web designs can vary, depending on the device used to view them. Some print designers struggle with the device dependency and fluidity of Web page designs. Some Web designers unnecessarily concern themselves about accommodating fluid or shifting content when designing a print advertisement.

Device Dependency and Fluidity

The main differences between print and Web design are related to device dependency and fluidity. Web pages are **device dependent**, meaning that the appearance of the page varies depending on the device (computer, cell phone, or PDA) on which they are viewed (Figure B–31). Discrepancies in monitor color calibration, screen resolution, and browser window size can affect how a Web page appears to the viewer. Colors can change, objects can shift, and text can wrap to a new line on different words from one device to another. In comparison, a newspaper or magazine looks the same no matter where it is purchased or where it is read.

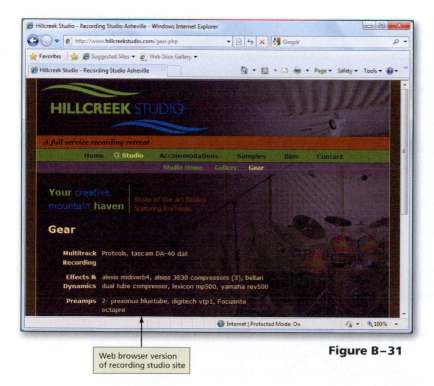

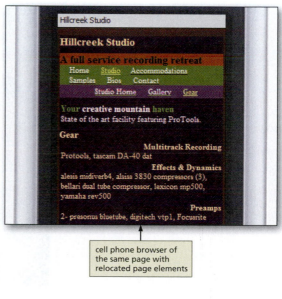

cell phone browser of the same page with relocated page elements

Web browser version of recording studio site

Figure B–31

Pixels, Dimensions, and Resolution

A pixel is the smallest element of a digital image. Magnifying an image reveals the individual pixels (Figure B–32). A pixel, unlike an inch or centimeter, is not an absolute measurement. The physical size of a pixel can change depending on device resolution.

As you learned in Chapter 1, resolution refers to the number of pixels displayed on a computer screen. More pixels gives greater detail. When referring to an image file, the phrase, document dimensions, is used to describe the number of pixels in the file. For example, an image may have the dimensions of 450 × 337, meaning it contains 450 pixels across and 337 pixels vertically, for a total of 151,650 pixels. File size is directly related to pixel dimension. The more pixels there are in a document, the larger the file size.

When used to describe an image file, the word, resolution, also is used to describe the printed output. The print resolution is given in pixels per inch (PPI); for example, 72 PPI or 300 PPI. PPI is a linear measurement: 72 PPI means that, when printed, the output will contain 72 pixels across every linear inch. If the document dimensions were 450 × 337, those 450 horizontal pixels would print in groups of 72 PPI, resulting in a printout just over six inches wide (Figure B–33). If the resolution, but not the dimensions, was

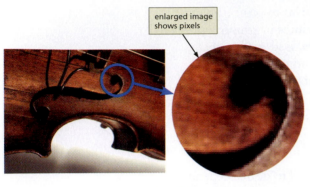

enlarged image shows pixels

Figure B–32

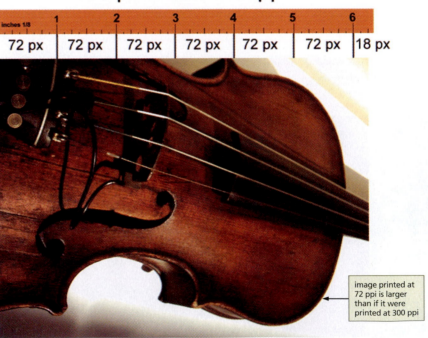

450 px wide at 72 ppi

inches 1/8	1	2	3	4	5	6
72 px	72 px	72 px	72 px	72 px	72 px	18 px

image printed at 72 ppi is larger than if it were printed at 300 ppi

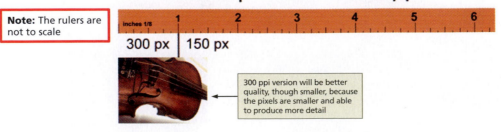

450 px wide at 300 ppi

Note: The rulers are not to scale

| inches 1/8 | 1 | 2 | 3 | 4 | 5 | 6 |

300 px | 150 px

300 ppi version will be better quality, though smaller, because the pixels are smaller and able to produce more detail

Figure B–33

increased to 300 PPI, then those same 450 pixels would print in groups of 300 per inch, producing a final output about 1.5 inches wide.

Key points to remember when working with resolution are:

- A pixel is not a static measurement. Pixels change in size. They get smaller or larger to fill an inch as defined in the PPI setting.

- Changing the resolution of an image file has no effect on the file size. It affects the physical size of the printed output.

- Changing the document dimensions does affect the file size.

When printing documents, printers create each individual pixel with a group of microscopic dots of ink (or toner or other pigment). The number of dots a printer can generate is measured in dots per inch (DPI). People sometimes incorrectly use the term DPI when they really mean PPI. A printer with a resolution of 2400 DPI means it can squeeze 2400 dots of ink (not pixels) into a single inch. The more dots used to create a pixel, the truer color each pixel can have — resulting in a higher quality print.

A common misconception related to creating image files is that all graphics for use on the Web should be created at a resolution of 72 PPI. However, because PPI affects the output of printing only, the PPI setting has no effect on the screen display of an image.

It is common practice to save Web images at 72 PPI, not because it optimizes images for the Web, but because the 72 DPI Myth so widely is believed, saving Web images at 72 PPI simply is very common.

> **BTW**
>
> **Resolution and Print Quality**
> The higher the resolution, the smaller the pixels and the printout, and the better the quality.

> **BTW**
>
> **PPI and Printing**
> An image with the dimensions of 800 x 600 at 72 PPI will look exactly the same on screen as the same image at 300 PPI. In fact, the file sizes will be identical. There will only be a difference when printed. For Web images, you can save them at 0 PPI, and they would work just as well, and have the same file size, as if you saved them at 1200 PPI. However, when printed, they will differ.

Working as a Graphic Designer

The business world offers many opportunities for people with creativity and an eye for design. From automotive design to fashion to advertising, the need for talented graphic artists is vast. Many industry experts believe there are generally three levels of professionals working in the graphics field: graphic artists, graphic designers, and people who own graphics editing/design software.

Graphic artists typically receive extensive schooling as art majors and know a lot about design principles and art history. However, schooling does not necessarily mean formal education in a school environment. A graphic artist can be self-educated. The key to the "artist" designation revolves around a personal need to creatively express oneself beyond that of producing commercial work for hire. While graphic artists work with software, they typically also produce art with more traditional media such as paints, pencils, fiber, metals, or other physical materials. Graphic artists may hold the same job as a graphic designer, but very often graphic artists will create and sell their own original artwork. This personal drive to create and the resulting independent production of original artwork is what distinguishes graphic artists from graphic designers.

The line separating graphic artists from graphic designers is a fine one. A **graphic designer** often is knowledgeable about design principles and may possess a wealth of information about art history, but not all graphic designers are graphic artists. They usually create design products for others, such as brochures, advertisements, or Web sites, using software, but do not create their own original works.

The third category of graphic designers includes people who own and use graphics design software for various purposes. This category, **software owners**, is not a true graphic design designation. Simply owning a copy of Photoshop or knowing how to use a certain software program does not make you a graphic artist/designer. Whereas artists and designers understand principles of design, effective use of color, and possess a certain degree of artistic ability or raw talent, design amateurs rely on the power of the software to help them create projects. Of course, it is possible for an amateur to become a professional designer or artist — but doing so requires education and training, not just purchasing a software suite.

Jobs in Graphic Design

An understanding of design principles and software skills opens the door to many opportunities in the professional graphics industry. Jobs for graphic designers range from freelance work and self-employment to full-time careers with advertising agencies, Web design firms, print houses, software companies, or the marketing team within an organization such as a school or commercial or nonprofit business. Perhaps the most important questions to ask yourself when considering a job in this field are:

- Do I want to work for myself or for someone else?
- Am I truly an artist? Am I creative? Or do I simply follow direction well, understand basic design principles, and know how to use graphics software?
- What is my preferred medium — physical (print) or electronic (Web, software interface)?

Once you have secured a position in the graphics field, you will be assigned projects that will call on your design skills and other abilities.

Design Projects

A successful project always begins with solid planning. Proper planning helps you to stay focused and reduces the potential for wasted time and money — both yours and your client's. A project plan must specify the following aspects of the project:

- Scope of design work
- Roles and responsibilities of designer and client
- Expectations and specifications for final product, including time frame

When you and your client agree on the scope of the work and are clear on what the final product should look like, you as the designer know exactly what it is you need to produce. It is better to take the time to plan a project before sitting down with Photoshop, so you have a good idea of what to do once you start the software.

Client and Designer Roles

Both the client and the designer have specific jobs. Defining and agreeing on these roles is crucial for the success of the collaboration.

Simply put, the client must clearly communicate his or her expectations. Clients often need help articulating their wants and needs, and the designer must be able to help draw this information from the client. Additionally, the client must be available to provide feedback when the designer offers a draft for feedback or proofing. A client's responsibilities include the following:

- Clearly communicate the needs of the project
- Provide timely and constructive feedback
- Trust the designer's expertise
- Pay the bills on time

Aside from the obvious (creating the product), the designer also is responsible for making sure the client knows their own responsibilities and avoids poor design choices. Sometimes, a client will request something that is just bad — like certain colors that do not work well together or make text unreadable. The designer is responsible for respectfully steering the client away from the bad options and toward a better alternative.

In a highly competitive job market, you must determine what sets you apart from your competition. A potential client might choose one designer over another not because one is a better or more creative artist, but simply because they like the other designer more.

Customer service is part of your job, as well. Treat your client and your client's time and money with respect, be personable, and appreciate your client, and you will have more to offer than your competitors will. In addition to meeting the responsibilities previously defined, you should do the following:

- Be on time to meetings
- Meet or beat your deadlines so you don't submit work late
- Treat your clients and their time and money with respect
- Be able to explain your design choices
- Ensure adherence to copyright law

Defining the Project

As a designer, you must understand you are acting in the role of a hired hand — not an artist with complete creative control. You are being hired to create what your client wants, not what you necessarily prefer. While you need to educate your client as to best practices in design, ultimately the client is paying the bill, so he or she has the final word when it comes to making decisions.

Specifying Project Details

Project details should be discussed with the client and agreed upon before any design work begins. One detail to consider is what the client needs for files. For example, does the client require a 300 PPI TIF file or a layered Photoshop file? How will the files be delivered? Will they be sent by e-mail, burned to a CD and mailed, or downloaded from a Web site or FTP server? Additionally, a timeline of deliverables should be stated. A first draft of the design should be sent to the client for approval by a certain date, and pending timely client feedback, the final version should be delivered by the project deadline. The client may have a desired time frame, and the designer must be able to deliver the work within that time frame. Sometimes a compromise must be reached.

BTW

Photos on CD or DVD
If possible, get photos and images on a CD or DVD. Many times a collection of photographs and other materials are too large to send by e-mail, and even if they are successfully sent, e-mails accidentally get deleted. Having all the materials on CD or DVD also guarantees you always have a backup of the original files as you modify copies with Photoshop or other software.

Collecting Materials

Existing materials help to speed up the design process. If you are hired to create a Web site or brochure, ask your client for copies of their existing promotional materials, such as a business card, letterhead, or logo. Ask your client what they like and dislike about these materials and if the product you are creating should be stylistically similar. This approach can prevent you from going down the wrong path, inadvertently creating something the client does not like or need. Additionally, you will need to collect any photographs your client has earmarked for the project.

Next, you must gather other assets for the project; specifically, high-quality artwork and photographs.

Original Artwork   If you have the raw artistic ability or own quality camera equipment, you can create your own original artwork or take your own photographs if you are a professional-level photographer. You can outsource some of this work to professional artists or photographers — just be sure to get your client's approval for the cost. Your other option is to use stock art.

Stock Art   Stock art includes existing artwork and photographs that can be licensed for use. The cost of a single picture can range from zero to several thousand dollars, depending on the source and license restrictions. Realistically, you should expect to pay between $5 and $40 for each print-quality digital file if you cannot find free sources.

Public Domain vs. Commercial Stock Art
Public domain stock art sites can be difficult to use because they do not have the funding for the more intuitive style of interface found on the commercial sites. You can often find exactly what you want in the public domain. However, sometimes it is worth the $5 to more easily find exactly what you want on a commercial Web site.

Stock art is commercially available from many companies, most with a Web presence — meaning you can download images or purchase whole collections of stock art on CD or DVD from a Web site. Thousands of companies sell commercial stock art online. Some of the most popular resources are fotosearch.com, corbis.com, and gettyimages.com.

When searching for stock art, be sure to seek out **royalty-free images**. Images that are royalty free can be reused without paying additional fees. For example, you could spend $100 to purchase an image that is not royalty free and use it on a Web site. If you want to use the same image in a brochure or another client's Web site, you might have to pay another fee to reuse the image. Royalty free means that once the initial payment is made, there are no re-usage fees.

If you do not want to pay anything for your images, look into finding **public domain** artwork or photographs. Images in the public domain are completely free to use. The only trick is finding quality artwork in the public domain. Whereas commercial stock art Web sites typically have millions of high-quality images from which to choose, public domain stock art Web sites often have far fewer choices. Public domain stock art sites include Flickr, Morgue File, and Uncle Sam's Photos.

Other Licenses   There are usage licenses allowing free unrestricted use of images, audio, video, text, and other content similar to that of the public domain. These licenses include Copyleft, Creative Commons, education use, fair use, GNU general public license, and open source. The definitions of these alternative licenses read like a law book, but it is helpful to recognize the names. Laws related to these licenses allow for limited use of copyright-protected material without requiring the permission of the copyright owner. If you find images or other content offered as one of these alternatives, there is a good chance it will be completely free to use.

Whatever the source for your images, be sure to read the license and usage rights and restrictions carefully. No matter your source for artwork, you need to document its origin. The documentation serves two important purposes. First, it provides a record of the image's origin in case you need to get additional similar artwork. Second, it provides peace of mind should you or your client ever face legal action for copyright infringement. The documentation does not have to be fancy; it can simply be a list of where an image is used in a project and where that image was acquired.

Summary

Successful design uses the principles of balance, contrast, dominance, proximity, repetition, closure, continuance, negative space, and unity. The properties of color include hue, saturation, shade, tint, and value. Color modes include RGB for Web images, CMYK for images you intend to print, and LAB for access to the largest color space possible when working with digital photographs. Adherence to Web-safe colors is unnecessary. Colors can have emotional implications and should be used in harmony with neighboring colors. Color schemes include monochrome, complementary, analogous, and split-complementary.

Typeface selections can affect text readability, as can line lengths. Typefaces are organized into several categories, including serif, sans-serif, script, and display. The same Web site can look different from one monitor or computer to another.

Pixels per inch (PPI) determines the number of pixels printed per inch and affects the printed size of an image only, not how it appears onscreen or its file size. Higher PPI settings produce better quality printouts but have no effect on how an image appears onscreen. Dots per inch (DPI) refers to printer capabilities and defines how many dots of ink a printer can print in a linear inch. Pixel dimensions, not image resolution, affect how large an image appears on-screen and the size of a file.

Working in graphic design can incorporate a range of creative roles; working with clients in a design role requires specifying project expectations and the responsibilities of both designer and client.

Appendix C

Changing Screen Resolution and Editing Preferences

This appendix explains how to change the screen resolution in Windows 7 to the resolution used in this book. It also describes how to customize the Photoshop window by setting preferences and resetting user changes.

Screen Resolution

Screen resolution indicates the number of pixels (dots) that the computer uses to display the graphics, text, and background you see on the screen. The screen resolution usually is stated as the product of two numbers, such as 1024 × 768. That resolution results in a display of 1,024 distinct pixels on each of 768 lines, or about 786,432 pixels. The figures in this book were created using a screen resolution of 1024 × 768.

To Change Screen Resolution

The following steps change your screen's resolution to 1024 × 768 pixels. Your computer already may be set to 1024 × 768 or some other resolution.

1

- If necessary, minimize all programs so that the Windows 7 desktop is displayed.

- Right-click the Windows 7 desktop to display the desktop shortcut menu (Figure C–1).

Figure C–1

2
• Click Screen resolution on the shortcut menu to open the Screen Resolution window. Maximize the window if necessary (Figure C–2).

Screen Resolution window

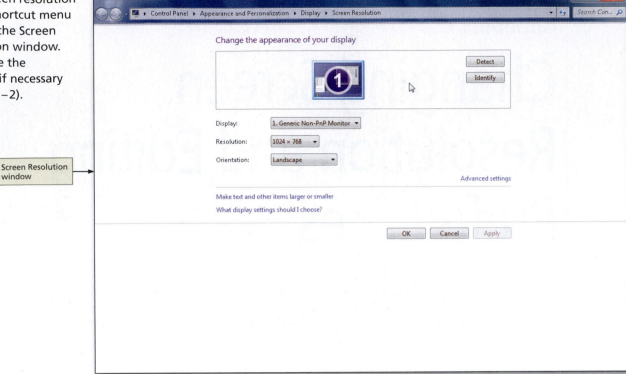

Figure C–2

3
• Click the Resolution button to display the list of available resolutions (Figure C–3).

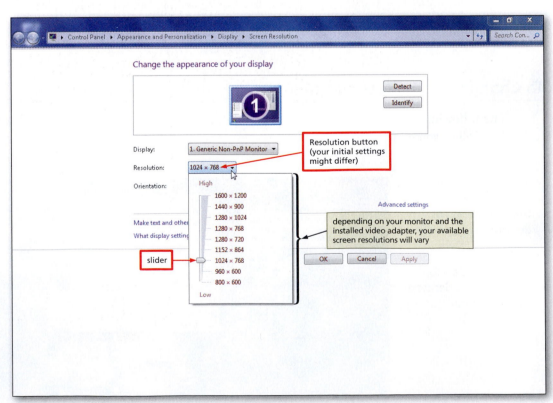

Figure C–3

4

• Drag the slider in the Resolution list so that the screen resolution changes to 1024 × 768, if necessary (Figure C–4).

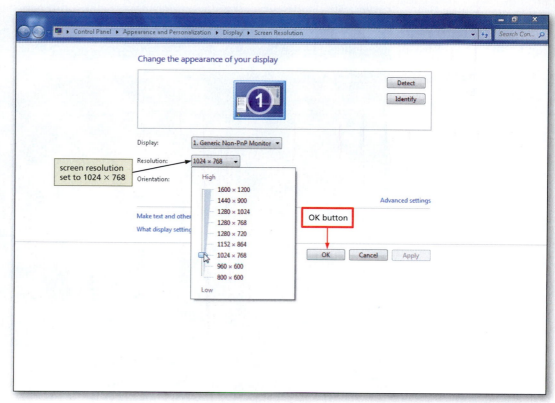

Figure C–4

5

• Click outside of the list to close the list. Click the OK button to change the screen resolution (Figure C–5).

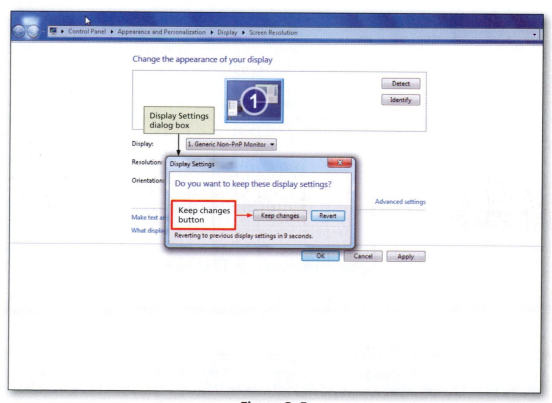

Figure C–5

6
- If Windows displays the Display Settings dialog box, click the Keep changes button to accept the changes (Figure C–6).

Figure C–6

BTW

Screen Resolutions
When you increase the screen resolution, Windows displays more information on the screen, but the information decreases in size. The reverse also is true; as you decrease the screen resolution, Windows displays less information on the screen, but the information increases in size.

Editing Photoshop Preferences

In Chapter 1, you learned how to start Photoshop and reset the default workspace, select the default tool, and reset all tools to their default settings. There are other preferences and settings you can edit to customize the Photoshop workspace and maximize your efficiency.

Editing General Preferences

General preferences include how Photoshop displays and stores your work. For example, you can change how many states are saved in the History panel, change the number of files shown on the Open Recent menu, or reset the display and cursors.

To Edit General Preferences

In the following steps, you will traverse through several Preferences dialog boxes to reset values and change preferences. You can access this set of dialog boxes by pressing CTRL+K or by clicking Preferences on the Edit menu.

1

- Start Photoshop CS5 for your system.

- Press CTRL+K to display the Preferences dialog box.

- Make sure the check boxes in the Options area are selected as shown in Figure C–7.

- Click the Reset All Warning Dialogs button, so your dialog boxes will match the ones in this book.

- When Photoshop displays a Preferences dialog box, click the OK button.

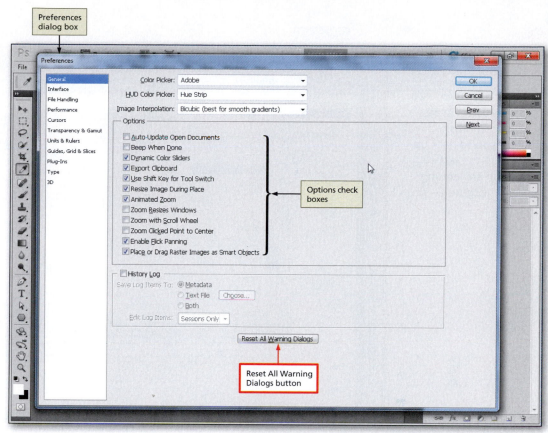

Figure C–7

2

- Click File Handling in the list of Preferences.

- Click the File Extension box arrow and then click Use Lower Case, if necessary, so Photoshop will use lowercase letters when saving.

- Make sure your check boxes are selected as shown in Figure C–8.

- Click the Maximize PSD and PSB File Compatibility box arrow and then click Ask, if necessary, so that Photoshop asks about saving files in PSD format.

- Type 10 in the Recent File List Contains box, if necessary, to specify that Photoshop will display the last 10 files.

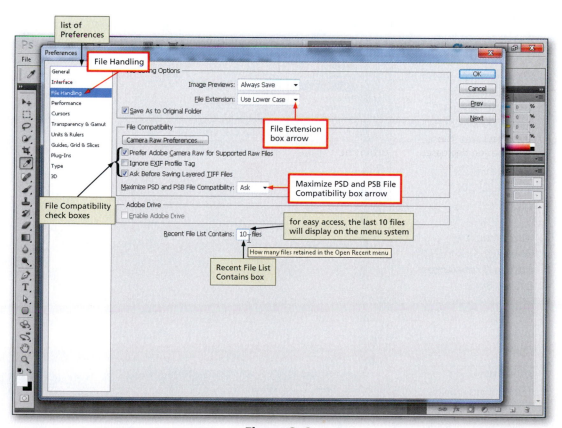

Figure C–8

3

- Click Performance in the list of Preferences.

- If necessary, type 2 0 in the History States box, so Photoshop will allow you to back up through the last 20 steps of any editing session (Figure C–9).

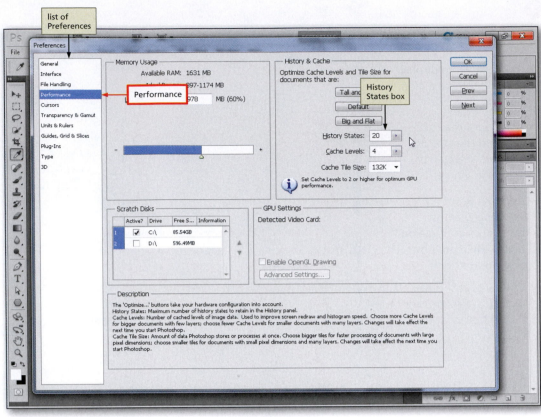

Figure C–9

4

- Click Cursors in the list of Preferences.

- If necessary, select Normal Brush Tip in the Painting Cursors area and Standard in the Other Cursors area, to reset those options back to their default values (Figure C–10).

5

- When you are finished, click the OK button (Preferences Dialog Box).

Other Ways

1. On Edit menu, point to Preferences, click General, select individual preferences

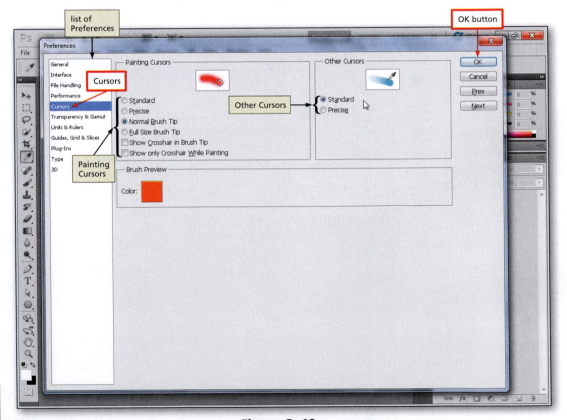

Figure C–10

The Preferences dialog boxes contain a variety of settings that can be changed to suit individual needs and styles. The Reset All Warning Dialogs button in Figure C–7 on page APP 27 especially is useful to display the dialog boxes if someone has turned them off by clicking the Don't show again check box.

In Figure C–10, Normal Brush Tip causes the mouse pointer outline to correspond to approximately 50 percent of the area that the tool will affect. This option shows the pixels that would be most visibly affected. It is easier to work with Normal Brush Tip than Full Size Brush Tip, especially when using larger brushes. A Standard painting cursor displays mouse pointers as tool icons; a Precise painting cursor displays the mouse pointer as a crosshair.

Menu Command Preferences

Photoshop allows users to customize both the application menus and the panel menus in several ways. You can hide commands that you seldom use. You can set colors on the menu structure to highlight or organize your favorite commands. Or, you can let Photoshop organize your menus with color based on functionality. If changes have been made to the menu structure, you can reset the menus back to their default states.

Hiding and Showing Menu Commands

If there are menu commands that you seldom use, you can hide them to access other commands more quickly. A hidden command is a menu command that does not appear currently on a menu. If menu commands have been hidden, a Show All Menu Items command will be displayed at the bottom of the menu list. When you click the Show All Menu Items command or press and hold the CTRL key as you click the menu name, Photoshop displays all menu commands, including hidden ones.

To Hide and Show Menu Commands

The following steps hide a menu command and then redisplay it.

1
- Click Edit on the menu bar, and then click Menus to display the Keyboard Shortcuts and Menus dialog box (Figure C–11).

BTW

Changing Preferences
If there is one particular setting you wish to change, you can open that specific Preferences dialog box from the menu. For example, if you want to change the color of a ruler guide, you can point to Preferences on the Edit menu and then click Guides, Grid & Slices on the Preferences submenu to go directly to those settings and make your edits.

BTW

Resetting Preferences
To restore all preferences to their default settings, you can press and hold ALT+CTRL+SHIFT as you start Photoshop, which causes the system to prompt that you are about to delete the current settings.

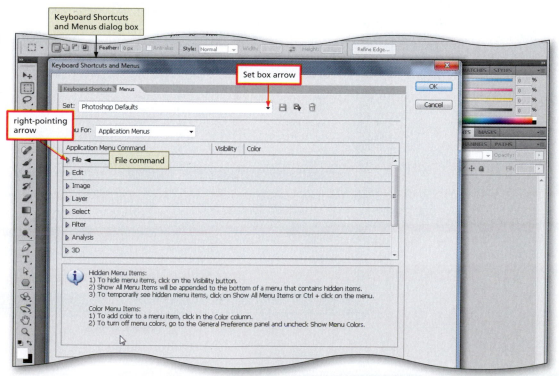

Figure C–11

2

• If necessary, click the Set box arrow and then click Photoshop Defaults.

• Click the right-pointing arrow next to the word File to display the File commands (Figure C–12).

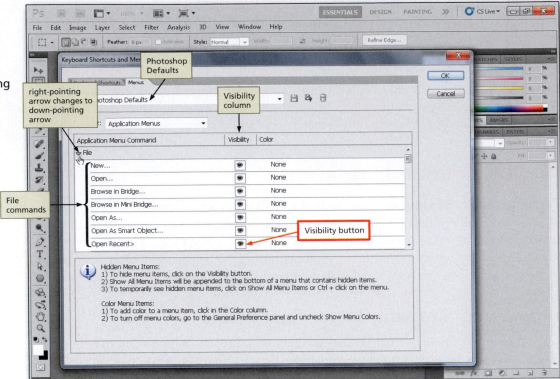

Figure C–12

3

• In the Visibility column, click the Visibility button next to the Open Recent command so it no longer is displayed (Figure C–13).

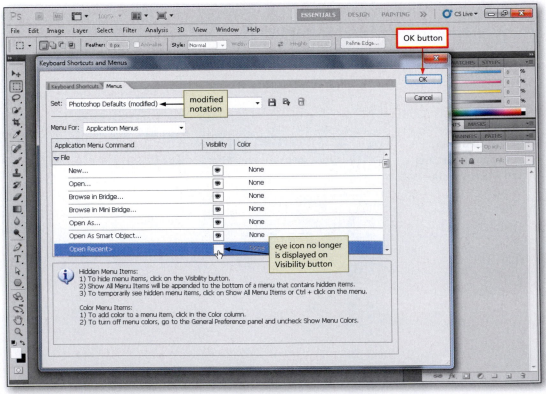

Figure C–13

• Click the OK button (Keyboard Shortcuts and Menus dialog box) to apply the settings.

• Click File on the menu bar to display the File menu (Figure C–14).

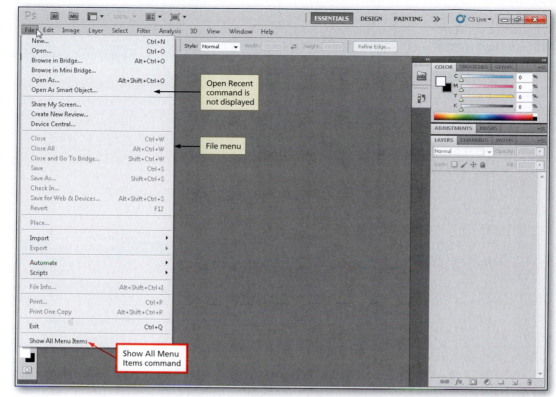

Figure C–14

• On the File menu, click Show All Menu Items to redisplay the command that you hid in Step 3 (Figure C–15).

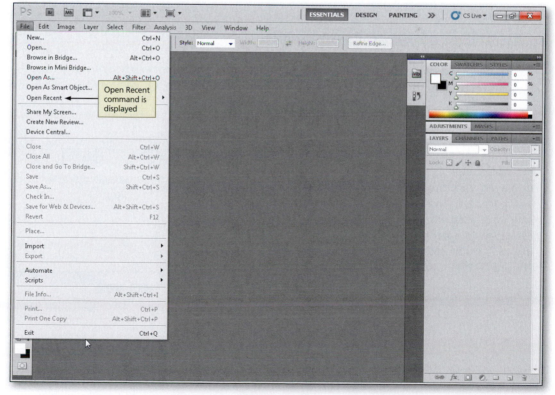

Figure C–15

6

- Click Edit on the menu bar and then click Menus to display the Keyboard Shortcuts and Menus dialog box again.

- If the arrow beside the word, File, is pointing to the right, click it to display the File list.

- Click the Visibility button next to the Open Recent command so it again is displayed (Figure C–16).

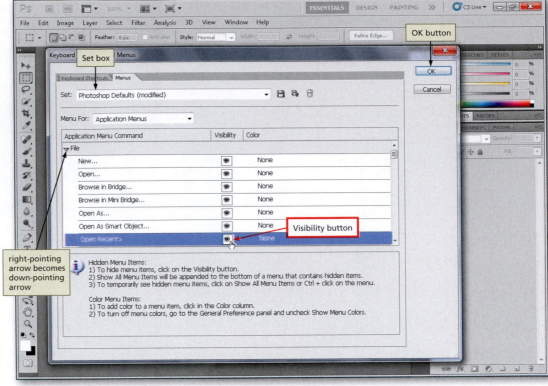

Figure C–16

Other Ways

1. On Window menu, point to Workspace, click Keyboard Shortcuts & Menus

2. Press ALT+SHIFT+CTRL+M

To Add Color to Menu Commands

You can add color to menu commands to help you find them easily or to organize them into groups based on personal preferences. The following steps change the color of the Open and Open As commands.

1

- With the Keyboard Shortcuts and Menus dialog box still displayed, click the word, None, in the row associated with the Open command to display a list of colors (Figure C–17).

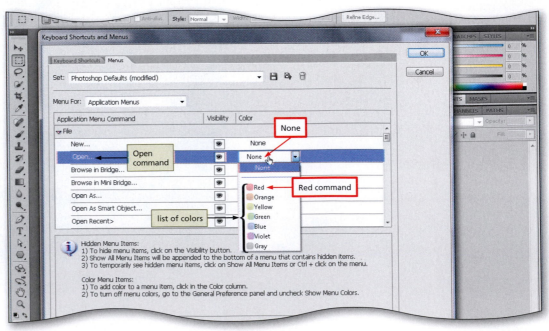

Figure C–17

- Click Red in the list to select a red color for the Open command.

- Click the word, None, in the row associated with the Open As command, and then click Red in the list to select a red color for the Open As command (Figure C–18).

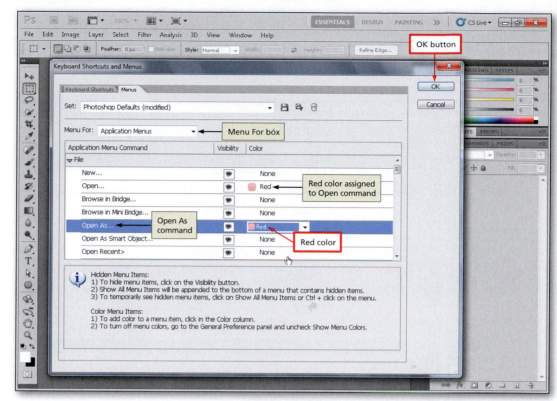

Figure C–18

- Click the OK button (Keyboard Shortcuts and Menus dialog box) to close the dialog box.

- Click File on the menu bar to display the new color settings (Figure C–19).

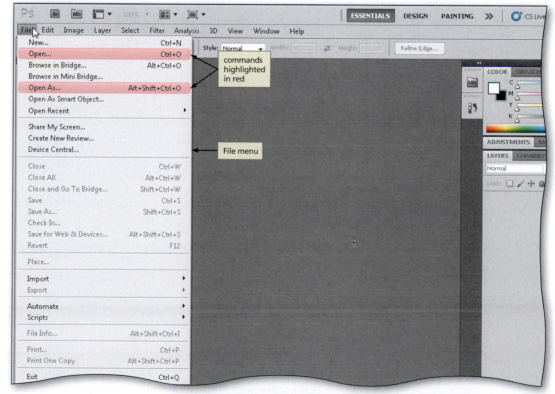

Figure C–19

BTW

Menu Box
The Menu For box
(Figure C–18 on the
previous page) allows
you to set options for
Application Menus or
Panel Menus.

The Set box (Figure C–20) lists three sets of stored menu commands: Photoshop Defaults, New in CS5, and Photoshop Defaults (modified), which you created in the previous steps. Choosing a set causes Photoshop to display related commands with color. For example, if you choose New in CS5, the commands on all menus that are new will appear in blue.

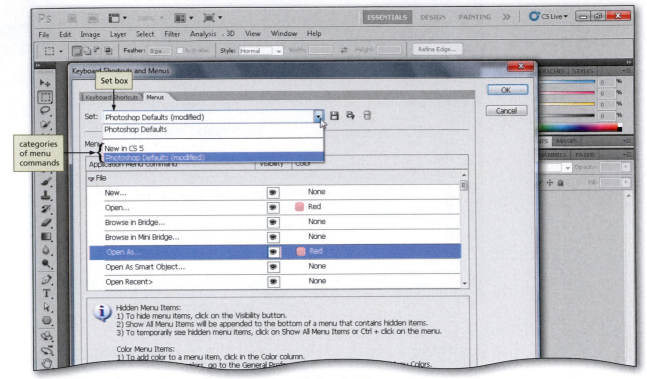

Figure C–20

To Reset the Menus

The following steps reset the menus, removing the red color from the Open commands.

1 Click Edit on the menu bar and then click Menus to display the Keyboard Shortcuts and Menus dialog box.

2 Click the Set box arrow and then click Photoshop Defaults in the list.

3 When Photoshop asks if you want to save your changes before switching sets, click the No button.

4 Click the OK button (Keyboard Shortcuts and Menus dialog box).

Resetting the Panels, Keyboard Shortcuts, and Menus

A **tool preset** is a way to store settings from the options bar. Besides the default settings for each tool, Photoshop contains tool presets for many of the tools that automatically change the options bar. For example, the Crop tool contains a preset to crop for a 5 × 7 photo. You can load other tool presets, edit current presets, or create new presets.

In a lab situation, if you notice that some tools are not working they way they are supposed to, or some presets are missing, someone may have changed the settings. The following steps reload all of the default tool presets.

To Reset Tool Presets

- On the options bar, click the current tool's Preset picker and then click the menu button to display the Tool Preset menu (Figure C–21).

- Click Reset Tool Presets.

- If Photoshop displays a dialog box, click the OK button to reload all of the default tool presets.

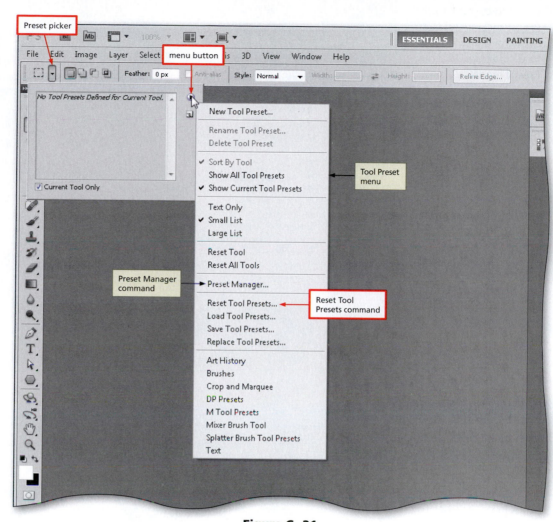

Figure C–21

Other Ways

1. From any panel menu, click Reset Tool Presets, click OK

Resetting Panel Components

Many panels, including the Brushes, Swatches, and Styles panels, display preset samples with preset shapes, colors, and sizes. A few options bars, including the Gradient and Shape options bars, as well as the Contours box in the Layer Style dialog box, also display similar components — all of which may need to be reset at some time.

You can reset these presets using the Preset Manager (Figure C–21), or each panel menu.

To Reset Panel Presets

The steps on the next page reset all panels that use presets.

- On the options bar, click the current tool's Preset picker and then click the menu button to display the Tool Preset menu.

- Click Preset Manager to display the Preset Manager dialog box.

- Click the Preset Type box arrow to display the list of panels that contain presets (Figure C–22).

- Click Brushes to select the Brush presets.

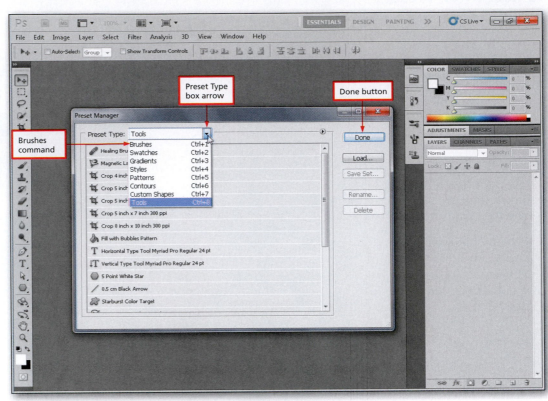

Figure C–22

- Click the Preset Manager menu button (Preset Manager dialog box) to display the list of commands and preset libraries (Figure C–23).

- Click Reset Brushes to reset the Brush presets. When Photoshop displays a confirmation dialog box, click the OK button.

- Repeat Steps 2 and 3 for each of the other panels that appear on the Preset Type box arrow list.

- When you are finished resetting all panels, click the Done button (Preset Manager dialog box) to close the dialog box.

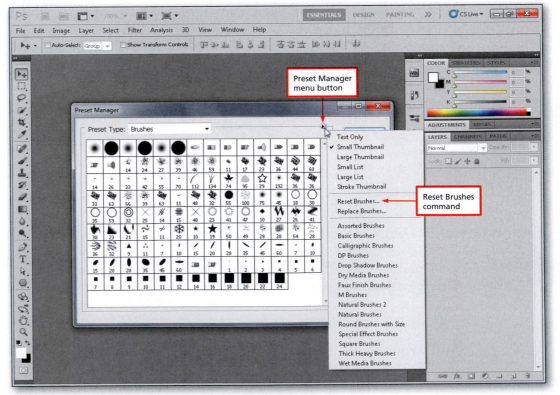

Figure C–23

Other Ways

1. On each panel menu, click Reset command, click OK button

Changing Preferences

Changing the Color and Style of Guides, Grid, and Slices

Instructions: You would like to use some different colors and styles for grids and guides because the current colors are very similar to the colors in your image, making them hard to see. You decide to change the color and style preferences on your system as described in the following steps.

1. Start Photoshop CS5.

2. On the Edit menu, point to Preferences, and then click Guides, Grid, & Slices.

3. When the Preferences dialog box is displayed, change the Color and Style settings as shown in Figure C–24.

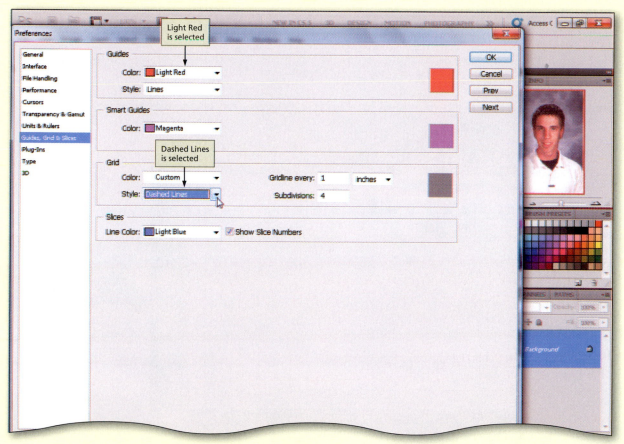

Figure C–24

4. Click the OK button.

5. Open any image file you have saved on your system and drag a guide from the horizontal ruler. Note the Light Red colored line.

6. On the View menu, point to Show, and then click Grid. Note the grid with dashed gray lines.

7. To clear the guides, on the View menu, click Clear Guides.

8. To hide the grid, on the View menu, point to Show and then click Grid.

9. To reset the colors and styles, either change the guide color back to Cyan and the grid style back to Lines, or quit Photoshop and then restart Photoshop while pressing ALT+CTRL+SHIFT. If Photoshop asks if you wish to delete the previous settings, click the Yes button.

Resetting Styles

Instructions: Someone has loaded many styles into the style box, making it difficult to find the common styles you are used to. You decide to reset the styles using the following steps.

1. Start Photoshop CS5.
2. On the Edit menu, click Preset Manager to display the Preset Manager dialog box.
3. Click the Preset Type box arrow to display the Preset list, and then click Styles in the list (Figure C–25).
4. Click the Preset Manager menu button to display a list of commands about the Styles Presets. Click Reset Styles in the list.
5. When Photoshop asks if you want to replace the styles with the default set, click the OK button.
6. Click the Done button to close the Preset Manager dialog box.
7. Quit Photoshop.

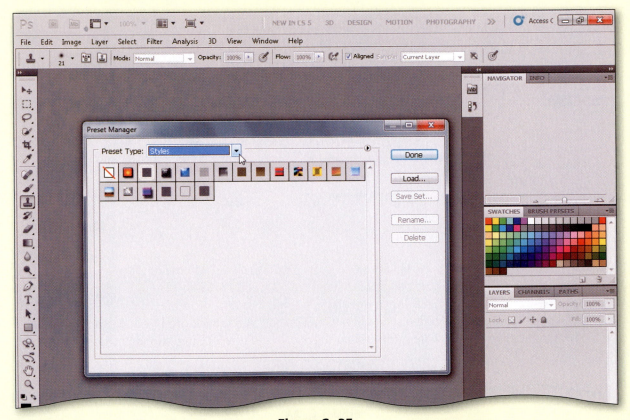

Figure C–25

Searching the Web

Instructions: You want to learn more about optimizing Photoshop settings and your computer system's memory by setting preferences for file size, history states, and cached views. Perform a Web search by using the Google search engine at google.com (or any major search engine) to display and print three Web pages that pertain to optimizing Photoshop CS5. On each printout, highlight something new that you learned by reading the Web page.

Appendix D
Using Photoshop Help

This appendix shows you how to use Photoshop Help. At anytime, whether you are accessing Photoshop currently or not, there are ways to interact with Photoshop Help and display information on any Photoshop topic. The help system is a complete reference manual at your fingertips.

Photoshop Help

Photoshop Help documentation for Photoshop CS5 is available in several formats, as shown in Figure D–1 on the next page. The first format is a Web-based help system that was introduced in Chapter 1. If you press the F1 key or choose Photoshop Help on the Help menu, Adobe Community Help appears in your default browser. You then can use the Web page to search for help topics. The Adobe Community Help page also contains many other kinds of assistance, including tutorials and videos. Your computer must be connected to the Web to use this form of Photoshop Help.

A second form of Photoshop Help is available as a PDF file. Again, pressing the F1 key or choosing Photoshop Help on the Help menu opens the Adobe Community Help page on the Web. Then, you can click the View Help PDF link to open a searchable help documentation, called Using Adobe Photoshop CS5, in book format. You can save this help file on your storage device, or continue to use it on the Web. Additionally, you can open a browser window and go directly to the Using Adobe Photoshop CS5 file by typing http://help.adobe.com/en_US/photoshop/cs/using/photoshop_cs5_help.pdf

Using Adobe Photoshop CS5 is packaged with Photoshop if you purchase the software on a DVD. To view the documentation, open the Documents folder on the installation or content DVD for your software, and then double-click Photoshop Help. If you prefer to view documentation in print form, you can print the Photoshop Help PDF file.

Photoshop Help displays two main panes. The left pane displays a search system. The right pane displays help information on the selected topic. Using Adobe Photoshop CS5 displays a chapter navigation system on the left, and pages from Photoshop Help documentation on the right.

Searching for Help Using Words and Phrases

The quickest way to navigate the Photoshop help system is through the **Search box** in the upper-left corner of the Adobe Community Help Web page. Here you can type words, such as *layer mask*, *hue*, or *file formats*; or you can type phrases, such as *preview a Web graphic*, or *drawing with the Pen tool*. Adobe Community Help responds by displaying search results with a list of topics you can click.

Here are some tips regarding the words or phrases you enter to initiate a search:

1. Check the spelling of the word or phrase.
2. Keep your search specific, with fewer than seven words, to return the most accurate results.
3. If you search using a specific phrase, such as *shape tool*, put quotation marks around the phrase — the search returns only those topics containing all words in the phrase.
4. If a search term does not yield the desired results, try using a synonym, such as Web instead of Internet.

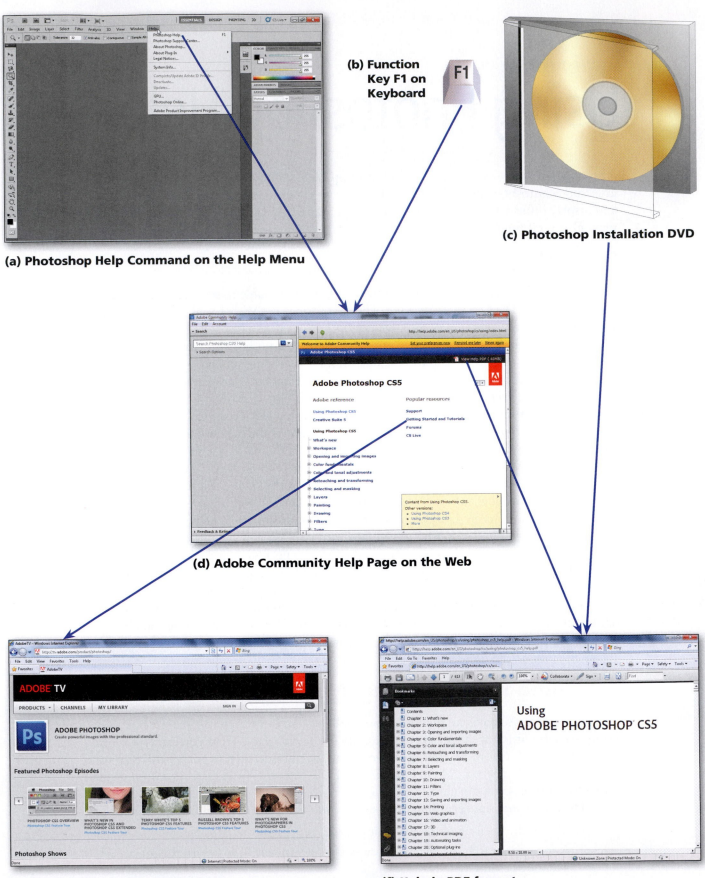

(a) Photoshop Help Command on the Help Menu

(b) Function Key F1 on Keyboard

(c) Photoshop Installation DVD

(d) Adobe Community Help Page on the Web

(e) Sample Video and Tutorial Page

(f) Help in PDF format

Figure D–1

To Obtain Help Using the Adobe Community Help Search Box

The following steps show how to open Adobe Community Help and use the Search box to obtain useful information by entering the keywords, ruler origin.

1

- With Photoshop running on your system, press the F1 key to display the Adobe Community Help window.

- When the Adobe Community Help window is displayed, double-click the title bar to maximize the window, if necessary.

- If the yellow informational slide-in tab is expanded, click the collapse button (Figure D–2).

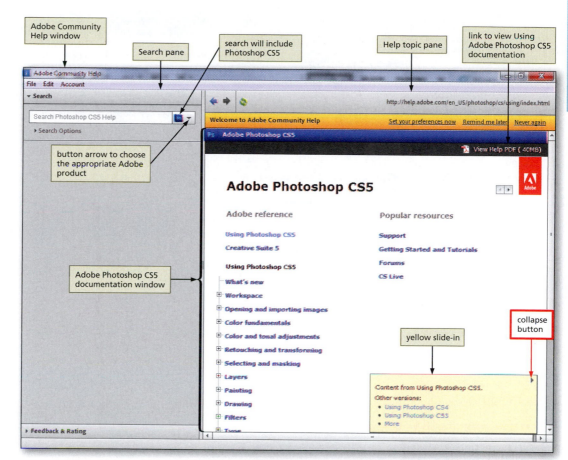

Figure D–2

I do not see a Search pane. Did I do something wrong?

No, someone might have closed the Search pane. To redisplay it, press CTRL+K, and then click the Off button in the Accessibility Mode area. Click the Done button to close the Preferences dialog box.

My help screen is asking me to download an update. Should I do that?

If you are in a lab situation, you should check with your instructor. If you are working on your own computer, the choice is yours. Downloading updates provide you with the latest help topics, videos, and tutorials, but the download takes time and disk space. You must be online to download the updates, and Photoshop may require you to restart your system.

2

- Click the Search box in the Search pane.

- Type `ruler origin` and then press the ENTER key to display the search results (Figure D–3).

- Click the Back button to return to the Adobe Photoshop CS5 page.

Q&A

What is the Adobe Community Help bar?

The Adobe Community Help bar contains links to assist you in setting Help preferences. If your system does not display a yellow bar, you can still set Help preferences by pressing CTRL+K.

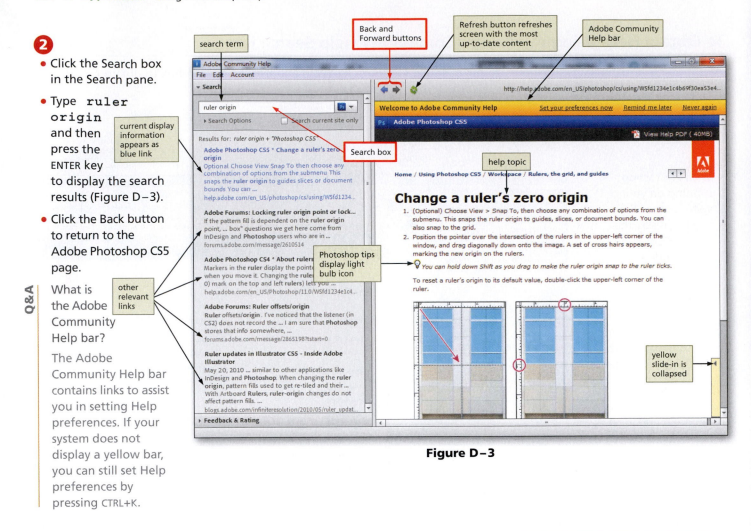

Figure D–3

On the right, Photoshop Help displays information about the topic, instructions, and a graphic. A light bulb icon indicates a Photoshop tip.

If none of the topics presents the information you want, you can refine the search by entering another word or phrase in the Search box. Or, you can click the Search Options button to filter or search other locations.

Adobe Community Help remembers the topics you visited and allows you to redisplay the pages visited during a session by clicking the Back and Forward buttons (shown in Figure D–3).

Using the Topics List

The Topics List is similar to a table of contents in a book. To use the Topics List, click any plus sign on the left side of Photoshop Help to display subtopics, as shown in the following steps.

To Use the Topics List

The following steps use the topics list to look up information about layers.

1

• In the Adobe Photoshop CS5 documentation window, scroll down and then click the plus sign next to the word, Layers, and then click the plus sign next to the words, Layer basics, to expand the list of topics (Figure D–4).

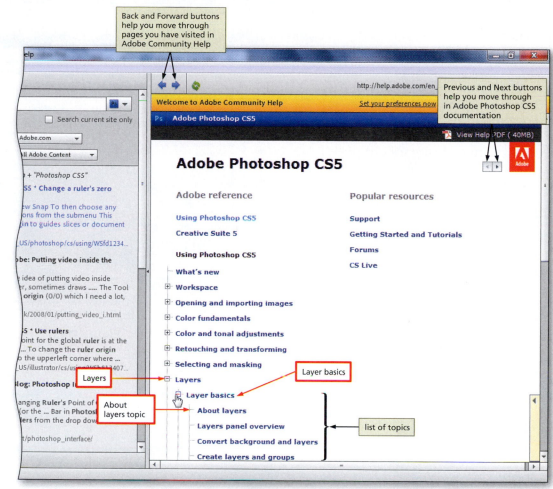

Figure D–4

2

- Click About layers to display information about Photoshop layers (Figure D–5).

Q&A

How do I get back to the table of contents?

Adobe Photoshop CS5's help documentation uses a breadcrumb trail navigation aid to help you see where you are within the documentation. A **breadcrumb trail** is a horizontal navigation that moves through the hierarchy of folders and files in a user interface. Click the Home link in the breadcrumb trail to return to the table of contents.

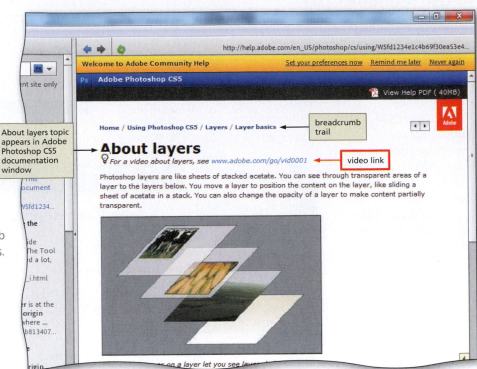

Figure D–5

To View a Video

Using Photoshop Help while connected to the Web, you can view online videos and tutorials, as done in the following steps.

1

- Click the video link www.adobe.com/go/vid0001 to start a video about creating layers (Figure D–6).

Figure D–6

2
- When the video is finished playing, click the Back button to return to the previous help topic (Figure D–7).

Q&A
Could I use the Close button on the Using Layers title bar?

The Close button closes the video and displays the Adobe Video Workshop home page.

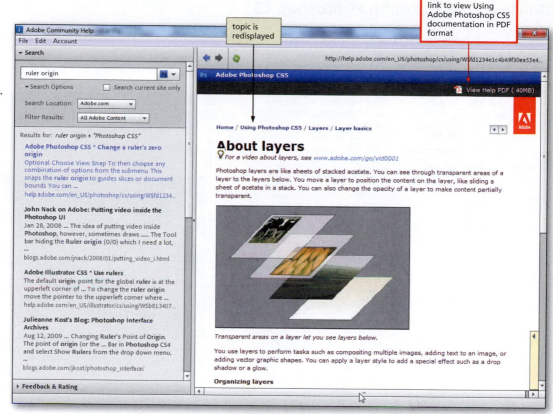

Figure D–7

Using Adobe Photoshop CS5 Documentation

Using Adobe Photoshop CS5 is a complete set of documentation for using Photoshop CS5. The PDF file is organized into 22 chapters with a table of contents like a regular book. You can access Using Adobe Photoshop CS5 by clicking the link on the Adobe Community Help page or by opening the file from the installation DVD.

To Open Using Adobe Photoshop CS5

The following steps open Using Adobe Photoshop CS5 from the Adobe Community Help page. You will use Adobe Acrobat to view the documentation.

1

• Click the link, View Help PDF in the upper-right corner of the Adobe Community Help window, to open the Using Adobe Photoshop CS5 documentation. (Figure D-8).

Q&A

The file would not open because I don't have Adobe Acrobat on my system.

See your instructor for ways to access the file.

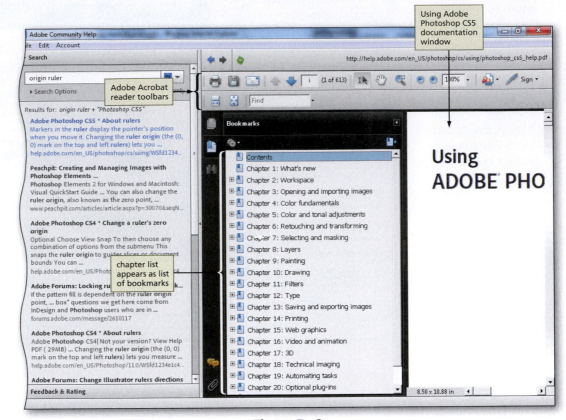

Figure D-8

To Navigate the Documentation by Chapter

The following steps use the left pane of the documentation window to find information related to color.

• With the Using Adobe Photoshop CS5 documentation file still displayed, click the plus sign next to the words, Chapter 4: Color fundamentals, and then click the plus sign next to the words, About color, to display the topics (Figure D-9).

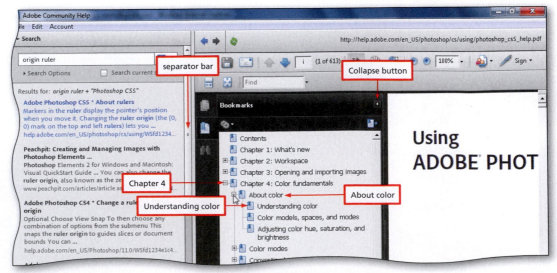

Figure D-9

2

• Click the words, Understanding color, to display the information on the right side of the window.

• Click the separator bar to hide the Search pane (Figure D–10).

Q&A

How can I redisplay the Search page?

Click the separator bar again to expand the pane.

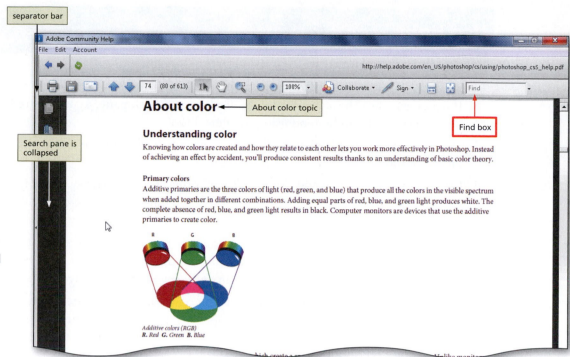

Figure D–10

To Use the Find Box

The following steps search the documentation information about the topic, knockout, using the Adobe Acrobat Find box.

1

• With the Using Adobe Photoshop CS5 documentation window still displayed, click the Find box in the Adobe Acrobat toolbar and then type **knockout**.

• Press the ENTER key to search for the term (Figure D–11).

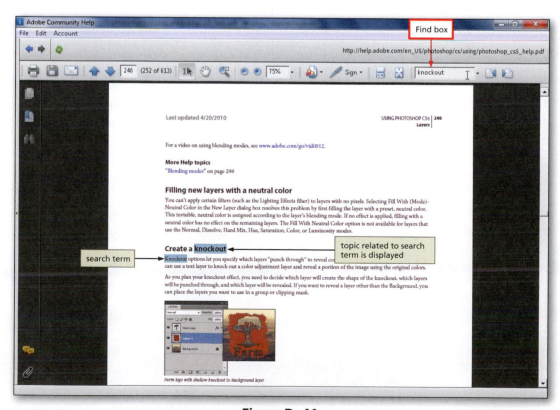

Figure D–11

Use Help

1: Using Adobe Help on the Web

Instructions: Perform the following tasks using Adobe Community Help.

1. If necessary, click the separator bar to display the Search pane. Type **pencil tool** in the Search box to obtain help on using the Pencil tool.

2. When the topics are displayed, click the topic, Adobe Photoshop CS5 * Paint with the Brush tool or Pencil tool.

3. One at a time, click two additional links and print the information. Hand in the printouts to your instructor. Use the Back to previous page and Forward to next page buttons to return to the original page.

4. Use the Search box to search for information on alignment. Click the Automatically align image layers topic in the search results. Read and print the information. One at a time, click the links on the page and print the information for any new page that is displayed.

5. Use the Search box to search for information on tutorials. Navigate to a tutorial of your choice and follow the directions. Write three paragraphs describing your experience, including how easy or difficult it was to follow the tutorial and what you learned. Turn in the paragraphs to your instructor.

6. Close Adobe Community Help.

Use Help

2: Using Adobe Photoshop CS5 Documentation

Instructions: Use the Using Adobe Photoshop CS5 documentation to understand the topics better and answer the questions listed below. Answer the questions on your own paper, or hand in the printed Help information to your instructor.

1. Use the Using Adobe Photoshop CS5 documentation to find help on snapping. Use the Find box, and enter **use snapping** as the term. Click the search result entitled, Use snapping, and then print the page. Hand in the printouts to your instructor.

2. Use the Using Adobe Photoshop CS5 documentation and expand the bookmarks, if necessary. Navigate to Chapter 10: Drawing, and then click the plus sign to expand the topic. Click the plus sign next to Drawing Shapes. One at a time, click each link and print the page. Hand in the printouts to your instructor.

Appendix E

Using Adobe Bridge CS5

This appendix shows you how to use Adobe Bridge CS5. Adobe Bridge is a file exploration tool similar to Windows Explorer, but with added functionality related to images. Adobe Bridge replaces previous file browsing techniques, and now is the control center for the Adobe Creative Suite. Bridge is used to organize, browse, and locate the assets you need to create content for print, the Web, and mobile devices with drag-and-drop functionality.

Adobe Bridge

You can access Adobe Bridge from Photoshop or from the Windows 7 Start menu. Adobe Bridge can run independently from Photoshop as a stand-alone program.

To Start Bridge Using Windows

The following steps start Adobe Bridge from the Windows 7 Start menu.

1

• Click the Start button on the Windows 7 taskbar to display the Start menu.

• Type `Bridge CS5` as the search text in the 'Search programs and files' text box, and watch the search results appear on the Start menu (Figure E–1).

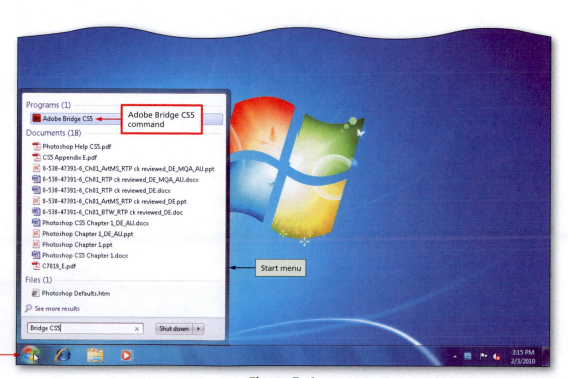

Figure E–1

2

- Click Adobe Bridge CS5 in the search results on the Start menu to start Bridge.

- When the Adobe Bridge window is displayed, double-click its title bar to maximize the window, if necessary (Figure E–2).

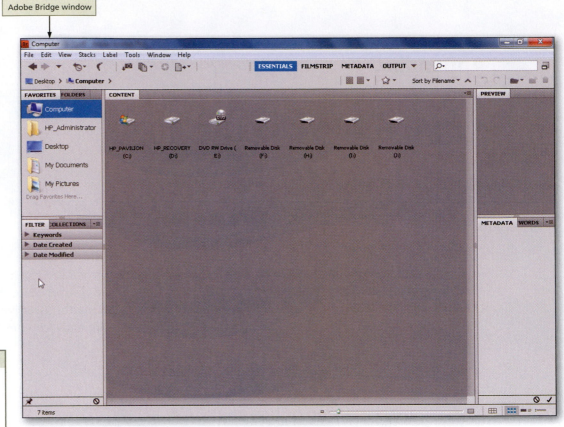

Figure E–2

Other Ways

1. In Photoshop, click File on menu bar, click Browse in Bridge

2. In Photoshop, click Launch Bridge button on Applications Bar

3. Press ATL+CTRL+O

To Reset the Workspace

To make your installation of Adobe Bridge match the figures in this book, you will reset the workspace to its default settings in the following steps.

1

- Click Window on the menu bar, and then point to Workspace to display the Workspace submenu (Figure E–3).

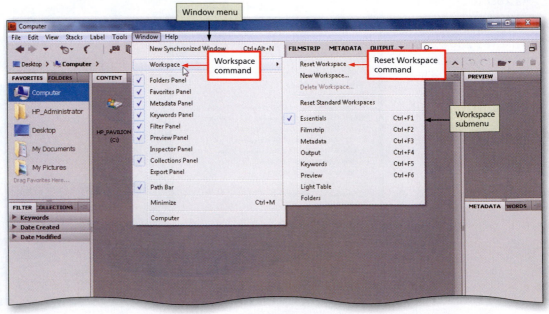

Figure E–3

2
- Click Reset Workspace on the Workspace submenu.
- In the Favorites panel, click Computer to display the files and folders, if necessary (Figure E–4).

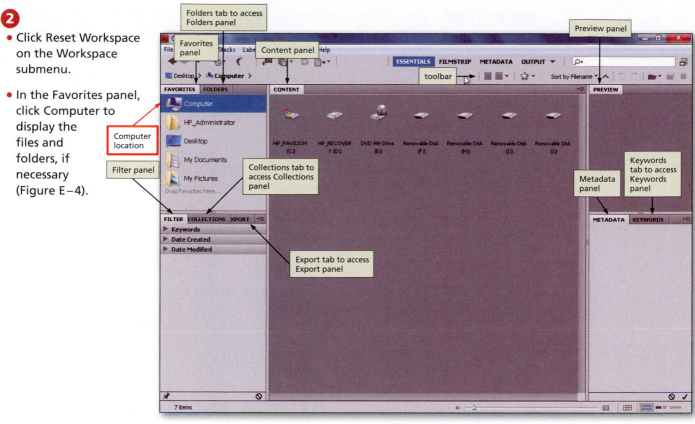

Figure E–4

Other Ways
1. Press CTRL+F1

The Adobe Bridge Window

The parts of the Adobe Bridge window are displayed in Figure E–4. The window is divided into panels and includes a toolbar and status bar.

The Panels

Several panels are displayed in the Bridge workspace in default view. To select a panel, click its tab. You can change the location of the panels by dragging their tabs. You can enlarge or reduce the size of the panels by dragging their borders. Some panels include buttons and menus to help you organize displayed information.

Favorites Panel   The Favorites panel allows quick access to common locations and folders, as well as access to other Adobe applications. Click a location to display its contents in the Content panel.

Folders Panel   The Folders panel shows the folder hierarchy in a display similar to that of Windows Explorer. Users click the plus sign to expand folders and the minus sign to collapse them.

Content Panel   The Content panel is displayed in a large pane in the center of the Adobe Bridge window. The content panel includes a view of each file and folder, its name, the creation date, and other information about each item. The Content panel is used to select files and open folders. To select a file, click it. To open a folder, double-click it. You can change how the Content panel is displayed on the Bridge status bar.

Preview Panel　The Preview panel displays a preview of the selected file that is usually larger than the thumbnail displayed in the Content panel. If the panel is resized, the preview also is resized.

Filter Panel　The Filter panel is displayed in the lower-left region of the Adobe Bridge window. The Filter panel includes many categories of criteria used to filter or control which files display in the Content panel. By default, three categories are displayed when you first start Bridge: Keywords, Date Created, and Date Modified. As you click files, the criteria categories change to include metadata that is generated dynamically depending on the file type. For example if you click an image in the Content panel, the Filter panel includes criteria such as camera data. If you click an audio file, the criteria include artist, album genre, and so on.

Collections Panel　The Collections panel is displayed in the lower-left region of the Adobe Bridge window. **Collections** are a way to group photos in one place for easy viewing, even if the images are located in different folders or on different hard drives. The Collections panel allows you to create and display previously created collections, by identifying files or by saving previous searches.

Export Panel　The Export panel is displayed in the lower-left region of the Adobe Bridge window. The panel helps with saving and uploading to photo-sharing Web sites, including Facebook, Flickr, and Photoshop.com.

Metadata Panel　The Metadata panel contains metadata information for the selected file. Recall that metadata is information about the file including properties, camera data, creation and modification data, and other pieces of information. If multiple files are selected, shared data is listed such as keywords, date created, and exposure settings.

Keywords Panel　The Keywords panel allows you to assign keywords using categories designed by Bridge, or you can create new ones. The keywords help you organize and search your images.

Toolbars and Buttons

Bridge displays several toolbars and sets of buttons to help you work more efficiently (Figure E–5).

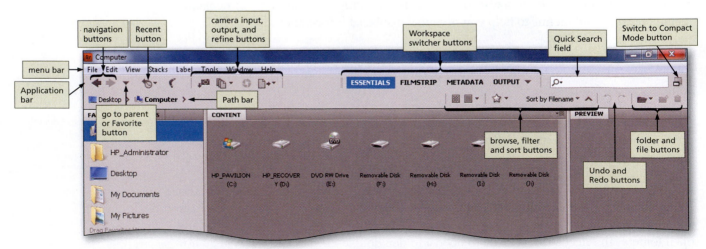

Figure E–5

Menu Bar   The menu bar is displayed at the top of the Bridge window and contains commands specific to Bridge.

Application Bar   Below the menu bar is the Application bar, which includes the navigation buttons, file retrieval and output buttons, buttons for switching workspaces, and other buttons to search for files.

Path Bar   The path bar displays the path for the current file. On the right side of the Path bar are shortcut buttons to help you work with your files. Browse, Filter, and Sort buttons change the display in the Content panel. The Create a new folder button inserts a new folder in the current location. The rotate buttons are active when an image file is selected in the Content panel. The Delete item button deletes the selected item.

Status Bar   At the bottom of the Bridge window, the status bar displays information and contains buttons (Figure E–6). On the left side of the status bar is information regarding the number of items in the current location and how many files are selected, if any. On the right side of the status bar, the Thumbnail slider sets the size of the thumbnails. To the right of the slider are four buttons used to change the display of the Content panel, including the 'Click to lock thumbnail grid' button, the 'View content as thumbnail' button, the 'View content as details' button, and the 'View content as list' button.

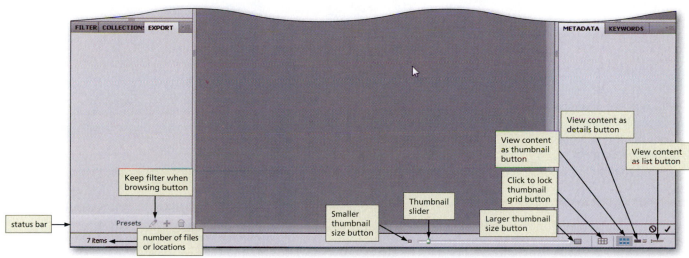

Figure E–6

Bridge Navigation and File Viewing

The advantages of using Bridge to navigate through the files and folders on your computer system include an interface that looks the same in all folders, the ability to see the images quickly, and the ease with which you can open the files in Photoshop or other image editing software. Besides the four kinds of displays represented by the Workspace switcher buttons on the right side of the status bar, Bridge offers several other configurations or layouts of the workspace accessible on the Workspace submenu on the Window menu (Figure E–3 on page APP 50).

To Navigate and View Files Using Bridge

The following step navigates to a CD to view files. Your instructor might specify a different location for these files. You then will use the Workspace switcher buttons to view the Content panel in different styles.

- Insert the CD that accompanies this book into your CD drive.

- After a few seconds, if Windows displays a dialog box, click its Close button.

- In the Content panel, double-click the CD icon associated with your CD drive.

- When the folders and files of the CD are displayed, double-click the Chapter 01 folder to display the files (Figure E–7).

Experiment

- One at a time, click each of the workspace buttons on the options bar and note how the Content panel changes.

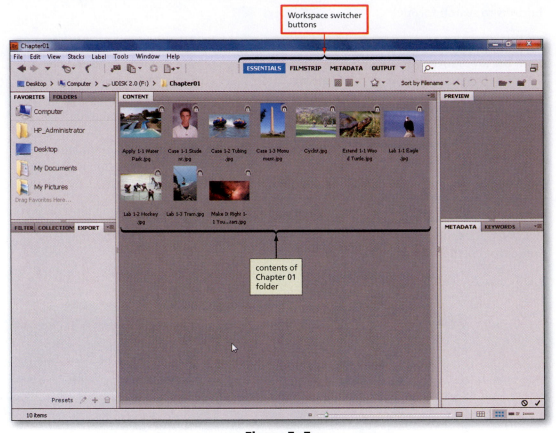

Figure E–7

Other Ways
1. To view Filmstrip workspace, press CTRL+F2   4. To view Keywords workspace, press CTRL+F5
2. To view Metadata workspace, press CTRL+F3   5. To view Preview workspace, press CTRL+F6
3. To view Output workspace, press CTRL+F4

BTW

Duplicating Files
Bridge also offers a Duplicate command on the Edit menu (Figure E–8) that makes a copy in the same folder. Bridge renames the second file with the word, Copy, appended to the file name.

Managing Files

If you want to move a file to a folder that currently is displayed in the Content panel, you can drag and drop the file. The right-drag option is not available. If you want to copy a file, you can choose Copy on the Edit menu, navigate to the new folder and then choose Paste on the Edit menu. At anytime you can press the DELETE key to delete a file or folder, or right-click and then click Delete on the context menu. To rename a photo in Bridge, right-click the file and then click Rename. Type the new name.

To Copy a File

The following steps copy a file from a CD to a USB flash drive using Bridge.

- With the Chapter 01 folder contents still displaying in the Content panel, click the Case 1-2 Tubing thumbnail to select it.

- Click Edit on the menu bar to display the Edit menu (Figure E–8).

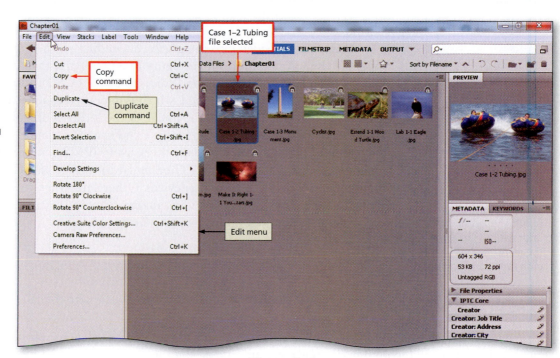

Figure E–8

- Click Copy on the Edit menu.

- In the Favorites panel, click Computer.

- When the Computer locations are displayed in the Content panel, double-click drive G or the drive associated with your USB flash drive.

- Click Edit on the menu bar, and then click Paste to display the copy in its new location (Figure E–9).

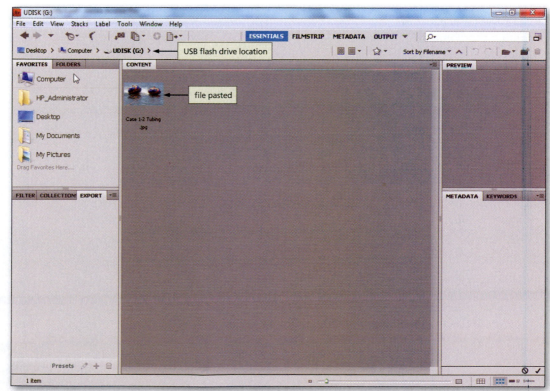

Figure E–9

Other Ways

1. To copy, press CTRL+C
2. To paste, press CTRL+V

BTW

Metadata
This extended set of metadata is particularly useful for large businesses, such as the newspaper industry, which contracts with many photographers and must maintain photo history.

BTW

Metadata Panel Menu
The Metadata panel menu button displays options to change the font size of the fields in the panel, options to set preferences, and ways to find and add new fields. For example, if your digital camera records global positioning system (GPS) information, you can use the menu to append that data to the digital photos.

Metadata

A popular use for Bridge allows you to assign metadata to files. Metadata, such as information about the file, author, resolution, color space, and copyright, is used for searching and categorizing photos. You can utilize metadata to streamline your workflow and organize your files.

Metadata is divided into categories, depending on the type of software you are using and the selected files. The category File Properties includes things like file type, creation date, dimensions, and color mode. IPTC Core stands for International Press Telecommunications Council, which is data used to identify transmitted text and images, such as data describing the image or the location of a photo. Camera Data (Exif) refers to the Exchangeable Image File Format, a standard for storing interchange information in image files, especially those using JPEG compression. Most digital cameras now use the Exif format. The standardization of IPTC and Exif encourages interoperability between imaging devices. Other categories may include Audio, Video, Fonts, Camera Raw and Version Cue, among others. You can see a list of all the metadata categories and their definitions by using Bridge Help.

To Assign and View Metadata

The Metadata Focus workspace makes it easier to assign or enter metadata for photos. In the Metadata panel, you can click the pencil icon to select fields of metadata, or you can move through the fields by pressing the TAB key. The following steps enter description and location information for the selected file.

1
- Click the Case 1-2 Tubing thumbnail to select it.

- In the Metadata panel, scroll down and if necessary, click the right-pointing arrow next to IPTC Core to display its fields.

- Scroll down to the Description field (Figure E–10).

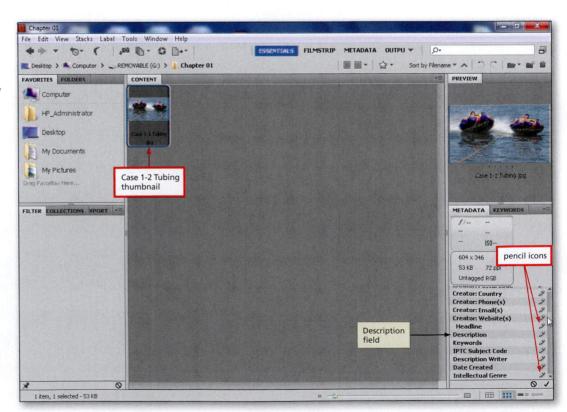

Figure E–10

2

- Click the pencil icon to the right of the Description field. Type **Tubing Adventure** as the description.

- Scroll as needed and then click the pencil icon to the right of the Sublocation field. Type **Raccoon Lake** as the location.

- Press the TAB key, Type **Rockville** as the city.

- Press the TAB key. Type **Indiana** as the state (Figure E–11).

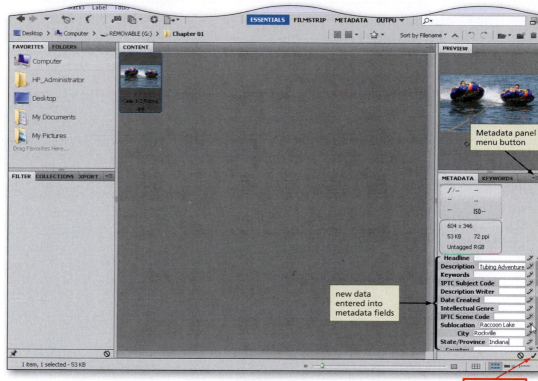

Figure E–11

Apply button

3

- Click the Apply button at the bottom of the Metadata panel to assign the metadata to the photo.

- Click File on the menu bar and then click File Info to display the Case 1-2 Tubing.jpg dialog box (Figure E–12).

- Click the OK button to close the dialog box.

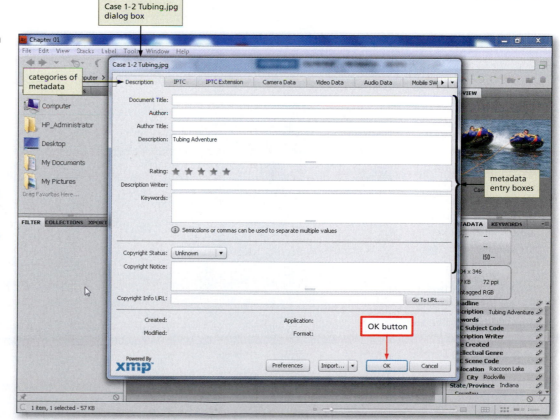

Figure E–12

Other Ways

1. Press CTRL+F4, enter data

To Enter a New Keyword

The Keywords panel lets you create and apply Bridge **keywords** to files. Keywords can be organized into categories called **sets.** Using keywords and sets, you identify and search for files based on their content. To assign keywords, you click the box to the left of the keyword in the Keywords panel, as shown in the following steps.

1

- With the Case 1-2 Tubing image still selected, click the Keywords tab to display the Keywords panel.

- Right-click the word, Places, to display the context menu (Figure E–13).

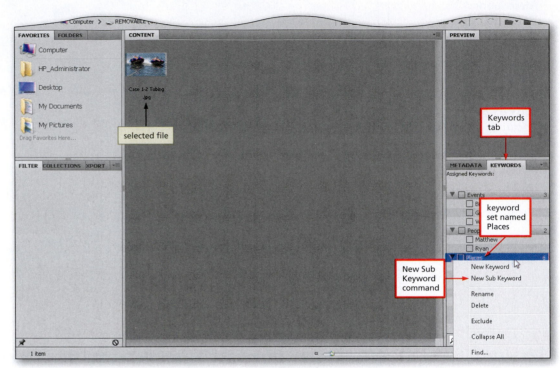

Figure E–13

2

- Click New Sub Keyword on the context menu.

- When the new field is displayed in the Keywords panel, type **Indiana** and then press the ENTER key to create the new item in Places.

- Click the check box to the left of Indiana to assign an Indiana keyword to the picture (Figure E–14).

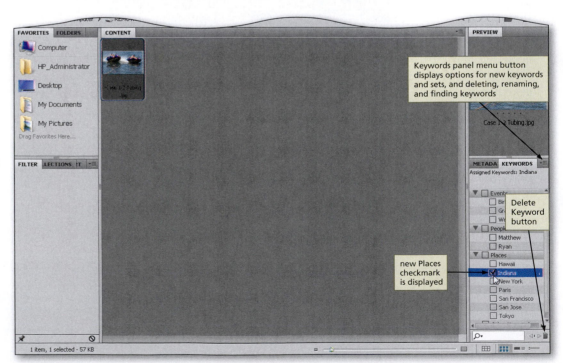

Figure E–14

To Rate a Photo

A rating system from zero stars to five stars is available in Bridge to rate your images and photos. A rating system helps you organize and flag your favorite, or best, files. Many photographers transfer their digital photos from a camera into Bridge and then look back through them, rating and grouping the photos. You can rate a photo using the Label menu or using shortcut keys. Once the photo is rated, stars are displayed below or above the file name depending on the workspace view. To change a rating, click Label on the menu bar and then either increase or decrease the rating. To remove all stars, click Label on the menu bar and then click No Rating. In some views, you can change a rating by clicking stars or dots that display below the thumbnail. You can remove the rating by clicking left of the stars.

The following step adds a rating to a photo file in Bridge.

1

- With the Case 1-2 Tubing image still selected in the Content panel, press CTRL+3 to assign a three star rating (Figure E–15).

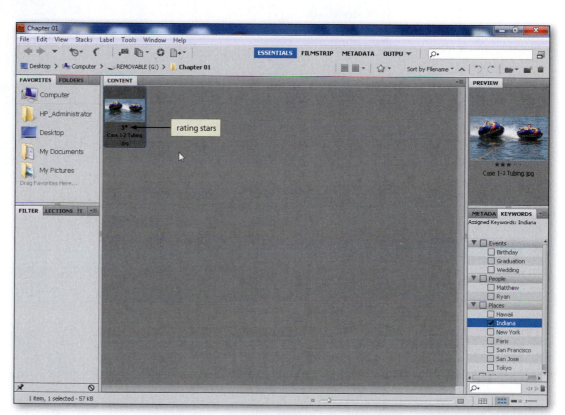

Figure E–15

Other Ways

1. On Label menu, select desired rating

To Label a Photo with Color-Coding

Another way to group photos in Bridge is to use a color-coding system. Bridge provides five colors with which users can label or group their photos. Each color has a category keyword that can be used to group photos. Keywords such as Approved, Second, or Review are used in photojournalism to indicate the status of the photo for future usage. Some companies use the colors for sorting and selecting only. The steps on the next page add a green color indicating approval to the Case 1-2 Tubing image using the menu system. Shortcut keys also are available for labeling photos with color-coding.

• With the Case 1-2 Tubing image still selected in the Content panel, click Label on the menu bar to display the Label menu (Figure E–16).

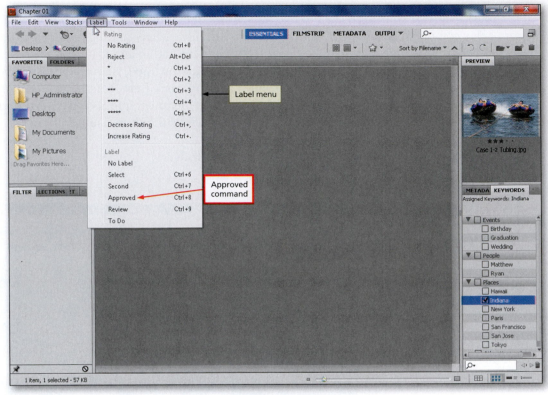

Figure E–16

• Click Approved.

• If Bridge displays a dialog box, click its OK button to apply the color (Figure E–17).

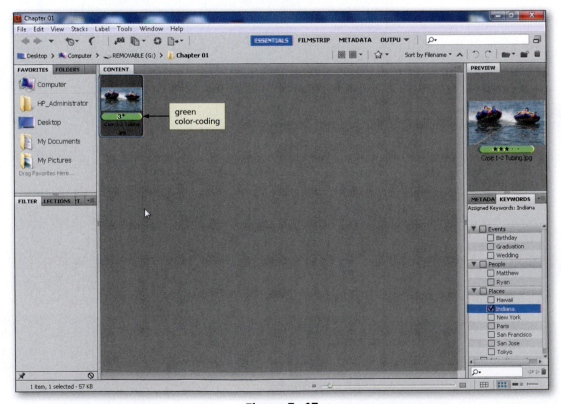

Figure E–17

Other Ways

1. Press CTRL+8

Searching Bridge

Searching is a powerful tool in Adobe Bridge, especially as the number of stored image files increases on your computer system. It is a good idea to enter keywords, or metadata, for every image file you store, to make searching more efficient. Without Adobe Bridge and the search tool, you would have to view all files as filmstrips in Windows, and then look at them a screen at a time until you found what you wanted.

Using the Find Command

In Bridge, you can enter the kind of data or field that you want to search, parameters for that field, and the text you are looking for using the Find command. For example, you could search for all files with a rating of three stars or better, for files less than 1 megabyte in size, or files that begin with the letter, m.

To Use the Find Command

The Find dialog box displays many boxes and buttons to help you search effectively. In the following steps, you will look for all files with metadata that includes the word, lake.

- Click Edit on the menu bar, and then click Find to display the Find dialog box (Figure E–18).

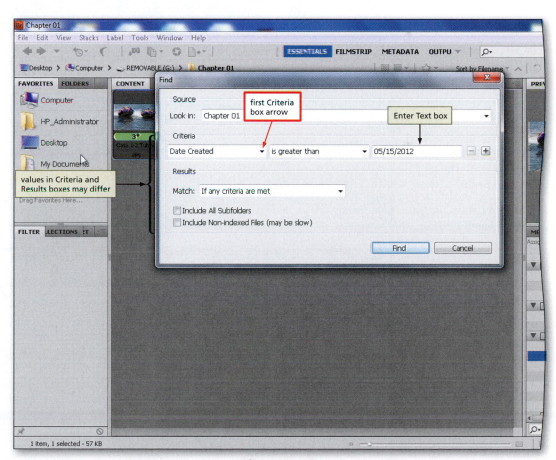

Figure E–18

● If necessary, click the first Criteria box arrow, scroll down as necessary, and then click All Metadata to search all of the metadata fields.

● Press the TAB key twice, and then type **lake** in the Enter Text box to enter the criteria (Figure E–19).

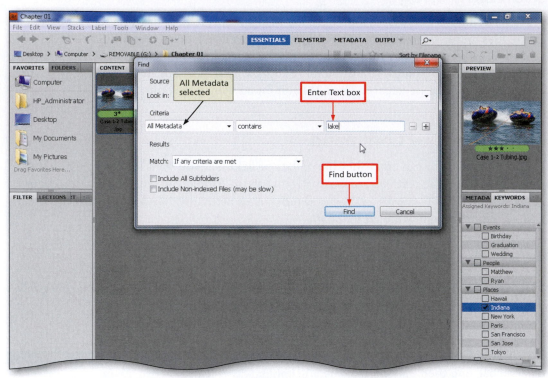

Figure E–19

③

● Click the Find button to display all files that have the word, lake, in any part of their metadata (Figure E–20).

● Click the Cancel button in the Search title bar.

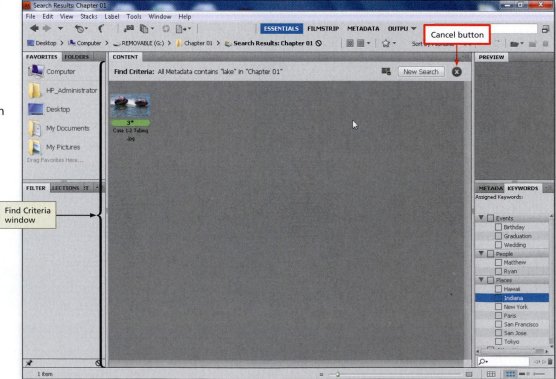

Figure E–20

Other Ways

1. Press CTRL+F, enter search criteria, click Find button

The plus sign to the right of the search boxes in the Find dialog box allows you to search multiple fields. When you click the plus sign, a second line of search boxes is displayed. For example, if you needed to find photos that were created last winter from your vacation in the Rockies, you could search for the date in the first line of boxes, click the plus button, and then enter the keyword to narrow your search even further in the second line of boxes (Figure E–21). When clicked, the Match box arrow allows you to match any or all criteria.

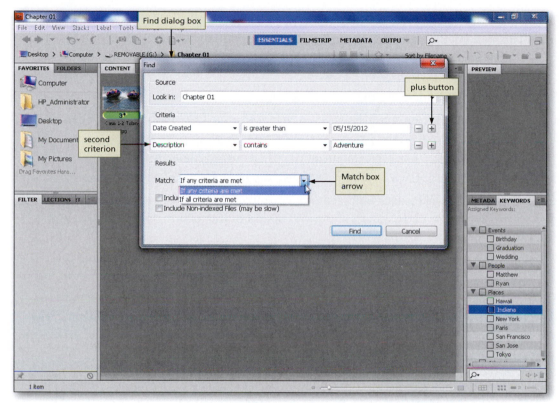

Figure E–21

Bridge offers you a way to save common searches as a **collection** for use later. For example, if you were working for a grocery wholesaler who stores many files for artwork in advertising, searching for pictures related to dairy products would be a common search. Looking through folders of images for pictures of milk or cheese would be very time consuming. Bridge then offers to name the search and store it. To display stored collections, click Collections in the Favorites panel. Then to perform the search again, double-click the collection. With metadata and collection searches, Bridge saves a lot of time.

To Quit Bridge

The final step quits Adobe Bridge.

1 Click the Close button on the Adobe Bridge title bar.

Using Bridge

1: Assigning Metadata

Instructions: You would like to assign metadata to some of the photos you worked on in previous chapters in this book. The photos can be found on the CD containing the Data Files for Students that accompanies this book, or your instructor may direct you to a different location. You will copy the photos from the CD to a local storage device and then assign metadata using Adobe Bridge.

1. Insert the CD that accompanies this book or see your instructor for the location of the data files.
2. Start Adobe Bridge on your system. When the Adobe Bridge window is displayed, on the Favorites tab, click Computer. In the Content panel, double-click the CD that accompanies this book, or navigate to the location specified by your instructor.
3. Right-click the Chapter 01 folder, and then click Copy on the context menu.
4. Using the Favorites tab, click Computer, and then navigate to your USB flash drive or other storage location.
5. On the Edit menu, click Paste. After a few moments, the Chapter 01 folder will appear in the right pane. Double-click the folder to open it. If necessary, click the Default button on the Bridge status bar.
6. Click the first photo. In the Metadata pane, scroll down and click the pencil icon next to the word, Description. In the description box, enter a short description of the picture. Click the Description Writer box. Enter your name.
7. With the first photo still selected, click the Keywords tab. When the Adobe Bridge dialog box appears, click Apply to apply the changes you just made in the Metadata pane. On the Keywords tab, click to place a check mark next to any keywords that apply to the photo.
8. Scroll to the bottom of the keywords list. Right-click the Other Keywords category and then click New Keyword on the context menu. When the new keyword box appears at the top of the panel, type a new keyword relating to the selected photo.
9. Repeat Steps 6 through 8 for each photo in the right pane of the Adobe Bridge window.

Using Bridge

2: Rating and Categorizing Photos

Instructions: You would like to rate and categorize some of the photos you worked on in previous chapters in this book. The photos can be found on the CD that accompanies this book, or your instructor may direct you to a different location.

1. If you did not perform exercise 1, Assigning Metadata, perform steps 1 through 5 from Exercise 1 to copy images to your storage location.
2. With the photos from the Chapter 01 folder displayed in the Content pane of the Adobe Bridge window, click the first photo. Assign a rating to the photo on a scale from 1 to 5 with 1 being the worst photo in the group and 5 being the best photo in the group. On the Label menu, click the number of stars that corresponds to your rating. Repeat the process for each of the photos in the folder.
3. Click the first photo again to select it. Click Label on the menu bar. Choose a label setting, such as Approved. Repeat the process for each of the photos in the folder, choosing different label settings.
4. Choose your favorite photo in the folder and right-click the image. Click Add to Favorites on the context menu.
5. Consult with at least three other members of your class to compare your ratings.

Quick Reference Summary

Adobe Photoshop CS5 Quick Reference Summary

Task	Page Number	Mouse	Menu	Context Menu	Keyboard Shortcut
Adjustment Layer	PS 187	Clip to Layer button on Adjustments panel	Layer | New Adjustment Layer		
Background Eraser Tool	PS 168	Background Eraser Tool button on Tools panel			SHIFT+E
Border, Create	PS 35–37		Select All | Edit | Stroke	Stroke	
Border, Modify	PS 38–40		Select | Modify | Border		
Brightness/Contrast, Adjust	PS 185	Brightness/Contrast icon on Adjustments panel or Create new fill or adjustment layer button on Layers panel | Brightness/Contrast	Layer | New Adjustment Layer | Brightness/Contrast		
Clone Stamp Tool	PS 192	Clone Stamp Tool button on Tools panel			S
Close	PS 42	Close button on document window tab	File | Close		CTRL+W
Commit Change	PS 118	Commit transform (Return) button on options bar			ENTER
Colors, Reset Default	PS 40	Default Foreground/Background Colors button on Tools panel			D
Colors, Switch Between Background and Foreground	PS 40	Switch Between Background and Foreground Colors button on Tools panel			X
Document Windows, Arrange	PS 152	Arrange Documents button on Application Bar	Window | Arrange		
Download Speed, Choose	PS 49	Select download speed button (Save for Web & Devices dialog box)	File | Save for Web & Devices		
Elliptical Marquee Tool	PS 80	Elliptical Marquee Tool button on Tools panel			SHIFT+M
Eraser Tool	PS 164	Eraser Tool button on Tools panel			E
Essentials Workspace, Select	PS 7	Essentials button on Application bar	Window | Workspace | Essentials		
Grid, Hide or Show	PS 101	View Extras button on Application bar	View | Show | Grid		CTRL+ APOSTROPHE (')
Guides, Create	PS 103	Drag from ruler	View | New Guide		
Guides, Hide or Show	PS 101	View Extras button on the Application bar	View | Show | Guides		CTRL+SEMICOLON (;)
Hand Tool	PS 27	Hand Tool button on Tools panel			H
Help	PS 58, Appendix D		Help | Photoshop Help		F1
History, Step Backward in	PS 93–94	Click state on History panel	History panel menu | Step Backward		CTRL+ALT+Z

Adobe Photoshop CS5 Quick Reference Summary *(continued)*

Task	Page Number	Mouse	Menu	Context Menu	Keyboard Shortcut
History, Step Forward in	PS 93	Click state on History panel	History panel menu | Step Forward		CTRL+SHIFT+Z
Hue/Saturation, Adjust	PS 185	Hue/Saturation icon on Adjustment panel or Create new fill or adjustment layer button on Layers panel | Hue/Saturation	Layer | New Adjustment Layer | Hue/Saturation		CTRL+U
Image, Crop	PS 33	Crop Tool button on Tools panel	Image | Crop		C
Image, Flatten	PS 195		Layer | Flatten Image or Layers panel menu | Flatten Image	Flatten Image	
Image, Resize	PS 44		Image | Image Size		ALT+CTRL+I
Keyboard Shortcuts, Create	PS 122		Edit | Keyboard Shortcuts		ALT+SHIFT+CTRL+K
Keyboard Shortcuts, Reset Default	PS 126		Edit | Keyboard Shortcuts | Photoshop Defaults		
Lasso Tool	PS 108	Lasso Tool button on Tools panel			L
Layer, Color	PS 148		Layers panel menu | Layer Properties | select color	Right-click Indicates layer visibility button | click color	
Layer, Create	PS 163	Drag new image into document window	Layer | New | Layer or Layers panel menu | New Layer		SHIFT+CTRL+N
Layer, Hide	PS 149		Layer | Hide Layers	Right-click Indicates layer visibility button | click Hide this layer	
Layer, Name	PS 148	Double-click layer name | enter new name on Layers panel	Layers panel menu | Layer Properties | enter new name	Layer Properties, | enter new name	
Layer, Show	PS 149	Indicates layer visibility icon on Layers panel	Layer | Show Layers		
Layer, Show Only Current	PS 163	ALT+click layer visibility icon on Layers panel			
Layers, Arrange	PS 171	Drag layer on Layers panel			CTRL+[or CTRL+]
Layer Effects, Hide	PS 190	Reveals layer effects in the panel button on Layers panel			
Layer Mask, Create	PS 174	Add layer mask button on Layers panel			
Layers Panel Options, Set	PS 145		Layers panel menu | Panel Options		
Layer Properties, Assign	PS 148, 154		Layer | Layer Properties or Layers panel menu | Layer Properties	Layer Properties	
Layer Style, Add	PS 189	Add a layer style button on Layers panel	Layer | Layer Style		
Layer Style, Copy	PS 187		Layer | Layer Style | Copy Layer Style	Copy Layer Style	
Layer Style, Paste	PS 187		Layer | Layer Style | Paste Layer Style	Paste Layer Style	
Layer Via Cut, Create	PS 147		Layer | New | Layer via Cut	Layer via Cut	SHIFT+CTRL+J
Levels, Adjust	PS 183	Levels icon on Adjustments panel or Create new fill or adjustment layer button on Layers panel | Levels	Image | Adjustments | Levels		CTRL+L
Magic Eraser Tool	PS 161	Magic Eraser Tool button on Tools panel			SHIFT+E
Magic Wand Tool	PS 110	Magic Wand Tool button on Tools panel			SHIFT+W
Magnetic Lasso Tool	PS 114	Magnetic Lasso Tool button on Tools panel			SHIFT+L

Adobe Photoshop CS5 Quick Reference Summary *(continued)*

Task	Page Number	Mouse	Menu	Context Menu	Keyboard Shortcut
Magnification, Change	PS 27	Enter number in Magnification box on status bar			
Menus, Edit	APP 29		Edit | Menus		ALT+SHIFT+CTRL+M
Mini Bridge, View Files	PS 54	Launch Mini Bridge button on the Application bar	File | Browse in Mini Bridge		
Move Tool	PS 84	Move Tool button on Tools panel			V
Opacity, Change	PS 18	Drag Opacity scrubby slider on Layers panel			
Open	PS 10		File | Open	Right-click document tab | click Open Document	CTRL+O
Open Recent	PS 43		File | Open Recent		
Panel, Collapse	PS 57	Collapse to Icons button on panel		Right-click panel tab | click Collapse to Icons	
Panel, Open	PS 55	Panel button on vertical docking of panels	Window | panel name		
Paste	PS 98		Edit | Paste	Paste	CTRL+V
Pattern Stamp Tool	PS 191	Pattern Stamp Tool button on Tools panel			SHIFT+S
Preview, Web	PS 48, 51	Preview button (Save for Web & Devices dialog box)	File | Save for Web & Devices		ALT+CTRL+SHIFT+S
Polygonal Lasso Tool	PS 105	Polygonal Lasso Tool button on Tools panel			SHIFT+L
Preferences, Edit	APP 26		Edit | Preferences | General		CTRL+K
Print	PS 47		File | Print		CTRL+P
Print One Copy	PS 47		File | Print One Copy		ALT+SHIFT+CTRL+P
Quick Selection Tool	PS 90	Quick Selection Tool button on Tools panel			W
Quit Photoshop	PS 60	Close button	File | Exit		CTRL+Q
Rectangular Marquee Tool	PS 83	Rectangular Marquee Tool button on Tools panel			M
Refine Edge	PS 96	Refine Edge button on options bar	Select | Refine Edge	Refine Edge	ALT+CTRL+R
Reset All Tools	PS 8			Reset All Tools	
Rule of Thirds Overlay, Position	PS 33	Drag overlay			
Rulers, Show or Hide	PS 30	View Extras button on Application bar	View | Rulers		CTRL+R
Save	PS 19		File | Save		CTRL+S
Save for Web	PS 52		File | Save for Web & Devices		ALT+SHIFT+CTRL+S
Save in PDF Format	PS 120		File | Save As | click Format box arrow | click Photoshop PDF (*.PDF; *.PDP)		
Save with New Name	PS 19		File | Save As | enter new name		SHIFT+CTRL+S
Screen Mode, Change	PS 28	Screen Mode button on Applications bar	View | Screen Mode | select mode		F
Select All	PS 36		Select | All		CTRL+A
Selection, Add To	PS 115	Add to selection button on options bar			SHIFT+drag
Selection, Deselect	PS 41	Click document window	Select | Deselect		CTRL+D
Selection, Distort	PS 86	Enter rotation percentage on options bar	Edit | Transform | Distort	Free Transform mode | Distort	
Selection, Duplicate	PS 98		Edit | Copy | Edit Paste		CTRL+ALT+drag
Selection, Flip Horizontal	PS 111		Edit | Transform | Flip Horizontal	Free Transform mode | Flip Horizontal	

Adobe Photoshop CS5 Quick Reference Summary *(continued)*

Task	Page Number	Mouse	Menu	Context Menu	Keyboard Shortcut
Selection, Flip Vertical	PS 111		Edit | Transform | Flip Vertical	Free Transform mode | Flip Vertical	
Selection, Free Transform	PS 86		Edit | Free Transform	Free Transform	CTRL+T
Selection, Grow	PS 107		Select | Grow		
Selection, Intersect with	PS 104	Intersect with selection button on options bar			
Selection, Rotate	PS 8	Enter degree rotation on options bar	Edit | Transform | Rotate	Free Transform mode | Rotate	
Selection, Rotate 180°	PS 86	Enter degree rotation on options bar	Edit | Transform | Rotate 180°	Free Transform mode | Rotate 180°	
Selection, Rotate 90° CCW	PS 86	Enter degree rotation on options bar	Edit | Transform | Rotate 90° CCW	Free Transform mode | Rotate 90° CCW	
Selection, Rotate 90° CW	PS 86	Enter degree rotation on options bar	Edit | Transform | Rotate 90° CW	Free Transform mode | Rotate 90° CW	
Selection, Scale	PS 99	SHIFT+drag corner sizing handle	Edit | Transform | Scale	Free Transform mode | Scale	
Selection, Skew	PS 8		Edit | Transform | Skew	Free Transform mode | Skew	
Selection, Snap	PS 106, 107	Drag selection near object or guide			
Selection, Subtract From	PS 110	Subtract from selection button on options bar			ALT+drag
Selection, Transform Perspective	PS 86		Edit | Transform | Perspective	Free Transform mode | Perspective	
Selection, Warp	PS 86	Warp button on Transform options bar	Edit | Transform | Warp	Free Transform mode | Warp	
Single Column Marquee Tool	PS 80, 82	Single Column Marquee Tool button on Tools panel			
Single Row Marquee Tool	PS 80, 82	Single Row Marquee Tool button on Tools panel			
Smart Object, Layer	PS 179		Layer | Smart Objects | Convert to Smart Object or Layers panel menu | Convert to Smart Object	Convert to Smart Object	
Smooth, Modify	PS 38, 39		Select | Modify | Smooth		
Snapping, Turn On	PS 107		View | Snap		SHIFT+CTRL+;
Transform Controls, Display	PS 84	Show Transform Controls checkbox on options bar	Edit | Free Transform		CTRL+T
Undo	PS 33, 34	Click previous state in History panel	Edit | Undo		CTRL+Z
Windows, Consolidate	PS 173	Arrange Documents button on Application bar | Consolidate All button	Window | Arrange | Consolidate All to Tabs	Right-click document tab | click Consolidate All to Here	
Zoom In	PS 23	Zoom In button on Navigator panel	View | Zoom In	Zoom In	CTRL+PLUS SIGN (+)
Zoom Out	PS 23	Zoom Out button on Navigator panel	View | Zoom Out	Zoom Out	CTRL+MINUS SIGN (−)
Zoom Tool	PS 23	Zoom Tool button on Tools panel			Z
Zoomify	PS 47		File | Export | Zoomify		

Index